STUDIES IN AFRICAN LITERATURE

Journeys Through the French African Novel

STUDIES IN AFRICAN LITERATURE: NEW SERIES

▼▼▼▼▼▼▼▼▼▼▼▼▼▼▼▼▼▼▼▼▼▼▼▼▼▼▼▼▼▼

▼▼▼▼▼▼▼▼▼▼▼▼▼▼▼▼▼▼▼▼

Journeys Through the French African Novel

MILDRED MORTIMER

University of Colorado

HEINEMANN
Portsmouth, NH

JAMES CURREY
London

Heinemann Educational Books, Inc.
361 Hanover Street   Portsmouth, NH 03801−3959
Offices and agents throughout the world

James Currey Ltd
54b Thornhill Square, Islington
London N1 1BE

Portions of chapter 5 also appear in *The French Review*, Vol. 64, no. 1 (October 1990).

Library of Congress Cataloging-in-Publication Data

Mortimer, Mildred P.
    Journeys through the French African novel/Mildred Mortimer.
       p. cm. − (Studies in African literature)
    Includes bibliographical references.
    ISBN 0−435−08042−3
    1. African fiction (French)−History and criticism. 2. Authors,
African−Journeys. 3. Africans−Travel−History. 4. Travel in
literature. I. Title. II. Series.
PQ3984.M58 1990
843.009′896−dc20   90−4416
                                                     CIP

British Library Cataloguing in Publication Data
Mortimer, Mildred
    Journeys through the French African novel.
    1. Fiction in French. African writers: Critical studies
    I. Title
    843

    ISBN 0−85255−526−1

Cover photo: Dogon statue from Mali (author's collection).
Designed by Jenny Greenleaf.
Printed in the United States of America.
90 91 92 93 94 9 8 7 6 5 4 3 2 1

*To Rob, who shared this journey,
and in memory of Mouloud Mammeri,
who showed me the path.*

Contents

▼▼▼▼▼▼▼

Acknowledgments

▼▲▼▲▼▲▼▲▼▲▼▲▼▲▼▲▼▲▼▲▼

I wish to thank the following friends and colleagues for their support and suggestions as the manuscript took shape: Elisabeth Mudimbe-Boyi, Valentin Mudimbe, Eric Sellin, Ken Harrow, Eileen Julien, Louis Tremaine, Hédi Bouraoui, Sonia Lee, Kristine Aurbakken, Monique Hugon.

I owe a debt of gratitude to the University of Colorado. Students in my francophone literature classes contributed directly and indirectly to this project; special thanks go to Nada Turk and Ann Scarboro. The University of Colorado has been most generous to me these past five years, awarding me grants from GCAH, IM PARTS, CRCW, and the Fund for the Promotion and Retention of Women and Minorities. I am very grateful to Sandy Adler for her critical eye as well as her impressive word processing skills.

I thank the National Endowment for the Humanities for a Summer Stipend and the American Institute of Maghribi Studies for a travel grant. Both contributed to my research in the initial phase.

At Heinemann, many thanks to Charlotte Bruner and John Watson and Donna Bouvier, my patient editors.

In addition to the support of friends in the United States, France, and Africa, I owe a debt of gratitude to my family — my husband Rob and our daughters Amy, Janine, Sylvie, and Denise. Each one of them has contributed in a special way to this journey through African texts.

Introduction

▼▼▼▼▼▼▼▼▼▼▼

Colonialism in Africa, a process of conquest by Europeans convinced of their civilizing mission, promoted voyages: European journeys to the African coast, across the Sahara, up the great rivers; African journeys away from remote villages to growing metropolitan areas such as Dakar and Lagos, and finally some as far as Europe. Focusing on voyages undertaken by Africans, this study, a thematic and structural analysis of the journey motif in representative works of francophone African fiction, privileges the African writer as the authentic voice and scribe for African societies.

Data suggest that several factors govern the African writer's choice of the journey motif. Rooted in African oral tradition, central to the European novel from its early beginnings, the journey motif also corresponds to African reality by reflecting a history of migrations and explorations as well as conquest. Given this multiple heritage, three factors emerge that critics have not yet studied in relation to one another: the importance of orature to African writing, the distinctions between men and women's journeys, and the literary bonds across the Sahara (links between Maghrebian and sub-Saharan fiction). Exploring these factors in addition to the thematic and structural elements of the journey motif, I will trace the development of a theme that the late Algerian novelist Mouloud Mammeri has called *l'itinéraire de lucidité* — the journey to self-understanding.

This study points to the importance of the spoken word to the emerging African novel, a genre created by the contact between African orature, or oral tradition, and French language and literature. The francophone African novel, like its anglophone counterpart, came into being because of dramatic political, social, and cultural transformations on the African continent; it is a product of colonialism. Initial explorations of the Portuguese along the Atlantic coast in the fifteenth century, followed by the establishment of European colonies four centuries later, resulted in many changes in African societies, not the least of which was the contact between European literacy and African orality.

In Africa, orality and literacy often inhabit the same space. In post colonial Africa, for example, where states established by European powers summarily disregarded ethnic divisions, sometimes one oral language is dominant, as in the case of Wolof in Senegal, or several, as in the linguistic inheritance in Côte d'Ivoire. Moreover, linguistic battles may represent new political struggles following the departure of the colonial power. In Algeria, for example, the campaign to promote Algerian Arabic as the national language has been to the detriment of the cultural and linguistic autonomy of Algerian Berbers.

What are the effects of literacy upon the individual and society? Individuals who have internalized writing speak literately; their oral expression reflects thought patterns and verbal patterns that distinguish them from members of oral cultures (Ong 56—57). In addition, literate cultures store quantities of information, whereas illiteracy results in selective memory, in retaining only information of social relevance. Thus, individuals in a literate culture probably cannot participate as fully in a cultural tradition as their counterparts in a nonliterate society. Finally, literacy establishes a more general and more abstract relationship between the word and its referent in a literate culture. One must conclude that literacy profoundly transforms the relationship of both the individual and society to language and history.[1]

Many an African writer has faced the problem of being a literate individual participating in a nonliterate or partially literate society. When Camara Laye depicts his Guinean childhood in *L'Enfant noir*, for example, he writes in French about a nonliterate Malinké society. Cheikh Hamidou Kane, in *L'Aventure ambiguë*, describes early Quranic training which predates his French colonial education; the former consists primarily of reciting and copying the Quran. The child, Samba, does not comprehend rationally the sacred book he is learning by rote memory.

Although Kane's traditional world is partially literate (in contrast to Camara Laye's, which is nonliterate), both writers are forced to straddle two worlds. Representative of most African writers of their generation, Camara Laye and Cheikh Hamidou Kane experience gains and losses. Acquiring literacy in French, they gain access to the colonizer's world. Learning the colonizer's language in the French colonial school, however, they abandon traditional education; the latter remains for them forever incomplete. Summing up the African writer's sense of nostalgia, of fragile links with one's irrecuperable past, the Nigerian critic Emmanuel Obiechina states: "For most Africans, life begins in the village, and wherever they go after that, they carry the village with them" (*Culture, Tradition, and Society in the West African Novel* 201).

The francophone African novelist adopts a European genre—the novel—as well as an imported language—French. Yet, unlike the colonizer's legacy of the European language and genre, the journey motif, taken from the African oral tradition, provides a way back to the village, to Laye's father's forge and Samba's Quranic school. By translating and transposing oral narrative to the printed page, Birago Diop provides his readers with adaptations of Senegalese Wolof tales. One such narrative, "L'Héritage" (see chapter 2), centers upon a journey that leads to lucidity, or self-understanding.

It would be misleading, however, to say that the journey as thematic element and structuring device occurs only in African tradition. On the contrary, the journey motif appears in European oral narrative and literature. Some heroes of European folktales (oral narratives committed to print) travel long distances: Hansel and Gretel leave a long trail of crumbs in the forest. Others travel short distances: Little Red Riding Hood meets up with the wolf because she takes a shortcut to her grandmother's cottage.

From the time of Cervantes' Don Quijote to the present, the protagonists of European novels have embarked on countless voyages. Reminding readers that the beginning of the modern European novel in Spain and England coincides with important navigational explorations and discoveries, Michel Butor affirms: "All fiction is thus inscribed in our space as a journey and we can say in this regard that it is the theme of all novels" (50).* Studying the origins of the European novel, Marthe Robert asserts that Cervantes and Defoe (fathers of two immortal itinerant heroes, Don Quijote and Robinson Crusoe) created the European novel.[2] Moreover, she claims that all nineteenth-century European novelists were brought up on both books; their reading could not have failed to influence their unconscious (104).

Where then does the journey motif that appears in African fiction originate? Do twentieth-century African writers who have adopted a European language and genre have the cultural framework of their European counterparts? My previous examples, Camara Laye and

---

* Toute fiction s'inscrit donc en notre espace comme voyage, et l'on peut dire à cette égard que c'est là le thème fondamental de toute littérature romanesque (50).

Kane, read the canonical French texts that formed the corpus of literary works studied in the French colonial school. On the other hand, they did not have a wide selection of European books neatly shelved in a family library. As youngsters they surely had greater contact with the oral tradition of their people than with the European literary masters Cervantes and Defoe.

In his study *Roman africain et tradition*, Mohamadou Kane expresses his belief that the journey motif has a dual origin:

> In this preeminence of the theme of the journey we must see the meeting of several traditions. The examination of texts of oral literature illustrates this very well. The tales of Bernard Dadié or Birago Diop or Ibrahima Seid allow us to evaluate its place and grasp its significance. The influence of the nineteenth century French novel (of the Balzacian type) must not be excluded since the approaches are connected. Here the French university background of a number of novelists comes into play. The intent to popularize new ideas, to challenge accepted opinions, leads us to suppose a more or less significant influence of the eighteenth-century novel. We know the position the journey holds and its equivalency with a philosophical or simply initiating purpose. (202)*

Kane thus makes the case for cultural blending, for African literature rooted in African orature and European literature. His study, which posits tradition as a dynamic rather than a static force in African society, encourages critics to seek elements of both oral narrative and European literature in the African novel. Acknowledging the importance of orature, the reader must also be aware of intertextuality. For example, thematic, stylistic, and structural elements of Zola's *Germinal* reappear in Ousmane Sembène's *Les Bouts de bois de Dieu*. Similarly, Montesquieu's *Lettres persanes* finds echoes in Bernard Dadié's *Un Nègre à Paris*.[3]

In African oral narrative, the protagonist sometimes leaves home voluntarily, in search of adventure, but quite often is either forced to

---

* Dans cette prééminence du thème du voyage, il faut voir la conjonction de plusieurs traditions. L'examen des textes de la littérature orale le montre à souhait. Les contes de Bernard Dadié ou de Birago Diop ou d'Ibrahima Seid permettent de mesurer sa place et de saisir sa signification. Une influence du roman français du XIXᵉ siècle (appartenant au type balzacien) ne doit pas être écartée tant les démarches s'apparentent. La formation universitaire française de nombre de romanciers entre en ligne de compte. Le souci de vulgarisation d'idées nouvelles, l'attitude contestataire au regard d'opinions tenues pour acquises, incitent à supposer une influence plus ou moins grande du roman français du XVIIIᵉ siècle. On sait la place que tient le voyage et son adéquation à l'intention "philosophique" ou plus simplement initiatique (202).

flee or sets out to complete a difficult if not impossible task. To the extent that the slave trade, military conscription, and work and study in African and European cities have caused African migrations at different historical moments, the journey motif in oral narrative expresses African reality.

Whether traveling heroes or heroines depart voluntarily or involuntarily, they almost always intend to return and, most important, view home as haven. As Daniel Kunene explains:

> Out there is a jungle. The hero who turns his back on the courtyards and cattle-folds and grazing fields of his home is entering this jungle with all its beasts and monsters. If he comes back alive and unscathed he will have learned some lessons of life. If he comes back scarred in body and soul, he will have tasted the hazards of being away from home, and will appreciate all the more the advantages of maintaining his links with family and his society. (189)

Returning to the initial point of departure, the travelers rejoin the community they call home. Moreover, the journey outward results in lucidity, in self-understanding. The heroes or heroines return wiser and, as more mature individuals, will assume their position within the community.

In traditional society, which emphasizes communal values, the journey is shown to benefit both the individual and the community. Having gained wisdom and maturity on the journey of initiation, the protagonists of oral narrative will take their place among the elders. In modern francophone African fiction, however, the "happy ending," depicted as a return to the bosom of the community, is often impossible. On the one hand, protagonists become acculturated to a modern world and no longer fit into traditional society. On the other hand, the stable society, an ideal represented in oral narrative, no longer exists in African society, which is caught up in the rapid transformation brought about by colonialism and postcolonialism. With reintegration impossible, Kane's protagonist, Samba Diallo, meets violence at the hands of a member of his own community upon his return home. Denying his protagonist reintegration, Mouloud Mammeri concludes *Le Sommeil du juste* with a similar but less violent example of rupture. Imprisoned by French authorities for nationalist activities, Arezki cannot return to his Algerian village. At the end of his journey, however, he is able to reestablish bonds with his family; Arezki shares their fate when he joins them in a prison cell. Hence, the clan is reunited — but in limbo — as the Algerian liberation struggle begins.

Arezki's itinerary leads him to political awareness. He gains the wisdom and maturity to struggle for political and social transformation. Whereas in oral narrative the journey's reward is reintegration, the novel expresses success in terms of self-understanding and group consciousness. With its emphasis upon transformation, the African novel is evolutionary (if not revolutionary); the oral narrative, in contrast, is fundamentally conservative.

Although various techniques of oral narrative reappear in the written tales of "literate" storytellers, the written text cannot truly convey the oral performance. Storytelling is an art usually confined to nightfall, to the hours when eerie sounds are heard, when mysterious creatures stalk the earth — at least in one's imagination. It is then that the verbal magician can relate tales of mystery and enchantment against the backdrop of the night. In the storyteller's performance, dialogue comes alive through voice and gesture. In addition, the audience at a live performance, unlike the reader of a written text, is in constant rapport with the storyteller.

Techniques used by "literate" storytellers include dialogue, repetition, songs and refrains, and questions to engage the audience.[4] Repetition (of words, phrases, situations) is an important mnemonic device of African oral narrative. When it reappears in written tales and novels, its purpose is to simulate orality and it is no longer an *aide-mémoire* for the storyteller. Similarly, songs and refrains that in the oral context allow the storyteller to engage the audience are used by the "literate" storyteller to emphasize the oral tradition, bringing African song and poetry into the French-language text.[5] In addition, by engaging the audience in dialogue through questions, the performing storyteller, involving the audience directly in the narrative process, succeeds in creating spontaneity. Although spontaneity is unattainable in a written text, questions posed to the reader simulate dialogue between the storyteller and the public, thereby encouraging the reader to participate vicariously in the narrative process.

In francophone Africa, the professional storyteller is often called a *griot*. Derived from the Wolof word *gewel*, the term originated with French anthropologists. The *griot* appears in African literary texts in two ways. In *Les Bouts de bois de Dieu*, Ousmane Sembène bestows upon the charismatic leader Bakayoko the *griot*'s power of persuasive speech; Bakayoko is a brilliant orator. At the same time, the novelist as narrator assumes the role of *griot*, professional storyteller and community historian. As Sembène transforms the individual journey to self-understanding into a collective one, he uses his mastery of the word to promote a new sense of communal identity.

Presenting a distinct voice in African fiction and a unique relationship to the literary genre, Ahmadou Kourouma adopts various elements of orature. In addition to employing oral narrative structures, *Les Soleils des indépendances* borrows freely from the *griot*'s bag of tricks, making use of dialogue, repetition, songs, proverbs, digressions, and questions to engage the audience. These techniques simulate the spontaneity of oral performance and alter the relationship between narrator and reader, and between the written and the spoken word.

Kourouma experiments with language; he infuses French prose with Malinké expressions in order to depict convincingly a traditional protagonist who has not acquired the French education that would ensure him a place among the elite in postcolonial Africa. Modifying both structure and language, the Ivoirian novelist adapts the European novel to African needs and specifications. Like Sembène, Kourouma attempts to find a common ground where distinctly different cultural heritages can meet.

The Ivoirian novelist does not "use" the language of the colonizer merely to prove that unlike Fama, the Malinké prince, he has mastered literacy. *Les Soleils des indépendances* reminds the reader that although the colonial language opens doors to the modern world, it may be viewed by former colonized peoples with ambivalence — as a tool of liberation *and* oppression. The language that provides a window on a new world, on modernity, bears traces of the blood of conquest. Kourouma's novel illustrates the process that Deleuze and Guattari call "deterritorialization."[6] Although the novelist writes in hegemonic French, he subverts or "deterritorializes" the language of the colonizer. Thus, Kourouma is representative of African writers who are struggling to transform and adapt the French language in order to express an authentic identity and worldview.

In its rejection of the French "civilizing mission," however, Kourouma's novel joins an earlier tradition. Among Caribbean and sub-Saharan African writers, the refusal of assimilation coupled with the valorization of African culture gave rise to the Negritude movement of the 1930s. In North Africa, the concept of assimilation was initially challenged by the Algerian poet Jean Amrouche in the late 1930s and pursued further by the "generation of 1954," writers espousing the cause of Algerian independence.

The beginnings of francophone African fiction, however, were predominantly assimilationist, embracing French culture with great enthusiasm. Turning to largely forgotten archives, the literary historian can trace the beginnings of francophone African fiction to the

1920s. In 1925, Abdelkader Hadj Hamou, assuming the pen name
A. Fikri, published *Zohra, la femme du mineur*, the first novel written
by an Algerian in French.[7] The first sub-Saharan francophone African
novel, Bakary Diallo's *Force-Bonté*, was published the following year.[8]
Bakary Diallo and Fikri (and later Fikri's Algerian compatriots, the
Zenatis) share a firm belief in French assimilation as well as a common
colonial language. In addition to the novels, French-language journals
appeared in the colonies, the first in 1913.[9]

A first-person linear narrative, *Force-Bonté* relates the life of a
Peul youth from his beginnings as a shepherd boy in a remote
Senegalese village to his experience as a soldier, a *tirailleur sénégalais*.
The youth, Bakary, is sent on a pacification mission to Morocco.
Wounded in combat, he is moved to a hospital in France. Although
Bakary wishes to acquire French citizenship, his hopes are dashed
when, despite his excellent war record, the request is denied. Firmly
patriotic toward France, Bakary blames French bureaucracy for
thwarting his dream but never wavers in his love for his adopted
country.

Readers of African fiction expecting to find disillusionment with
European values, a search for authenticity, and a clear rejection of
colonialism in francophone African fiction are surprised by Bakary's
expression of dependency. The protagonist's attitude is illustrated in
the closing pages of the novel. Upon noticing a French woman
feeding birds in a park, he exclaims: "Oh! How sweet to see this! For
it seems to me that we are these birds, the Blacks who wish to love,
and that this woman is France!" (207).* Proclaiming the inferior
status of the African, Daillo's novel was doomed to oblivion by
subsequent generations embracing Negritude. In similar fashion,
Maghrebian writers cast aside the assimilationist writings of Fikri
and the Zenati brothers.[10]

Force-Bonté is the first francophone African novel to introduce
the journey motif. The structure of the novel anticipates later texts
such as *L'Enfant noir* and *L'Aventure ambiguë*, in which the novelist
traces a journey outward, from the African village to France. Moreover, Bakary's itinerary also leads to the psychological transformation
that foreshadows the rupture with traditional life that occurs in both
later works. His experience in France leads Bakary to exclaim, "I

---

* "Ah! Que c'est doux à voir. Car il me semble que ces oiseaux, c'est nous, les noirs
qui désirent aimer, et que cette Dame est la France!" (207).

swear that you (the French) have transformed me, head, heart, spirit, and soul" (205).*

Like Camara Laye and Kane, Diallo emphasizes autobiographical elements of the narrative by giving his own name to the protagonist (Kane, however, creates ambiguity: only the informed reader will know that Samba Diallo is his name in Poular). Thus, Diallo anticipates the autobiography and mimesis that become important elements in the fiction of the 1950s and 1960s, when African writers find inspiration in their own lives and cultures and imitate this reality. Most important, *Force-Bonté* points to the seductive power of the written word. In an attempt to learn to write, the protagonist scribbles on a whitewashed wall. Bakary's efforts to master writing foreshadow Laye's awe before the blackboard (*L'Enfant noir*) and Samba's fascination with the European alphabet (*L'Aventure ambiguë*).[11] Despite its assimilationist message, *Force-Bonté* anticipates later African fiction. Diallo discovers the power of the pen, an instrument that future generations will craft into a subversive weapon of "deterritorialization."

In this exploration of the journey motif, the emphasis is upon process rather than product. Although we may choose to categorize journeys to lucidity or self-understanding as successful, ambiguous, or thwarted, I maintain that the process is inherently successful. The physical and/or spiritual experience of the journey rather than its destination, engage the reader's interest and provide an approach to African fiction. Nevertheless this study poses a dual dialectic: successful vs. thwarted journeys on the one hand, outer journeys vs. enclosure on the other. A comparative study of Kateb Yacine's *Nedjma* with Ousmane Sembène's *Les Bouts de bois de Dieu* (in chapter 3) illustrates the first dichotomy; a discussion of African women's writing (the novels of Mariama Bâ, Assia Djebar, Ken Bugul, and Leïla Sebbar in chapters 5 and 6) explores the second.

Using historical confrontations as a frame for individual and collective maturation, Kateb focuses upon Algerian uprisings in Sétif and Guelma in 1945; Sembène depicts the Dakar-Niger railway strike of 1947. In *Nedjma*, Kateb portrays four protagonists who can escape neither from the spell of the mysterious Nedjma nor from the circle of violence that surrounds them. In colonial Algeria, these men

---

* Vous [les Français] m'avez changé, je vous le jure, la tête, le coeur, l'esprit et l'âme (205).

journey from construction site to prison and back, their lives marked by an absence of itinerary. Kateb links the spatial dialectic, itinerary vs. aimless wandering, to temporal conflict of past, present, and future. The very concept of itinerary is lacking and can only return to the lives of these individuals when Algeria wins independence and the nation emerges from the colonial past. Kateb depicts transformation through defeat: the Algerian uprising of 1945, a foreshadowing of the liberation struggle in the next decade, is harshly repressed by the French authorities. The nationalist struggle, however, continues. Sembène's novel, in contrast, portrays political victory: the successful railway workers strike. Moreover, the women's march to Dakar, a collective demonstration that successfully challenges colonial authority, initiates the general strike that results in the railway workers' triumph.

By projecting African women toward political action, *Les Bouts de bois de Dieu* challenges societal norms. This novel "deterritorializes" space just as *Les Soleils des indépendances* "deterritorializes" language. Sembène not only writes African women into fiction two decades before the emergence of sub-Saharan francophone women writers; he also gives several female protagonists — Ramatoulaye, Penda, Maimouma — revolutionary scripts. Therefore, the *griot*-narrator confirms the iconoclastic nature of Penda's role as political organizer: "It was the first time in living memory that a woman had spoken in public in Thies..." (255)*. When she proposes the women's march to Dakar, Penda is responding to a community crisis, the railway workers' strike, by moving women into public space. Her actions, both the fiery speech and the march, foreshadow a demand for freedom to enter public space that marks later Maghrebian and sub-Saharan African women's fiction.[12]

A Berber proverb succinctly expresses the spatial limitation traditionally placed on women's freedom of movement: "Man is the outer lamp; woman is the inner lamp." Since men are given the opportunity to make the journey outward, returning home wiser for the experience, and women are usually barred from doing so, this study will explore the implications of gender-based spatial norms in African fiction. It will test the premise that novels written by African male writers present their conquest of public space formerly reserved

---

* De mémoire d'homme c'était la première fois qu'une femme avait pris la parole en public à Thiès...(289).

to the colonizer, hence the journey outward, whereas the African women writers' fiction depicts an inner journey initiated by enclosure. In the chapters exploring women's fiction, I will be seeking answers to the following questions: If the journey and its concomitant rewards of maturity and self-understanding have been primarily an option reserved for men in African society, how do women compensate for the restriction upon travel?[13] Do traditional restrictions have a positive value? In other words, do they result in a rich inner life? Annis Pratt states that women's escape through imagination is not escapist but strategic, a withdrawal into the unconscious for the purpose of personal transformation (177). What strategies of escape occur in francophone African women's fiction?

Because of the dominance of African male writers, critics have tended to approach African literature from the point of view of male experience. As I focus upon women's experience of enclosure and escape in the concluding chapters, I urge the reader to bear in mind that enclosure in male fiction (Kateb Yacine's protagonist locked in a circle of violence, for example) differs from enclosure in women's fiction; the former originates in colonialism, the latter in both colonialism and patriarchy.

Readers of African literature must be conscious of cultural elements that writers introduce in their works, including culturally specific aspects of patriarchy. However, feminist critical methodologies (both Western and non-Western) can prove extremely useful to the study of African fiction. A case in point is Sandra Gilbert and Susan Gubar's study of British and American women writers, *The Madwoman in the Attic.* Exploring the texts of women from Jane Austen and Charlotte Brontë to Emily Dickinson, Virginia Woolf, and Sylvia Plath, they find recurrent images of enclosure and escape:

> Both in life and in art, we saw, the artists we studied were literally and figuratively confined. Enclosed in the architecture of an over-whelmingly male-dominated society, these literary women were also, inevitably, trapped in the specifically literary constructs of what Gertrude Stein was to call "patriarchal poetry." For not only did a nineteenth-century woman writer have to inhabit ancestral mansions (or cottages) owned and built by men, she was also constricted and restricted by the Palaces of Art and Houses of Fiction male writers authored. We decided, therefore, that the striking coherence we noticed in literature by women could be explained by a common, female impulse to struggle free from social and literary confinement through strategic redefinitions of self, art, and society. (xi—xii)

Despite the fact that patriarchal structures of Victorian England and contemporary Africa are not identical (and that patriarchy varies within the African continent as well), the images of enclosure as well as the impulse to break free which Gilbert and Gubar discover in Victorian literature correspond to patterns in francophone African women's fiction. Exchanging one archetypal victim of enclosure for another, with the image of the slave woman buried alive replacing Rochester's mad wife in the attic in Charlotte Brontë's *Jane Eyre*, Florence Stratton introduces the possibility of a universal female literary tradition. Her study of archetypes in African women's writing reveals a psychological and artistic response to patriarchy that transcends cultural specificity.[14]

My study of African women's fiction similarly discloses the psychological and linguistic effects of enclosure upon women's creative work. I will show that just as the outer journey leads the traveling hero or heroine to lucidity and self-understanding, the inner journey — which includes personal thoughts, past memories, the collective experience of the family or the clan — helps the African female protagonist develop the inner strength necessary in a twofold struggle against the vestiges of colonialism and the present grip of traditional patriarchy. The Senegalese writer Mariama Bâ places this struggle within the West African Islamic context. Her novel *Une si longue lettre* illustrates the positive aspects of enclosure, that is, of private space used as refuge. Assia Djebar's most recent novels, *L'amour, la fantasia*, and *Ombre sultane*, distinguish between the comforting haven conducive to female bonding and threatening confinement, where woman is victim. Nevertheless, Bâ and Djebar both express the need to "struggle free from social and literary confinement" (Gilbert and Gubar). They lay claim to public space; at the same time, they view the act of writing, empowerment through language, as an important process that leads to liberation and transformation.

In her work, Djebar depicts the three traditional forms of female enclosure of the Arab world: the *harem* (women's secluded quarters), the *haïk* (veil), and the *hammam* (bath). Emphasizing the importance of the freedom to circulate in public space, Djebar views the harem and veil as threatening confinement, but the hammam as comforting refuge. Her fiction illustrates Fatima Mernissi's sociological findings concerning the significance of spatial boundaries in Islamic societies.

In *Beyond the Veil*, the Moroccan sociologist explores the effects of gender-based spatial division in Muslim society: the universe of men — the *umma* or public sphere — and the universe of women — the private or domestic sphere. Traditionally, when women entered public space they were trespassing on men's territory; hence, in some parts of the Muslim world, women could only enter public space veiled. Mernissi calls attention to the fact that the term for a woman who is not veiled is "nude" (*aryana* in Moroccan Arabic); the Arabic language confirms her vulnerability. Although Mernissi calls for the liberty to circulate without constraints in public space, she is fully aware that the demands of modernization conflict with traditional patriarchy. Her more recent study, *Le Harem politique*, is a direct challenge to traditional patriarchy by documenting that incorrect interpretations of religion have been used to prohibit women from entering public space.[15] Novelists Ken Bugul and Leïla Sebbar, who depict female protagonists in flight and exile, are similarly challenging tradition. In their portrayal of the traveling heroine, these writers adapt the conventions of the picaresque, a male literary tradition. Bugul and Sebbar's affirmation of the outward trajectory traditionally denied women runs counter to the rules of patriarchy.

In exploring the journey motif in francophone African fiction, this study points to bonds across the Sahara. The "dry sea," often perceived as a barrier, has in fact been a major trade route for Africans. Although the Maghreb was spared the European slave trade, the experience of nineteenth-century colonialism as well as the impact and importance of Islam link North Africa to sub-Saharan Africa. In the early 1950s, Maghrebian and sub-Saharan African writers, formed by a common French colonial school system, began to describe the life of the African hybrid whose double acculturation — European and African — resulted in an ambiguous adventure. It is not surprising that Camara Laye's *L'Enfant noir*, as a cultural document of a vanishing Africa and a psychological portrait of a cultural hybrid, bears a striking resemblance to an Algerian autobiographical novel of the same era, Mouloud Feraoun's *Le Fils du pauvre*. Both works express the writer's debt to oral tradition. Camara Laye remembers the Malinké *griot* who, by singing the blacksmith's praises, inspired his craftsmanship. Feraoun recalls his aunt's stories of crafty M'Quidech, who outwits his evil opponents; the Algerian novelist concludes that Khalti's gift to him of dream and imagination was crucial to his later development as a writer (50–51).

I have noted that a comparative study of Sembène's *Les Bouts de bois de Dieu* and Kateb's *Nedjma* illustrates the dialectic of successful vs. thwarted journeys. Both novelists, one Senegalese, the other Algerian, use historical confrontations between colonizer and colonized as a frame and a catalyst for individual and collective maturation in the period leading to independence. In Sembène's text, the successful Dakar-Niger railway strike of 1947 profoundly alters the lives of the protagonists, giving rise to a communal political consciousness. In Kateb's work, the Algerian uprisings that occur a decade before the beginning of the Algerian Revolution, although harshly repressed, similarly transform the lives of the participants. Finally, both novels express a national identity rooted in precolonial history and transcending a tribal and colonial past.

Turning to the postcolonial era, I do not claim that Kourouma's *Les Soleils des indépendances* and Mammeri's *La Traversée* reflect an identical reality, but rather that disillusionment in postcolonial Africa coupled with allegiance to a threatened culture result in their shared preoccupation with death. Kourouma and Mammeri, one Ivoirian, the other Algerian, are both committed to exposing corruption, repression, hypocrisy, Kourouma's Fama uncovers pervasive corruption in the course of his travels from the city to the village and back. Mammeri's Mourad loses all illusions as he travels through the Sahara. For both protagonists, the journey to lucidity results in the recognition of their marginality as well as disillusionment.

The purpose of juxtaposing Maghrebian and sub-Saharan fiction in four of the six chapters of this book is to disclose affinities between texts. While I do not attempt in depth contrastive analyses in this study, I hope that my initial efforts will encourage critics to explore a neglected path.[16]

In addition, I hope that my choice of texts will not appear arbitrary to readers.* I have chosen works in which the physical journey is a key thematic element and structuring device. With one exception, each journey to self-understanding, from Conrad's *Heart of Darkness* to Sebbar's *Les Carnets de Shérazade*, originates in a physical voyage.[17]

Finally, I urge the reader who joins me on this journey through the texts to bear in mind the multiple heritage reflected in the African writer's choice of the journey motif. The adventures of traveling heroes and heroines are rooted in both the African oral tradition and the European novel. Furthermore, journeys correspond to African

---

* The translations are my own, except where otherwise indicated.

reality, reflecting a history of migrations, explorations, and conquest. With this multiple heritage in mind, I will put forth two arguments in this study: first, the appropriateness of the journey motif as a means of understanding and appreciating the modern francophone African novel; second, the importance of cultural blending in a literary tradition that owes a great debt to the spoken word.

Chapter 1

▼▼▼▼▼▼▼

From the Colonialist to the African Novel

JOSEPH CONRAD, *Heart of Darkness*
CAMARA LAYE, *L'Enfant noir*

Marlow's Quest

Literary expression of the journey, which for many became a maturing experience resulting in greater political and psychological awareness, is a theme shared by colonizer and colonized. In European fiction, for example, Joseph Conrad's *Heart of Darkness* presents the seaman Marlow, who gains insight into himself as he makes his way up the Congo River to meet the enigmatic Kurtz. In francophone African fiction, Camara Laye's *L'Enfant noir* recounts a young boy's initiation into both traditional and Western ways as he moves from Kouroussa, a town in Guinea, to Conakry, the Guinean capital, and finally to Paris.

The journey of the European outsider, Marlow, who is taking part in the historical process of colonial expansion, is quite different from Laye's. Whereas Laye will recall with nostalgia the years of childhood and youth that represent a gradual moving away from his father's forge and his mother's hut, Marlow will remember nightmare, disillusionment, and finally ultimate hypocrisy embodied in "the lie" he fabricates for Kurtz's fiancée. In contrast to the African child's formal and informal initiation into adult Malinké society, the uninitiated Marlow has no prior preparation on either continent, Europe or Africa, for the situations that he will confront on his journey. Ian Watt, however, views Marlow's visit to the trading company in Brussels as a progressive initiation and even Marlow's approach through unfamiliar streets to the building as the beginning of the rite of passage. When Marlow meets the director and sees the two knitters in the office guarding the door of Darkness, the scene offers a symbolic interpretation of the narrative as a descent into hell. As Watt explains:

> When the scene ends we can look back and see that Marlow is left with a sense of a doubly fraudulent initiation; the company has not told him what he wants to know: but since Marlow has been unable to formulate the causes of his formal discomfort, much less ask any authentic questions or voice any protest, his own tranced submission has been a betrayal of himself. These implications pre-figure what we are to see as one of the larger and more abstract themes of the story—the lack of any genuine reciprocal dialogue: even Marlow cannot or does not speak out. (194)

Marlow has the technical skills necessary to navigate up the Congo River but is not equipped with the interpersonal skills needed to comprehend his surroundings as he does so. He states: "The prehistoric man was cursing us, praying to us, welcoming us—Who could tell? We were cut off from the comprehension of our surroundings" (96).[1] Unable to comprehend because he is unable to communicate with the indigenous Africans, Marlow can never bring himself to view them, fellow pilgrims on life's journey, as human beings like himself. He sees Africans as total strangers and describes their "otherness" as primitive, prehistoric, inferior.

Offended by the depersonalization of Africans in the novella, the Nigerian novelist Chinua Achebe has called Conrad "a bloody racist" (9) for describing Africans leaping and howling in the bush and for portraying Kurtz as someone once "civilized" who then degenerates mentally and physically in Africa. Whether Conrad is endorsing a stereotyped vision of Africa or treating it ironically, one point to acknowledge is that Marlow's physical journey results in an inner one. Despite the spectacle of natives howling, shouting, attacking the steamboat with spears, and provoking the boat's gunfire, Marlow's journey is one of self-discovery, Albert Guérard notes that at the beginning of the novella Marlow does not know himself; at the end he is a mature man (9). Linking maturity to humanist values, Peter Nazareth concludes that Marlow's maturity results in the erosion of an inherited racist framework (177).

The reader learns that Marlow, in his quest, appears as an outsider, ill at ease with the Europeans he mocks and with the Africans he cannot fathom. What communication is possible between Marlow and the creatures who howl and grunt? To Marlow's ears, unaccustomed to the sounds of African languages, the Africans "exchange short grunting phrases" (103). Speech belongs to the civilized, to the Europeans, as we see in the following exchange between Marlow and a native crewman: "'Catch 'em' he snapped with a bloodshot widening of his eyes and a flash of sharp teeth — 'catch 'im. Give 'im to us'. 'To you, eh?' I asked: 'what would you do with them?' 'Eat 'em!' he said" (103). This conversation reinforces in Marlow the fear of falling victim to cannibals.[2] Conrad then tantalizes the reader with the possibility of another exchange between European and African. As Marlow's wounded helmsman lies dying, Marlow says, "I declare it looked as though he would put to us some question in some understandable language" (112). The helmsman dies in silence, a deep frown crossing his face. Towards the end of the novella, the manager's boy, described as insolent and contemptuous, will announce in pidgin English, "Mistah Kurtz — he dead" (150).

Unable to engage in meaningful dialogue and having no friends among the Europeans, Marlow longs to talk to Kurtz, to hear the voice of the ivory collector about whom he has heard so much. The voice more than anything else beckons Marlow up the river. Yet all Marlow learns from this dying man is "the horror! the horror!" (194), words that acknowledge the collapse of the colonial dream. Kurtz, the man with great intentions, has become, in Marlow's words, "hollow at the core" (131).

Marlow leaves Africa with no fond memories of the voyage and with a profound sense of disillusionment. In this, the protagonist indeed reflects the attitude of the author. Conrad as a child had dreamed of traveling to Africa. Yet when his childhood fantasy materialized, he discovered great loneliness in the heart of the continent. For Conrad, Africa was first conceptualized as a blank, a "blank darkness" that Christopher Miller finds to be consistent with the prevailing view of Africa in the nineteenth century,[3] and one that Conrad's biographer Gérard Jean-Aubry traces back to Conrad's childhood:

> It was in 1868, when nine years old or thereabouts, that while looking at a map of Africa of the time and putting my finger on the blank space then representing the unsolved mystery of the continent, I said to myself with absolute assurance and an amazing audacity which are no longer in my character now:
> "When I grow up I shall go *there*."
> And of course I thought no more about it till after a quarter of a century or so an opportunity offered to go there — as if the sin of childhood audacity was to be visited upon my mature head. (153)

Yet after traveling *there*, Conrad writes from Stanley Falls in 1890:

> A great melancholy descended on me. Yes, this was the very spot. But there was no shadowy friend to stand by my side in the night of the enormous wilderness, no great haunting memory, but only the unholy recollection of a prosaic newspaper "stunt" and the distasteful knowledge of the vilest scramble for loot that ever disfigured the history of human realities of a boy's daydreams. I wondered what I was doing there, for indeed it was only an unforeseen episode, hard to believe in now, in my seaman's life. Still, the fact remains that I have smoked a pipe of peace at midnight in the very heart of the African continent, and felt very lonely there. (169)

In *Heart of Darkness* Conrad returns to his early memories of a child's fascination with the map of Africa. His boyhood fantasy, however, is significantly transformed. Marlow states:

> At that time there were many blank spaces on the earth, and when I saw one that looked particularly inviting on a map (but they all look that) I would put my finger on it and say, when I grow up I will go there. . . . True, by this time, it was not a blank space anymore. It had got filled since my boyhood with rivers and lakes and names. It had ceased to be a blank space of delightful mystery — a white patch for a boy to dream gloriously over. But there was in it one river especially, a mighty big river, that you could see on the map, resembling an immense snake uncoiled, with its head in the sea, its body at rest curving afar over a vast country, and its tail lost in the depths of the land. (52)

The blank places are now named and settled by Europeans who in their Eurocentrism are unaware that Africans had given place-names to land and water before the arrival of Europeans.[4] As for the river, it is an *uncoiled* snake because Marlow's journey into the "heart of darkness," the center of Africa, is a linear one. He travels up the river to meet Kurtz and travels back down again before heading home to Europe. Of course, the snake as symbol of temptation is all too clear, enticing Marlow to take a bite of the colonial apple.

Once Marlow has met Kurtz and realizes that the man has been destroyed by the colonial venture, he has no choice but to leave. The would-be empire builder wears the mask of death. Recognizing Kurtz in himself, Marlow must depart before the same demons — greed, debauchery, violence — attack him as well.

Conrad criticizes the colonial venture in Africa, not only as a vile scramble for loot, but for its cruel exploitation of Africans. In a frequently quoted passage that reveals Conrad's humanitarian impulses, he shows Africans dying because of the colonial venture. Europeans are working them to death. Marlow states: "They were dying slowly — it was clear. They were not enemies, they were not criminals, they were nothing earthly now — nothing but black shadows of disease and starvation, lying confusedly in the greenish gloom" (66). Then, in a humanitarian gesture, he gives one a biscuit, using the word *man* for the first and only time in the passage: "The *man* seemed young — almost a boy — but you know with them it's hard to tell" (67, emphasis mine).

Just as he is about to acknowledge kinship with the sick man, Marlow draws back, distancing himself. He notices that the African has a bit of wool yarn around his neck. Because he does not understand the purpose of the yarn and suspects that it is a sign of superstition, Marlow is disconcerted. A moment later, Marlow is "horror-struck" to see that another sick African "went off on all-fours towards the river to drink. He lapped out of his hand" (67). Having acknowledged the native as a man, Marlow now draws back once more and creates distance by showing the latter's animal-like behavior. We may conclude from this brief episode that the one biscuit offered a starving human being is all the charity that Marlow — and perhaps Conrad — is able to muster.

The colonial experience that Conrad came to know in Central Africa in the 1890s was physically dangerous for Europeans. On Conrad's voyage from Kinshasa to Stanley Falls, his boat picked up a dying agent, Georges-Antoine Klein, who provides one model for Kurtz in the novella. According to Jean-Aubry, the two men, Klein and Kurtz, were quite alike (170). Jean-Aubry also notes that a study of Conrad's original manuscript reveals that Conrad had, in one place at least, changed the words Monsieur Klein to read Mr. Kurtz.[5] Watt states, however, that except for his illness, death, and international origins, Klein was not a convincing model. Other names — Arthur Eugene Hodester, Emin Pasha (Eduard Schniter), Major Edmund Musgrave Barttletot, and Charles Henry Stokes — are all possibilities. These men all have in common the fact that they went "fantee," adopting native customs, and died violent deaths in Africa (144).

Some colonialists died violently; others died of fever. Moreover, the colonial venture that proved dangerous also became degrading. In the alien environment where a European could live with little or no external controls on behavior, he could become a megalomaniac like Kurtz. Conrad depicts the latter worshipped as a deity by natives whom he rules by terror. In addition, this colonial venture is sharply defined by gender; only white males embark on the journey of conquest in the name of the civilizing mission.

In the interior, Kurtz, the colonial agent, has an African mistress. She is portrayed by Conrad as a wild and mysterious apparition:

> She walked with measured steps, draped in striped and fringed cloths treading the earth proudly, with a slight jingle and flash of barbarous ornaments. She carried her head high; her hair was done in the shape of a helmet; she had brass leggings to the knee, brass wire gauntlets to the elbow, a crimson spot on her tawny cheek, innumerable necklaces of glass beads on her neck; bizarre things, charms, gifts of witch-men, that hung about her, glittered and trembled at every step. She must have had the value of several elephant tusks upon her. She was savage and superb, wild-eyed and magnificent; there was something ominous and stately in her deliberate progress. And in the hush that had fallen suddenly upon the whole sorrowful land, the immense wilderness, the colossal body of the fecund and mysterious life seemed to look at her, pensive, as though it had been looking at the image of its own tenebrous and passionate soul. (135–36)

This woman is temptress, not maternal goddess. There are even hints of the Amazon about her—her vitality, helmet headdress, leggings. Yet the crimson spot on her cheek, a fantasy of the author, is a bit of exotic make-up primarily for the romantic fantasies of the armchair traveler. The faithful reader of *Blackwood's Magazine* in England, eager for tales about natives, ivory traders, and beautiful native women, would never be able to check the imaginary against the real.

In her world in which whites have come to dominate blacks, the European ivory trader's mistress retains a certain authority and preserves some dignity. Nevertheless, the "African Princess" is presented according to Conrad's formula. She too presumably grunts and howls. We never hear her words. We know that she talks to Kurtz and we are informed of one conversation. However, the actual words never reach either us or Marlow because the only witness, Kurtz's Russian assistant, does not understand the dialect. (Africans never speak languages, only dialects, in colonialist literature!) In his portrait of this African woman as she stands on the shore watching the boat pull away, Marlow studies her body movements and her facial expressions. Since the boat has come to take Kurtz away, her face predictably and understandably registers sorrow and pain. Conrad gives her a "*fierce* aspect of *wild* sorrow and *dumb* pain" (136, emphasis mine). The author clearly wants her to appear as the sister of the poor African who went off on all fours. She too is a wild thing with animal instincts. It is not clear whether the "wild and gorgeous apparition of a woman" (135) has lured Kurtz into his world of evil; I see her rather as concrete proof of his fall. Yet M. M. Mahood concludes: "She and the wilderness are one. The call of the wild comes from the Africans themselves and tribal life is presented in this part of the story as an agent of demoralization" (29).

Conrad also claims the inferiority of the natives by portraying them as children. He writes: "I don't think a single one of them had any clear idea of time as we at the end of countless ages have" (103). Miller concludes: "These people are thus stuck in time, prior to time and outside it, in a 'perpetual childhood'" (179). Conrad wants his readers to believe that the natives locked in their "perpetual childhood" are capable of accepting Kurtz as a deity just as the African child, Laye, later views his father, the Malinké blacksmith, a man with special gifts, almost as a divine figure. This view that Conrad presents is highly inaccurate. On the one hand, Africans did not open their secret societies and religious practices to European Christians. On the other hand, African religion consistently taught a social code. Furthermore, as Mahood explains: "No African religion that has been put on record could accurately be described as devil worship" (27).

More in keeping with reality, however, is Conrad's acknowledgment of respect for the power of the word in African societies. Conrad presents Kurtz as a European who understands and speaks the indigenous language and who uses it skillfully as a technique for domination. Journalist, poet, and orator—Kurtz gains power among the natives because of his ability to make magic, a fetish, out of language (Miller 180). Language becomes a key actor in Conrad's binary world. Yet Africans are depicted without a language; they grunt and howl. Moreover, Kurtz, the colonizer, not only has the power of speech but speaks *eloquently*.

In contrast to Kurtz settled on the mainland, Marlow is aboard ship most of the time. As a traveler, not a settler, Marlow does not have the close contact with African village life that would allow him to learn their language and their customs. Yet, in the long term, the traveler is more fortunate than the settler. Marlow is spared the physical isolation that proves so damaging to Kurtz's psyche. One time, Marlow is tempted to go ashore, "for a howl and a dance," but refrains from doing so. Interjecting the work ethic, he formulates an excuse. He is too busy repairing his ship to be tempted by native drums.

Thus, although Marlow is fascinated by Kurtz, he is very different from him. Whereas Marlow can impose self-control and takes pride in himself as a worker, Kurtz reveals a progressive lack of restraint. As he disintegrates physically and psychologically, Kurtz's empire building takes the form of making empty speeches and forcing others, the Africans, to collect ivory for him.[6]

When Conrad visited the Congo in 1890, he found it less primitive than the region depicted in *Heart of Darkness*. Conrad's diary, from June 13 to August 1, 1890, reveals a region where missionaries, soldiers, explorers, ships' captains, and commercial agents were all involved in bringing "civilization" to the country. The Inner Station was a large settlement. By 1893, it included various elements of European organizations—a hospital, a police barracks, and a prison. In addition, a railway was under construction at the time. It is interesting too that Conrad's novella makes no mention of the conflict between the Belgian authorities and the Arabs who were raiding the local villages of the region for slaves and ivory. The Arabs, like Kurtz, posed a threat to official commercial interest (Watt 141). We must assume that the contrast between Conrad's experience in a region that was more organized and developed than the world surrounding both Kurtz and Marlow is intended to heighten the isolation of his characters. Conrad stresses the physical and spiritual isolation of both men by placing them in a wilderness for the symbolic descent into hell. But in so doing, he distorts reality.

Kurtz, the greedy ivory hunter in the remote outpost, keeps shrunken heads on doorposts to decorate his compound. Although startled by Kurtz's savagery, Marlow resolves to protect the reputation of the company agent to the bitter end. Remaining faithful both to Kurtz and to his own nightmare, Marlow lies to Kurtz's fiancée and assures her that he was indeed a fine person. One can only wonder: Is the lie meant for Europe as well? Just as Marlow is disturbed by Kurtz's violence, readers may be troubled by the possibility that Conrad may be endorsing the very colonial venture he criticizes for its cruelty, hypocrisy, absurdity. Is Marlow unable to tell the truth in Brussels because Kurtz has indeed become a hero to him?

Susan L. Blake states, "Kurtz, devil that he is, becomes a hero to Marlow because he acknowledges his deviltry; heroism becomes a matter of individual consciousness unrelated to its effect on other people" (403). I do not believe that Kurtz has become Marlow's hero and I question Blake's use of the term; Marlow has discovered that Kurtz is a hollow man. Marlow had gone up the river to meet a god but had, in fact, come face-to-face with Satan. Having confronted Kurtz, Marlow is then obsessed with the latter's deviltry. By telling his story, and by telling it precisely to men with whom he shares a bond (namely fellow sailors who chart the seas), Marlow attempts to exorcise his demons, not to create a legendary hero.

As I mentioned previously, Achebe has attacked Conrad as a racist. Achebe also questions whether the novel, in its treatment of Africans as creatures who are only the remote kin of civilized Europeans, ought to be considered a literary classic. For Achebe the answer is no. My answer is a qualified yes. On the one hand, *Heart of Darkness*, as Achebe admits, does reveal the evils of colonialism as a negative experience for Europeans. Kurtz becomes a man consumed with a greed for ivory, a man without restraint. Unfortunately, Conrad's novella also implies that Kurtz, as the colonialist prototype, is corrupted by his contact with Africans. In this, Jonah Raskin sees Conrad echoing a common belief of his time, and notes that had Conrad embraced the message of J.A. Hobson's *The Psychology of Jingoism*, published in 1901, one year before *Heart of Darkness*, he would have presented the more enlightened view that colonialism, and not the native, was responsible for the corruption (117).

One danger of the text lies in its potential influence upon an uninformed reader who may accept the unjust and inaccurate colonialist bias. The novella presents two distinct sets of negative biases, one racist, the other sexist; two major flaws challenge all readers. The first is one of depersonalization; the other, of omission. Marlow depersonalizes Africans and in so doing renders them mute. He also ignores women. In Conrad's world, women, like the Africans, appear primarily as prisoners of silence. Furthermore, women are usually absent. For example, Kurtz's fiancée remains in Brussels, far removed physically from the colonial venture. She does not participate in it at all.

The sea, Marlow's world, is a man's world. Open seas and unchartered rivers have historically remained off-limits to women. As often portrayed in nineteenth- and twentieth-century fiction, women spend their lives in dimly-lit drawing rooms enclosed with heavy curtains. Kurtz emphasizes the stereotype of woman as weaker vessel when he says "They—the women I mean—are out of it— should be out of it—We must help them to stay in that beautiful world of their own, lest ours gets worse" (115). The choice to bring them in or keep them out, however, becomes Marlow's following the death of Kurtz. Marlow chooses not to inform Kurtz's intended about "the horror! the horror!", not to tell her about the collapse of Kurtz's dream, his fine intentions gone askew. Were Marlow to tell her the truth, he would presumably still not reveal the existence of her rival, the African princess. Yet it is Marlow in the darkened parlor in Brussels who remembers the African woman on the riverbank. Kurtz's fiancée, stretching her arms across a windowpane, reminds the seaman of her. One woman in a closed and darkened room in the "civilized" world, her fair hair set against the backdrop of her dark mourning clothes, reminds Marlow of the other in the wilderness, "stretching bare brown arms over the glitter of the infernal stream, the stream of darkness" (160–61). Portraying the African woman as a wild thing viewed from afar is one stereotype; portraying the intended as a hothouse flower, unable to grasp the ugly reality of the scramble for loot in the wilderness, is yet another.[7]

The story that Marlow tells to his fellow seamen is a tale told among men. Yet it ends with an inconclusive and ambiguous dialogue between a man and a woman. Marlow and the Intended are two strangers who have never met before but are linked by their attachment to a man buried in a remote corner of the "uncivilized" world. He, Marlow, knew Kurtz too well; she, the Intended, sure that she knew him best, knew him least of all. This story, built upon the framework of racial inequality and lack of communication between races, black and white, ends with yet another gap of communication, one between men and women. Marlow refuses to communicate reality, for it is cruel, and instead chooses to say, "the last word he pronounced was your name" (161). He prepares us for this act early in the novella, after bidding his aunt farewell: "It's queer how out of touch with truth women are. They live in a world of their own and there has never been anything like it, and never can be. It is too beautiful altogether, and if they were to set it up it would go to pieces before the first sunset" (59).

One might well question whether Kurtz did not seek to construct for himself an inverted version of this very world described as a female sphere. He replaces beauty with greed. The world quickly becomes one of depravity. In his thirst for ivory, Kurtz destroys the balance of nature. In his greed, he kills animals. He also murders natives and puts their heads on stakes. Transgressing the laws of man and nature, Kurtz finds that his kingdom goes to pieces before the first sunset.

In this study of francophone African fiction, I have chosen to discuss in detail *Heart of Darkness*, Conrad's novella written in English, for two reasons. First, African fiction is a response to colonialist literature. The latter depersonalizes colonial subjects just as the colonial political structure dispossesses them of political rights. Unable to speak up and thereby correct a distorted image, the colonized as object becomes the projection of the colonizer's fantasy. Hence, when African writers take up the pen, they will write *against* the stereotype depicted in colonialist literature. Second, despite a significant body of French colonialist literature written during the period of colonial expansion, from 1871 to 1914, *Heart of Darkness* (*Au coeur des ténèbres* in French) has no counterpart in French literature. Although the French colonialist writer Pierre Loti (the *nom de plume* of Julien Viaud) has received critical attention, studies by Léon Fanoudh-Siefer, Martine Astier-Loutfi, and, more recently, Alec Hargreaves attest to the intellectual and artistic limitations of Loti and his successors. Lacking the depth and complexity of Conrad, they appear more blatantly racist.

In his study of French colonialist literature, Fanoudh-Siefer emphasizes Loti's role in creating the distorted myth of Africa and Africans. Although Loti saw only a small part of Africa, living in Dakar from November 1873 to May 1874 and traveling back and forth to Saint-Louis, he generalized his particular experience: it became representative of all Africa. In Loti's view, Africa is a hostile inferno in which sun, heat, and fever destroy the Europeans taking part in the colonial endeavor. Fanoudh-Siefer explains that Loti presents his readers with "a Black Africa that is desolate, dreadful, strange, mysterious, infernal, a Saturnian land, a land of melancholy and death. It is the land of Ham, a land that is cursed and forsaken by God" (79).[*] Furthermore, Loti's European transplanted to Africa is not only threatened by a hostile climate, either a barren desert or a dense jungle, he is menaced by Africans. Jean Peyral, the protagonist of Loti's novel *Le Roman d'un spahi* (1881), a courageous and upright youth from rural France, is seduced by the sensual and primitive Fatou-Gaye. Proof of her lack of moral conscience is revealed when Fatou repeatedly steals Jean's money and belongings.

---

[*] Une Afrique noire désolée, épouvantable, étrange, mystérieuse, infernale, une terre saturnienne, une terre de mélancolie et de mort. C'est la terre de Cham, une terre maudite et oubliée de Dieu (79).

To prepare the reader for the young Senegalese girl's weakness of character, Loti compares her physically to a monkey. We read "In her little head, as crafty as a young monkey's" (88)* and learn that Jean is disturbed by her black hands with their pink palms; they remind him of *pattes de singe*, monkey's paws (116). Since Fatou's language never evolves beyond pidgin French, she cannot eloquently challenge her French lover's racist biases. When he calls her his *petite fille singe*, Fatou exclaims: "Oh! Tjean! You no say that, my white man! First, a monkey, he not know way to speak — and me know very well!" (118)† Jean never wavers from his belief that Africans are not quite human. When Fatou gives birth to their mulatto child, he is delighted that his son is fair-skinned: "The child had rejected his mother's blood; he resembled Jean completely — he was tanned, but white like the Spahi; he had big deep eyes, and was handsome like him" (216).‡

Finally, Jean shares Kurtz's fate: he dies in Africa, killed in battle with his fellow Spahis, French troups fighting against the army of an African king. In his last moments, Jean prays to the Virgin Mary. Unlike Marlow, who matures in the course of his African odyssey and survives to recount the tale, Loti's protagonist dies as a faithful son of the Cévennes and a loyal colonial soldier.

For Jean Peyral there is no *prise de conscience*, no awareness of the horror of the "civilizing mission" that Kurtz and Marlow both finally acknowledge. Jean probes neither the motives nor the effects of the colonial endeavor on the African continent. Loti keeps his protagonist from ever penetrating the surface of his colonial experience. As the studies of Fanoudh-Siefer and Hargreaves both confirm, the writer's political role in the colonial venture was significantly greater than his literary accomplishment; promoting the dual image of the inferior African and the inhospitable land, Loti granted Europeans an easy conscience.

In contrast, Conrad's novella, which Miller terms a "self-conscious meditation on misunderstanding" (171), initiates the subsequent critique of colonialism as it projects the colonial fantasy. In

---

* Dans sa petite tête, rusée comme celle d'un jeune singe (88).

† "Ah! Tjean! Toi n'y a pas dire ça, mon blac! D'abord, singe, lui, n'y a pas connaît manière pour parler — et moi connais très bien!" (118)

‡ L'enfant n'avait pas voulu du sang de sa mère; il était tout entier de celui de Jean; — il était bronzé, mais blanc comme le spahi; il avait ses grands yeux profonds, il était beau comme lui (216).

other words, Conrad deals in African stereotypes, but also turns the tables on the colonizer when he reveals Kurtz to be the demonic self-destructive prince of darkness. Miller argues that the novella's "self-consciousness...places it at a highly significant crossroads between an old and a new mode of Africanist expression" (171). Therefore, African writers of francophone as well as anglophone fiction have been able to dismiss Jean Peyral and his ilk easily but have had to reflect more seriously upon Kurtz and Marlow, the two looming shadows of Conrad's creation. The first, in the name of progress and civilization, caused evil on the African continent. The second, with a misplaced sense of loyalty, chose to remain faithful to a nightmare, and to perpetuate the lie.

Camara Laye in Quest of a Vanishing Self

When Camara Laye picked up his pen and wrote, "I was a little boy playing around my father's hut" (11),[8]* he was far removed in space and time from the actual scene.[9] Laye was in Paris studying at a technical engineering school and working in an automobile factory rather than in the village of his birth, Kouroussa, in Guinea. In addition, Laye, the son of the village blacksmith, had appropriated modern European technology. As an engineer, a technocrat, he could no longer assume a role in the life of the village that he recalled.

Published in 1953, Laye's autobiographical novel has received considerable international attention in subsequent years for several important reasons. First, it is a challenge to the colonialist novelist's premise that Africa is uncivilized, without culture, a blank darkness. Second, it proves that the indigenous oral culture has become a literate one, with the writer assuming the language of the colonizer. Third, it establishes the African writer as the authentic voice and scribe for a society known intimately from within. Finally, in contrast to the colonialist novel, which is written exclusively for Europeans, Laye's novel is written for Africans and Europeans. The African reading public, quite small when the novel was first published, has grown considerably as Africans throughout the continent have had greater access to schooling. Classics of African literature such as *L'Enfant noir* have become part of the curriculum in African schools.

There was a fifty-year gap between the publication of *Heart of Darkness* in 1902 and *L'Enfant noir* in 1953. Conrad described the

---

* J'étais enfant et je jouais près de la case de mon père (9).

Belgian Congo at the turn of the century; Camara Laye depicted Guinea during the 1930s and early 1940s. By the 1940s the African continent had become home, permanent or temporary, for a significant number of Europeans. Yet they do not figure in young Laye's experience; most lived in cities rather than villages. Thus, Marlow would have encountered more Europeans in Africa had he made his journey thirty years later. In the same vein, Kurtz would have had difficulty finding so isolated a camp in the intervening decades. Critics such as Watt and Raskin, however, explain that even in 1902 Conrad chose to make the landscape more "primitive" than it actually was in order to emphasize Kurtz's spiritual and psychological isolation.[10] Nevertheless, Conrad's armchair traveler, the devotee of *Blackwood's Magazine*, would accept Conrad's exoticism in 1902 more easily than the better-informed reader in 1953.

Agreeing with Abdul JanMohamed that "Conrad systematically uses the Western notion of Africa as an evil place, bereft of social order, where the darker side of human nature can be played out" (3), I would like to examine Laye's novella as a response to Conrad and, by extension, as a response to other colonialist works. In my view, Laye sets himself a twofold task. He wishes to show that the culture ignored and/or denigrated by colonialists, labeled "pagan" or "primitive," is in fact *different* from but not inferior to European culture. He also wishes to define himself, to ask the question, "Who am I?"

In his introduction to the English translation by James Kirkup and Ernest Jones of *L'Enfant noir*, Philippe Thoby Marcelin states, "What gives it its charm, in my opinion, is the aura of dignity with which he surrounded his family and people" (7). As Richard N. Coe points out, however, to affirm the dignity of his Malinké culture, Laye depicts a very happy childhood spent during the colonial period (226–27). This idyllic childhood was the theme that brought the work under attack by African writers such as Mongo Béti, who criticized Camara Laye for ignoring the political realities of the colonial period. The title of Béti's article (published under his real name, Alexandre Biyidi, in *Présence Africaine* in 1955) states his position clearly: "Afrique noire, littérature rose."

If we turn back to *Heart of Darkness*, to one last glimpse of the shoreline as the steamboat leaves Kurtz's outpost, we see through Marlow's eyes an undifferentiated mass of Africans:

> When next day we left at noon, the crowd, of whose presence behind the curtain of trees I had been acutely conscious all the time,

flowed out of the woods again, filled the clearing, covered the slope
with a mass of naked, breathing, quivering bronze bodies. (96)

Laye's task will be to take this mass and differentiate it. To do
so, he begins at the center, presenting his world, his family, and his
childhood experiences. Laye's narrative reflects specific choices. He
chooses to present autobiographical episodes that refer to his individual
maturation process, to his coming of age in Malinké society. Yet
Laye, the individual, is part of a larger community; he is emotionally
attached to his parents, siblings, and to other members of the village.
Evoking his strong bonds to family and community, the narrator
depicts the magical quality of life in his village community. He views
his parents as the most important people in his life and he sees them
both as human beings with supernatural powers. In this vein, Laye
relates a conversation with his father concerning the little black snake
responsible for his father's special powers. The snake warns the
blacksmith about future events. Laye's father tells him:

> "You can see for yourself that I am not more gifted than any other
> man, that I have nothing which other men have not also and even
> that I have less than others, since I give everything away and would
> even give away the last thing I had, the shirt on my back. Neverthe-
> less, I am better known than other men, and my name is on
> everyone's tongue and it is I who have authority over all the
> blacksmiths in the five cantons. If these things are so, it is by virtue
> of this snake alone, who is the guiding spirit of our race. It is to this
> snake that I owe everything, and it is he likewise who gives me
> warning of all that is to happen." (18−19)*

In this episode, Laye views his father with awe and admiration.
The village as well as Laye believe that the man has supernatural
powers and considers him an important man in the community, who
holds sway over "all the blacksmiths in the five cantons." Moreover,
as a blacksmith, Laye's father has the special powers that all Malinké
smiths have. As Mircea Eliade explains, "The blacksmith is the
principal distributing agent of mythologies, rites, and metallurgical

---

* "Tu vois bien toi-même que je ne suis pas plus capable qu'un autre, que je n'ai rien de
plus que les autres, et même que j'ai moins que les autres puisque je donne tout, puis
que je donnerais jusqu'à ma dernière chemise. Pourtant je suis plus connu que les
autres, et mon nom est dans toutes les bouches, et c'est moi qui règne sur tous les
forgerons dans cinq cantons du cercle. S'il est ainsi, c'est par la grâce seule de ce
serpent, génie de notre race. C'est à ce serpent que je dois tout, et c'est lui aussi qui
m'avertit de tout" (19).

mysteries" (*Forgerons et Alchimistes*, 19).* Laye's father, as Sonia Lee notes, is aware of his special status within the community, as a link between the natural and the supernatural world. She adds: "He believes, as his ancestors had believed, and has been chosen to attest to the fact that the visible world is but a small part of the true world, and that one does not need to understand in order to believe" (*Camara Laye*, 22). Thus, were the young Laye to remain with his father, he would learn more than the craft of the blacksmith; the father would share important secrets with his son. Laye would be educated into his father's belief system.

Laye also tells the reader of his mother's impressive magic powers. She is forewarned of the future in dreams and never fears a crocodile because it is her totem. The son remembers how the mother, by means of her powers, once coerced a recalcitrant horse to obey her. Laye concludes: "I have told in very simple language, but very precisely, what I saw that day, saw with my own eyes; and to my mind the thing is incredible; but the event was just as I have described it: the horse got up without any further delay and followed his master. If he had refused to follow him, my mother would have intervened once more, until she had achieved the desired effect" (59–60).†

Thus, in a subtle and indirect way, by depicting his village as a kind of magical kingdom, Laye is giving a new definition to exoticism. He is positing a different but not an inferior culture. It seems clear that Laye wishes to correct prejudices his European readers may have concerning African women. First, he dedicates the novel to his mother, writing: "Black woman, woman of Africa, O my mother, I am thinking of you..." (5).‡ To Laye his mother represents all African mothers who, he insists, are important members of their community. Laye defends the role of women in Malinké society:

> I realize that my mother's authoritarian attitudes may appear sur-
> prising; generally the role of the African woman is thought to be a
> ridiculously humble one, and indeed there are parts of the continent
> where it is insignificant; but Africa is vast, with a correspondingly
> vast diversity of types. In our country, the woman's rule is one of
> fundamental independence; she has great personal pride. We despise

---

* Le forgeron est le principal agent de diffusion des mythologies, des rites, et des mystères métallurgiques (19).

† Je dis très simplement, je dis fidèlement ce que j'ai vu, ce que mes yeux ont vu, et je pense en vérité que c'est incroyable, mais la chose est bien telle que je l'ai dite: le cheval se leva incontinent et suivit son maître; s'il eût refusé d'avancer, l'intervention de ma mère eût eu pareil effet (75).

‡ Femme noire, femme africaine, ô toi ma mère je pense à toi...(7).

only those who allow themselves to be despised; and our women very seldom give cause for that. (58)[*]

As he describes his family, Laye describes his village's social organization and beliefs. Through the young African boy's eyes, the outsider (the non–Malinké reader) becomes acquainted with a society imbued with Islamic and pre-Islamic traditions. Laye depicts a cohesive society with a strong social and spiritual fabric. He is responding indirectly to the colonialist novel, implying that it would be impossible for members of his village to submit to the power of a European despot such as Kurtz. There is no place for the "unspeakable rites" that Conrad hints at but never describes.

In contrast to the rites that Conrad only suggests for fear of offending the sensibilities of his European reader, Laye records in detail the initiation rites of adolescent boys in Malinké society. He depicts the night of Konden Diara, when young boys prepare for the rite of circumcision by conquering their fear, and he describes the circumcision ritual itself. In these scenes, Laye is both participant and observer. He had participated in the Malinké ritual more than ten years before. As a writer, he recalls the event later, filtering the experience through the pane of memory. When Laye recalls the preparatory exercise, the Konden Diara, the night of the roaring lions, he remembers the conversation with his father preceding the ceremony:

> "I too, went through this test," said my father.
> "What happens to you?" I asked.
> "Nothing you need really be afraid of, nothing you cannot overcome by your own will-power. Remember: you have to control your fear, you have to control yourself. Konden Diara will not take you away; he will roar; but he won't do more than roar. You won't be frightened, now, will you?"
> "I'll try not to be." (80−81)[†]

---

[*] Je sais que cette autorité dont ma mère témoignait, paraîtra surprenante; le plus souvent on imagine dérisoire le rôle de la femme africaine, et il est des contrées en vérité où il est insignifiant, mais l'Afrique est grande, aussi diverse que grande. Chez nous, la coutume ressortit à une foncière indépendance, à une fierté innée; on ne brime que celui qui veut bien se laisser brimer, et les femmes se laissent très peu brimer (73).

[†] "Moi aussi, je suis passé par cette épreuve," dit mon père.
"Que se passe-t-il?" dis-je.
"Rien que tu doives vraiment craindre, rien que tu ne puisse surmonter en toi. Rappelle-toi: tu dois mater ta peur, te mater toi-même! Konden Diara ne t'enlevera pas; il rugit; il se contente de rugir. Tu n'auras pas peur?"
"J'essaierai." (105)

Having conquered his fear of the roaring lions and having learned that the noise was made by special wooden instruments, not by lions at all, Laye is ready to face the true physical and psychological test, circumcision, with other members of his age group in the village. As Laye confesses:

> It was not without misgivings that I approached this transition from childhood to manhood; the thought of it really caused me great distress, as it did those who were to share the ordeal. Of course, the ceremony itself, the visible part of it at least, was familiar to us, for each year we would watch the candidates for circumcision dancing in the town's main square. But the important, the essential part of the ceremony remained a secret, and we only had a very vague notion of how it was carried out, though we knew that the operation itself was a painful one. (93)[*]

Despite the anticipation of physical suffering, Laye is anxious for the reward, to be acknowledged a man in the community — "I wanted to be born, to be born again" (94).[†] He describes the public celebrations, the singing and dancing preceding the rite of circumcision, as well as the specific costumes the boys wear, and he finally depicts the rite in the bush.[11] The observer again becomes participant: "I did not have time to be afraid. I felt something, like a burn, and I closed my eyes for a fraction of a second. I do not think I cried out. No I cannot have cried out; I certainly did not have time to do that either. When I opened my eyes, the operator was bent over my neighbour. In a few seconds the dozen or so boys there were that year became men" (103).[‡] At this point, Laye feels he is firmly attached to his African community. Having been very close to his mother, he recognizes that the relationship with her will have to change now as he assumes

---

[*] Je n'étais pas sans crainte devant ce passage de l'enfance à l'âge d'homme, j'étais à dire vrai fort angoissé, et mes compagnons d'épreuve ne l'étaient pas moins. Certes, le rite nous était familier, la partie visible de ce rite tout au moins, puisque, chaque année, nous avions vu les candidats à la circoncision danser sur la grande place de la ville; mais il y avait une part importante du rite, l'essentielle, qui demeurait secrète et dont nous n'avions qu'une notion extrêmement vague, sauf en ce qui regardait l'opération même que nous savions douloureuse (124).

[†] Je voulais, renaître! (125).

[‡] Je n'ai pas eu le temps d'avoir peur: J'ai senti comme une brûlure, et j'ai fermé les yeux une fraction de seconde. Je ne crois pas que j'aie crié: je n'ai sûrement pas eu le temps non plus de crier! Quand j'ai rouvert les yeux, l'opérateur était penché sur mon voisin. En quelques secondes, la douzaine d'enfants que nous étions cette année-là sont devenus des hommes (139).

his new role in the village. For one thing, he will no longer live in her hut but will have his own dwelling.

In his study of autobiographies of childhood, Coe mentions that Laye's experience of moving into adulthood, which is viewed as a community rite, is a very healthy way of making the transition to adulthood. He contrasts it with the anguish and solitude of the European adolescent at the same juncture. What distinguishes Laye's experience from those of most of his village companions, however, is that this integration into the adult world precedes a painful departure. Laye soon leaves his village for the city of Conakry. There a second initiation awaits him. The French colonial school system leads him through a different set of tasks and hurdles. By the end of the novel, Laye has been initiated into his society and has also acquired the skills necessary to allow him to work in the modern sector.

Examining the structure of the novel, one finds that Laye uses the journey motif in a way similar to Conrad. *L'Enfant noir* can be viewed as an African *Bildungsroman*, with a requisite journey to maturity and self-understanding. Guérard's appraisal of Marlow can be applied to Laye; both protagonists arrive at the end of their journey with greater maturity. Nevertheless, their points of departure and arrival are in contrast to one another. At the end of the journey, Marlow is home in England; he has traveled from Europe to Africa and back. Laye, on the other hand, is leaving Africa, his home, for Europe, a new land, at the end of his narrative.

Laye's journey begins at the very center of his childhood universe, at his father's hut. First, he recounts his earliest childhood memory: playing with a dangerous snake at the age of five or six. Except for summer holidays when he visits his grandmother and other members of his mother's family in a nearby village, Laye's itinerary leads him farther and farther from this center, from the village of his birth. The various moves are necessary to secure an education within the French colonial school system. Although Laye's father is convinced that the endeavor is a worthwhile one, his mother is of the opposite opinion. The boy's return home always implies another painful departure. Parting becomes increasingly difficult for the young man so attached to his family and friends and for those who have to watch him go away. His mother, more than the other members of his family, expresses the pain.

Critics such as Mongo Béti who have faulted Camara Laye for a nostalgic picture of bygone days have ignored the subversive text, the traces of alienation that run through the novel. The young boy often questions the wisdom of those who send him away from his father's forge. As an adult, he emphasizes the fact that his comprehension of village life and ways is forever incomplete because he left his father's forge too soon. In Tindican, his grandmother's village, where he spends periods of his childhood working in the fields with his uncles, Laye says sorrowfully, "My life did not lie here...nor in my father's forge, either. Then what sort of life was I going to lead?" (49).*

Laye's journey has been potentially one of double acculturation. One set of initiation rites, both formal and informal, is to prepare him for life as an adult Malinké; the other is to prepare him for the modern world — one beyond the confines of the village. The writer shows how the African child is progressively initiated into both. Nevertheless, writing his autobiography years later, the adult Laye questions whether it is truly possible to fuse both worlds.

It is clear that the act of writing is an attempt on the part of the writer to preserve the memories of the traditional world when he is far fom home and, indeed, when the very word *home* is fraught with ambiguity. Since the novel ends on a new opening — Laye on board a plane heading for Paris — the reader is left with a series of unanswered questions. Will Laye be richer for the double culture? Will he be able to move in both worlds? Will he feel a disquieting sense of alienation? Will he be a stranger in two worlds?

In a review of the novel in *Le Figaro littéraire* shortly after its publication, Jean Blanzat wrote of Camara Laye: "He places confidence in White men, but nothing that he learns from them touches his inner life. He has no intellectual uncertainty. His faith is total. He does not feel separated from his people by any inner distance, but only by geographical space. In his mind he does not separate what he will keep from what he will reject; he keeps everything, for if his mind was able to change, his spirit remained the same" (16).†

I disagree with Blanzat's interpretation, for Laye's life has been profoundly touched by his contact with European civilization. The episode that shows this most clearly concerns the death of his friend

---

* Ma vie n'était pas ici...et elle n'était pas non plus dans la forge paternelle. Mais où était ma vie? (61).

† Il fait confiance aux Blancs mais rien de ce qu'il apprend d'eux ne touche sa vie profonde. Il n'y a chez lui aucune inquiétude intellectuelle. Sa fidelité est totale. Il ne se sent pas séparé des siens par aucune distance intérieure, mais seulement par l'espace géographique. Il ne fait dans son esprit aucun tri pour garder ou rejeter: il garde tout, car si l'esprit a pu changer, l'esprit est resté le même (16).

Check. When Laye is studying in Conakry, he comes home every summer vacation to Kouroussa. There he rejoins his friends Check and Kouyate. Both friends also live away from home, one in Dakar, the other in Popodra; they are both studying to be teachers. One summer, however, Check returns ill. His mother at first takes him to a traditional medicine man, a *guérisseur*. Later, Check is brought to the European hospital. Neither African nor European medicine saves him. Check dies, leaving Laye and Kouyate to grieve.

When Check is first treated by the medicine man, Laye comments:

> I don't know whether Check had very great confidence in the medicine-men; I rather think he had very little: we had by now spent too many years at school to have complete faith in them. Yet our medicine-men are not charlatans; many of them have great knowledge and can perform real cures; and certainly Check was aware of that. But he must have realised that this time their remedies were not working; and that is why he said, "It will probably go as quickly at it came." putting more faith in the passage of time than in massage and infusions. (148)*

Laye recognizes that he and his friends, having spent so much time in the European school, have lost faith in all the traditional practices, i.e., traditional medicine. When Check dies, Laye views him as a victim caught between two worlds. Moreover, Laye identifies with Check; he too is a similar victim. Check's death signifies the mark of Laye's own vulnerability and mortality as well as the loss of a dear friend. Laye, however, affirms his own spiritual beliefs: "I think of those past days, and now quite simply I think that Check has gone before us along God's highway, and that all of us will one day walk along that highway, which is no more frightening than the other... The other?...Yes, the other: the highway of life, the one we set foot on when we are born, and which is only the highway of our momentary exile" (150).†

---

* Je ne sais si Check avait grande confiance dans les guérisseurs, je croirais plutot qu'il en avait peu; nous avions maintenant passé trop d'années à l'école, pour avoir encore en eux une confiance excessive. Pourtant tous nos guérisseurs ne sont pas de simples charlatans: beaucoup détiennent des sécrets et guérissent réellement; et cela, Check certainement ne l'ignorait pas. Mais il avait aussi dû se rendre compte que cette fois, leurs remèdes n'agissaient pas, et c'est pourquoi il avait dit: "Cela partira sans doute comme c'est venu," comptant plus sur le temps que sur les tisanes et les massages (205–6).

† Je songe à ces jours, et très simplement je pense que Check nous a précédés sur le chemin de Dieu, et que nous prenons tous un jour ce chemin qui n'est pas plus effrayant que l'autre...L'autre?...L'autre, oui: le chemin de la vie, celui que nous abordons en naissant, et qui n'est jamais que le chemin momentané de notre exil (209).

Thus, Laye's spiritual beliefs remain untouched—he never loses his faith in God—but his apprenticeship to the world of scientific learning has certainly weakened his ability to embrace the magic that was at the heart of his parents' experience in life.

I have spoken about Laye's double initiation into the traditional and the modern world. It is possible to find within the novel a third form of initiation, that of the artist. James Olney suggests that Laye's novel is "an autobiography with the double motivation of the man remembering his happy childhood and the artist creating his ideal world" (127). These two themes fuse when Laye, as a very young child, watches his father, the blacksmith, turn gold dust into a beautiful jewel. In the child's mind the crafting of the jewel is a magical rite: "The operation that was going on before my eyes was simply the smelting of gold; but it was something more than that: a magical operation that the guiding spirits could look upon with favour or disfavour; and that is why there would be all round my father that absolute silence and that anxious expectancy" (26).* It is significant that the goldsmith works in silence, although his lips move silently as he addresses incantations to magic spirits. The craftsman becomes, as Lee notes, "a priest, a translator, and a mani-pulator of supernatural powers and vital energies" (*Camara Laye*, 24). This ritual, the gold smelting and the incantations, is followed by the performance of the *griot*, the praise-singer, the poet whose spoken words encourage the craftsman and whose powerful song, the *douga*, closes the ritual: "Indeed, the praise-singer participated in a curious—I was going to say direct, effective—way in the work. He, too, was intoxicated with the joy of creation; he declaimed his rapture, and plucked his harp like a man inspired; he warmed to the task as if he had been the craftsman himself, as if the trinket had been made by his own hands" (3).†

Laye views his father as an artist as well as a man imbued with magic. In his view, both go together. Moreover, the boy who left his father's forge too soon to learn to communicate with the magic

---

* C'était une fusion d'or, assurément c'était cela, mais c'était bien autre chose encore: Une opération magique que les génies pouvaient accorder ou refuser; et c'est pourquoi, autour de mon père, il y avait ce silence absolu et cette attente anxieuse (29).

† Au vrai, le griot participait curieusement—mais j'allais dire: directement, effective-ment—au travail. Lui aussi s'enivrait du bonheur de créer; il clamait sa joie, il pinçait sa harpe en homme inspiré; il s'échauffait comme s'il eût été l'artisan même, mon père même, comme si le bijou fût né de ses propres mains (34).

snake and to create beautiful pieces of jewelry goes on to apprentice himself to a different craftsman. He follows the *griot*. But rather than becoming a Malinké poet, a *maître de la parole* (master of the spoken word), Laye became a master of the written word, transforming his native speech, *la parole malinké*, into the written word, *l'écriture française*. This apprenticeship first began in the primary school in Kouroussa. Laye explains how intimidated and yet challenged he felt at first sight of the blank blackboard: "This blackboard was our nightmare. Its dark, blank mirror was the exact reflection of the amount of our knowledge. We knew very little, and the little we knew was very shaky: the slightest thing could upset it" (66).* The blank surface was eventually covered with signs adopted from the colonial system. In his attempt to answer Montaigne's question, "Qui suis-je?", Laye turns to a twentieth-century version of Montaigne's language.

Laye's literary masters are primarily French realists. The Guinean novelist has acknowledged studying Flaubert's style when writing *L'Enfant noir* (Gavronsky 843). The African voice is altered, assimilated to the European one, when Laye writes: "The sea is very beautiful, seen from the corniche, and shot with brilliant colours: it is opaque at the edges, mingling the blue of the sky with the shining green of the coco and palm trees on the shore, and fringed with foam—a rainbow fringe; farther out, it has a pearly lustre" (137).†

It is not surprising that Laye would look to Flaubert as a master of literary technique. The author of *L'Education sentimentale* and *Un coeur simple* skillfully expressed nostalgia. Laye's *L'Enfant noir* and Flaubert's *Un coeur simple* recreate in different times and places comparable worlds of innocence. In addition, Laye, like Proust, attempts to recall to mind and preserve in prose "the bitter-sweet charm of something vanished forever" (137).‡ With respect to Flaubert, it is interesting that whereas Laye learns to fill the blank blackboard at school—to speak, read, and write in French, the colonizer's language—

---

* Ce tableau noir était notre cauchemar: son miroir noir ne reflétait que trop exactement notre savoir; et ce savoir souvent était mince, et quand bien même il ne l'était pas, il demeurait fragile; un rien l'effarouchait (84–85).

† La mer est très belle, très chatoyante, quand on la regarde de la corniche: elle est glauque sur les bords, mariant le bleu du ciel au vert lustre des cocotiers et des palmiers de la côte, et frangée d'écume, frangée déjà d'irisation; au-delà elle est entièrement nacrée (190).

‡ le charme doux-amer des choses à jamais enfuies (189).

Flaubert's Norman peasant, Félicité, remains illiterate in French. The greater contrast, however, lies in the fact that Flaubert's Félicité experiences loss as her world grows smaller and as the people she loves die—"the little circle of her ideas grew smaller" (50)[*]— whereas Laye experiences loss as his world grows larger. He embarks on the journey outward with conflicting emotions.

In her study of Camara Laye's writings, Sonia Lee considers the Guinean writer's expression of his *déchirement* an indirect criticism of colonialism. In her view, had the French school not come to the village, Laye would have followed his father's footsteps. He would have become a blacksmith, learned his father's magic secrets, learned to speak to the snake, and taken his place among the village elders. He would never have acquired other skills, those necessary to write this book that Lee and other critics view as a successful attempt to capture a vanishing world (*Camara Laye*, 17). I believe it is more appropriate to view *L'Enfant noir* as Laye's attempt to capture a *vanishing self* and in the process to become a new kind of *griot*, a master of the written word.

L'Enfant noir is an important novel because it places an African on center stage as a thinking, speaking, feeling *subject*. No longer projections of the colonizer's fantasy, the African man, woman, and child cannot be depicted as distorted images of shrieking, howling savages in Marlow's nightmarish journey to a fictional kingdom quite inappropriately called "the heart of darkness."

---

[*] le petit cercle de ses idées se rérecit (50).

Chapter 2

▼▼▼▼▼▼▼

Cultural Conflict During the 1950s and 1960s

MONGO BETI, *Le Pauvre Christ de Bomba*
CHEIKH HAMIDOU KANE, *L'Aventure ambiguë*

In oral tradition the *griot*, mediator between tale and audience, relates the exploits of others; he does not tell his own story. When Camara Laye composed his autobiographical novel, for example, he turned to his African heritage for his subject matter but to European literature for literary techniques. Flaubert, master of French realism, then became an important influence upon the Guinean novelist. The *Bildungsroman*, the novel of initiation that had begun with Goethe in Germany in the late eighteenth century, had been adopted by French and English novelists in the following century. Conrad's *Heart of Darkness* provides such a model. As we have already noted in the previous chapter, Marlow's journey is one of self-discovery.

To view the emerging African fiction in the 1950s and 1960s from an exclusively Eurocentric perspective, however, is to ignore an important dimension of the work. Moreover, this myopic vision ignores recent scholarship. The critical writings of Mohamadou Kane and Eileen Julien have established the importance of traditional narrative elements in African fiction. They both focus on the work of Birago Diop, a contemporary Senegalese writer who in the mid-1940s began to reconstruct and transpose Wolof folktales. Transforming the oral legacy to the printed page, Diop made the collection of tales available to a wide audience of non–Wolof speakers, and he validated his own cultural heritage for a European public that consistently has shown greater respect for writing than orality.

In this chapter, I will trace traditional narrative themes and structural elements in two representative novels of the 1950s and

1960s that center upon cultural conflict. Because the importation of church and school caused acute conflict in African communities, I have chosen novels that use these as settings for the struggle between colonizer and colonized. Mongo Beti's *Le Pauvre Christ de Bomba* deals with the missionary presence; Cheikh Hamidou Kane's *L'Aventure ambiguë* depicts the problems posed by the French colonial school. Whereas Camara Laye focuses on the traditions of his Malinké childhood and presents the conflicts he experiences between African and European values as an indirect criticism of colonialism, Beti and Kane heighten the tension created by the colonial presence: they deal directly with the threat that colonialism poses to African culture.

Both Beti and Kane begin their narratives in childhood. Beti's Denis and Kane's Samba are children who mature in the time span of the novel and who live in societies in which religion is an important element — one to be embraced, challenged, or rejected. In Beti's *Le Pauvre Christ de Bomba* and Kane's *L'Aventure ambiguë*, the protagonist, like the hero or heroine of the oral narrative, makes a circular journey, leaving home for an unknown place and then returning. This experience results in lucidity, in self-understanding. Both circular journeys reflect autobiographical elements. Beti was a student at a mission school in Cameroun; Kane began his studies at the Quranic school before entering the French colonial school in Senegal.

In order to trace the thematic and structural elements of traditional narrative that appear in these two works, I propose first to examine an example of a traditional narrative that illustrates the journey of initiation. I have chosen "L'Héritage," a folktale that appears in Birago Diop's collection *Les Contes d'Amadou Koumba*.

An old man named Samba dies bequeathing three sacks to his three sons, Momar, Birame, and Moussa. The first sack contains sand; the second, pieces of rope; and the third, gold. Unable to decipher the meaning of their peculiar inheritance, the three sons seek the advice of the wise man in their village. He sends them away in search of Kem Tanne, "the man who knows everything." On their journey, the three sons come across a succession of six mysterious animals: a warthog disguised as a marabout, a goat struggling with a log, a sturdy bull covered with sores, a skinny cow in a lush prairie, a fat cow in a sparse field, and finally a three-legged doe. With each puzzling encounter, Samba's sons repeat, "Whoever travels a long time, sees a lot."*

---

* "Qui marche longtemps, voit beaucoup."

The three brothers finally arrive at Kem Tanne's village and meet the wise man, who is disguised as a child. Kem Tanne first explains the symbolic meaning of each animal encountered on the trip. The three-legged doe, for example, symbolizes life with its ups and downs, including the happy days we wish to lengthen and the sorrowful ones we would like to shorten. Kem Tanne then unravels the mystery of Samba's legacy to his sons. Since Moussa's gold cannot be eaten, it is no more valuable than Momar's sand (symbol of their father's land) nor Birame's bits of rope (representing Samba's herds of cattle). The wise man tells the three sons to put away their sacks, continue working the land as their father had done before them, and never to forget this journey.

The journey motif offers the hero or heroine of the folktale—and the audience—an understanding and appreciation of community values as well as respect for individual wisdom; the journey leads to lucidity. The moral lesson—the virtue of diligent labor in agricultural society—that is communicated to Samba's three sons and, by extension, to the *griot* Amadou Koumba's audience, is less important for our purposes than the role of Kem Tanne. The sage interprets the riddle of the inheritance *after* deciphering the hidden meaning of the six encounters with mysterious animals. By means of carefully structured repetition, Kem Tanne initiates the naïve sons into the importance of probing surface reality. At the same time, this experience—the journey in search of Kem Tanne—teaches them the importance of intercessors. They need the help of a wise person in their village to send them in search of the sage and they must seek out Kem Tanne. Throughout the journey they believe, and rightly so, that the puzzling sights will be explained by the sage. Yet, as Mohamadou Kane explains, Kem Tanne does not solve mysteries by providing a single key to a puzzle. He does not explain away allegory but interprets it. Moreover, he remains open to further interpretations ("Document pédagogique" 27).

An important outcome of the journey of Momar, Birame, and Moussa is that in addition to their having acquired wisdom (both the work ethic and a new approach to reality), they, in their maturity, return and re-establish themselves within their community as wiser and therefore better citizens. In their journey to self-understanding, however, protagonists of contemporary African fiction are often not able to rejoin the community they left when they embarked upon the journey. *L'Enfant noir*, for example, ends with the hero, Laye, aboard a plane heading for Paris. He does not know when he will return to the point of departure, his Guinean village. We will see that in both

Beti's *Le Pauvre Christ de Bomba* and Kane's *L'Aventure ambiguë* lucidity gained by means of the journey results in rupture, not re-integration.

The Christian Mission: *Le Pauvre Christ de Bomba*
Against the backdrop of the Catholic church in Africa, Beti sets two individuals on parallel but separate journeys: one, a middle-aged man trying to save his beliefs; the other, an adolescent groping toward maturity by learning to decipher the behavior of European and African adults. Unlike Momar, Birame, and Moussa, searching for the key that will solve the enigma of their father Samba's bequest, the French missionary Father Drumont and his mission boy Denis are not engaged in the same quest, although their physical voyage is identical; they leave the Bomba mission for the Tala region and return together.

In this novel, Beti sets in motion the journey of an outsider, the European missionary, and that of an insider, an African child. Father Drumont and Denis meet because the colonial structure is now in place in Cameroun in the 1930s, and missionaries like Father Drumont nurture a dream, the civilizing mission in Africa, ill conceived though it may be. The journey is initiated by Father Drumont, who chooses Denis to accompany him on a two-week inspection tour (from February 2 to 15, 193–) of villages in the back country that the priest has not visited in two years.

Upon their return to Bomba, both the European man and the African child are transformed. For Denis, the trip results in a new maturity; both his naïveté and his virginity are shed in the bush. For Father Drumont, however, the journey ends in defeat. The missionary returns to Bomba to acknowledge a series of personal failures: his tour through villages in the bush was not enthusiastically received by the villagers; his mission, plagued by scandal, is abandoned, and with it goes his dream to contribute to a Christian empire in Africa. All at once, Drumont loses the mission, his followers, and his vocation. With the collapse of the mission, Drumont returns to France; Denis, no longer employed by the missionary, plans to go to work for a Greek merchant.

Presented as a first-person narrative, as a diary written by Denis on the tour, *Le Pauvre Christ de Bomba* (1956), like *L'Enfant noir*, introduces a child-narrator who experiences the break with tradition, but with substantial differences. Laye has no contact with Christianity and minimal contact with Europeans. He is initiated, albeit imperfectly, into a traditional African belief system that blends Malinké animism with Islam. Moreover, Laye attempts to adopt European technology and the French language without renouncing Malinké beliefs. Denis, on the other hand, is handed over to Father Drumont by his father, a convert to Catholicism, and therefore breaks with traditional African beliefs.

Laye's reverence for his parents and belief in their supernatural powers stems from his close contact with his family. The contrast with Denis's life is very clear. Bereft of a mother, who died when he was a small child, and sent off to the white man by a rather indifferent father, Denis is an orphan. To remedy the loss of both parents, the boy attaches himself to Father Drumont, a false father. In his innocence and search for love, Denis identifies with the missionary: "It seems to me that I stand in his very shoes and that the two of us form a single man" (12).[1*] Denis, as observer and narrator, appears naïve and blind, giving unqualified support to Drumont. He is as blind to the true character of Drumont as is the missionary in his rigid and unsympathetic treatment of the villagers. Whenever Father Drumont comes into conflict with tradition, such as the African acceptance of polygamy, Denis supports the missionary without question. Denis becomes the classic unreliable narrator whom Beti uses to poke fun at Father Drumont and indeed the whole colonial system.

In her study of the orphan motif in folklore and the francophone fiction of Cameroun, Susan Domowitz reveals that novelists Ferdinand Oyono and Mongo Beti are both natives of Camerounian regions in which orphan tales are a familiar part of the oral tradition (352). Examining *Le Pauvre Christ de Bomba*, she emphasizes the circularity of the journey, beginning and ending at the Bomba Mission with the requisite initiation of Denis into adulthood. According to Domowitz, "these circular journeys in the tales and novels may be seen as metaphors for the initiation process in which candidates leave the village for the bush, where they are initiated before returning to the village as adult members of the community" (355).

Both Oyono in *Une Vie de boy* and Beti in *Le Pauvre Christ de Bomba* place their orphan-heroes in the care of priests who act as protectors and guides in the novels in the way that the intercessors give protection and usually important advice to orphans in the folktales. The latter are necessary in the folktales so that the orphans can

---

[*] Il me semble que lui et moi ne formons qu'un même homme (22).

successfully complete the initiation process. In Oyono's and Beti's novels, priests bridge the gap between Europe and Africa; they live among Africans and, unlike other colonialists, speak their language. They also serve to initiate the orphans into the colonial world and its cruelty and violence. Once the mission has collapsed and Father Drumont has left, it is quite possible that Denis, without his protector, will find himself on the road gang.

Thus, the tragic dimension of the novel sets it apart from the folktale. In contrast to the orphans in the oral tradition who, although marginal and often living in misery, nevertheless triumph through courage and obedience, to be re-integrated into society as adults, Beti's novel does not end in such victory; Denis, without his protector, Father Drumont, is vulnerable in a hostile colonial world and may fall victim to colonialist injustice.

Although Denis appears to be the victim of patriarchy, abandoned at the beginning of the novel by his biological father and at the end by his adopted one, his remembrances of a dead beloved mother play an important role in his eventual maturity. Denis is forever in search of her and invokes her name whenever he is in need. Denis even imagines that he and Father Drumont share a similar legacy, that they are both orphans: "Perhaps he lost his mother when a boy, just like me" (47).* He hypothesizes this while acknowledging that the missionary has replaced his own father in his heart: "And just now I certainly love him more than my own father" (46).†

When he is afraid to confess to Father Drumont that he has slept with Catherine (girlfriend of the cook, Zacharie), Denis expresses his feelings of solitude and his longing for maternal comfort: "Oh mother, dear, dear mother!...Poor lost mother...I feel so alone...Why haven't I got a mother like all the other boys my age? Perhaps if I had a mother I wouldn't be so unhappy. Perhaps I would tell her everything. And what would she say? Oh, she wouldn't be severe with me. More likely she would console me. That's what a mother is for, to console her child. How wretched I am!" (81).‡

The encounter between Denis and Catherine results in the transformation of the young boy's adoration for Father Drumont into mature love for the priest, Catherine, and others (Porter 105). Never-

---

* Peut-être a-t-il perdu sa mère en bas age tout comme moi (68).

† Et il est certain qu'en ce moment j'aime le R.P.S. bien plus que mon propre père (68).

‡ "Oh! mère, ma mère...Pauvre mère disparue! Je me sens si seul!...Pourquoi n'ai-je

theless, the young woman's role as a maternal figure should not be forgotten. Having seduced Denis one night, Catherine bathes and dresses him like a child the following morning: "She tied the laces of my shoes as if I had been her child" (88).* In this scene, Catherine in part replaces the lost mother and at the same time affirms sexual initiation as only one step along the road to maturity for Denis. The morning after, Denis is still a child; he will become an adult when his eyes are fully opened to the colonial situation and to his adopted father's role as an active agent of colonial rule.

Denis does not have to smash patriarchal idols, for Father Drumont self-destructs. The tour failed, the mission destroyed, the colonial administration initiating a program of forced labor in the region, Father Drumont acknowledges defeat and returns to France. In the final pages of the novel, Denis, who has not heard from the missionary since his return to Europe, renews ties with his "real" father, who now considers his son to be a man: "He seems to regard me as an adult now" (218).† Denis has been initiated, albeit in an original, eclectic manner, into adulthood. Yet he cannot remain at home because, as his father warns him, the risk of being taken into the road gang is too great. Thus, colonialism, the modern political structure in Cameroun, conflicts with tradition, and Denis, like Laye before him, embarks on another journey. The fact that the mission boy decides to seek employment with a Greek merchant is yet another failure for the missionary.

Critics disagree with respect to Beti's portrayal of European missionaries in Africa. Thomas Cassirer insists that the Camerounian novelist treats them with ambivalence, refuting their claim to leadership in modern Africa but also presenting them sympathetically. To Cassirer, Father Drumont is portrayed as a man of ideals struggling against conservatism and materialism (227). The critic emphasizes the missionary's naïveté: "Mongo Beti's missionaries have come to Africa inspired by what one might call a 'primitivist' Christian faith, a belief in the childlike virtues of the African which should allow him

---

pas une mère comme tous les garçons de mon age?...Si j'avais aussi une mère, peut-être que je ne serais pas si malheureux. Peut-être que je lui avouerais tout. Et qu'est-ce qu'elle me dirait, elle?...Oh! elle ne me parlerait pas durement. Elle me consolerait plutôt. Une mère, c'est fait pour ça, pour consoler son enfant. Ça doit être fait pour ça, une mère. Comme je suis malheureux!" (113).

* Elle a noué les lacets de mes chaussures de toile comme si j'avais été son enfant (122).

† On dirait qu'il me considère comme un homme adulte (281).

to enter the Kingdom of Heaven far more easily than the white man once he has accepted the Christian message" (225). Drumont's naïveté is all too evident when he is convinced that the Tala villages will greet him warmly after a two-year absence.

Thomas Melone, on the other hand, views the priest as a crazed fool: "Mongo Beti presents Father Drumont as a kind of crazy person, a megalomaniac who thinks he is Christ and a miracle worker, who speaks to his flocks in a language from another world, becomes agitated when he speaks, scolds, or laughs, dissipates all his energy menacing or cursing the natives, becomes irritated and winds up duped in the process" (*Mongo Beti, L'homme et le destin* 36).* According to Melone, Drumont is unable to acknowledge a pre-Christian tradition. Blind to African gods, he views Africa as a *tabula rasa*.²

There are three key episodes in the reader's evaluation of Father Drumont: the first involves the destruction of musical instruments (77–81); the second concerns a power struggle with the sorcerer Sanga Boto (98–110); the third centers on the interrogation of the women in the *sixa*, the institution to prepare young women for Christian marriage. In the first two instances, Drumont reveals himself to be blind to community values; it is only with the third and most dramatic incident, when the sixa scandal breaks, that he is able to see clearly.

In the first episode, Father Drumont attempts to stop a dance because it is taking place on the first Friday of the month. Angered by this behavior that he considers offensive to Christians, Father Drumont becomes so enraged that he tries to break the musicians' instruments and succeeds in smashing the xylophones. Denis is delighted to see the missionary take a firm stand: "I love to see him decisive: it is always when he storms, when he pushes them around that the folks obey him" (74, my translation—Moore omits this passage).† The village chief holds a different point of view and must be physically restrained from attacking the priest. One wise man asks the missionary a pertinent question: "Suppose the whites were dancing

---

* Mongo Beti nous présente le Père Drumont comme une sorte de fou, un mégalomane qui se prend pour le Christ et pour un thaumaturge, qui parle pour ses ouailles un langage d'un autre monde, s'excite quand il parle, gronde, ou rit, dépense toutes ses énergies à menacer ou à maudire les indigènes, s'irrite ou pour finir est dupe de tout.

† J'adore le voir aussi décidé: c'est toujours quand il tonne, c'est toujours quand il les bouscule que les gens lui obéissent (74).

here tonight instead of us and you were passing by, would you rush in and break their trumpets and their guitars?" (55–56).* Drumont's answer reveals his weakness: "But I didn't come to this country for the whites. I came for you, the blacks. I'm not concerned with the whites. They are bad men and will go to Hell like all bad men" (56).†

Father Drumont is blind to his misguided endeavor. His own European society having failed him in its materialism, the missionary has come to Africa to save the souls he deems worthy of saving. He lacks the maturity to understand that he is interfering in a society that has its social and religious structures in place. Deaf to the truth that non-Christians cannot be expected to observe a Christian holiday, that the "pagan" villagers have every right to dance on a Friday night, and that he is imposing his will by force, not reason, Father Drumont becomes an absurd figure whose actions are puzzling to the very community he is trying to influence. He is unaware as well of the subversive forces that surround him. For example, Zacharie, his pragmatic cook, continues to whistle the popular tune that was played on the xylophones before Father Drumont destroyed them (108). Zacharie makes the subversive message clear to the reader, if not to the priest; traditions live on in spite of an angry missionary's violence against a few sticks of wood.

In his struggle with Sanga Boto, Father Drumont appears at first to gain the upper hand. The missionary surprises the sorcerer in his hut. Witness to Sanga Boto's capture and emotionally involved in the event, Denis writes, "We surprised Sanga Boto in his very nest of deviltries and lusts" (73).‡ Father Drumont humiliates Sanga Boto by dragging him half-naked through the village and then calling him a devil in public: "Sanga Boto!...So there you are, Sanga Boto! I've been looking for you for a long time and now, here you are, the incarnation of Satan! You came here to deceive my Christians, the children of God" (75).§

---

* Suppose que des Blancs aient dansé ce soir à notre place; suppose que tu aies eté près de leur fête, est-ce que tu serais allé briser leurs trompettes et leurs guitares? (80).

† Mais je ne suis pas venu dans ce pays pour les Blancs. Je suis venu pour vous, pour les Noirs. Les Blancs, ça ne me regarde pas. Ils sont mauvais, les Blancs, ils iront en enfer comme tous les hommes mauvais (80).

‡ Nous avons surpris Sanga Boto dans son antre de sataneries et de lubricité (102).

§ Sanga Boto!!!...Ah, te voilà, Sanga Boto! J'ai toujours souhaité de te rencontrer, et te voilà, toi, l'incarnation de Satan! Tu étais venu dans ce pays pour tromper les chrétiens, les enfants de Dieu" (105).

Father Drumont's initial victory is overshadowed by his subsequent near-drowning, an event that Sanga Boto later boasts as his doing. With the two leaders winning only one part of the struggle, the outcome remains ambiguous.[3]

It is clear that Drumont's near-drowning creates doubt in his mind concerning Sanga Boto's true powers and his own capacity to convert the population to Christianity. The near-tragic incident disturbs Denis greatly, for the mission boy fears the people will see the river accident as the sorcerer taking his revenge. Hence this incident, like the previous one in which Father Drumont smashed the xylophones, repeats the pattern of a Pyrrhic victory. Whenever the missionary believes he has gained control of people and events, he finds the victory to be an illusory one.

The final and most dramatic episode involves Father Drumont's discovery that the *sixa*, the institution for the training of future Christian wives, has become a bordello; to make things worse, most of the young women are infected with syphilis. This scandal is the final blow to the missionary's dream.

To get at the truth, however, Father Drumont becomes an inquisitor. With his assistant cook wielding the whip, Father has each woman of the *sixa* beaten to get her to confess. With each confession, he turns to his vicar, witness to the interrogation, and exclaims, "Ah! What a people"! (178)[*] or simply "What a race!" (178).[†] Only when the full story is told does Father Drumont look inward for the culprit. The story that emerges of women forced into prostitution is an ugly one. It leads Father Drumont to realize the folly of his actions. Sorrowfully, he states at last: "The guilty party in this whole affair is me. Do you hear? ME!" (204)[‡] Having constructed the *sixa* twenty years before, he had not even thought of inspecting the facility in the following two decades.

Once the scandal breaks at Bomba, both Father Drumont and Denis see the world in a new way. Father Drumont recognizes his failings and takes the blame. Having already inflicted pain and hardship on his parishioners, he cannot remain in a region that is about to build a new road with indigenous forced labor. Denis, on the other hand, recognizes his former naïveté: "When I think of the severity

---

[*] "Ah? ça, c'est une race!" (230).

[†] "Quelle race!" (231).

[‡] "Le seul coupable dans cette histoire, c'est moi, vous entendez, moi!" (263).

with which I judged the Tala during our fortnight's journey! I thought of them as real monsters. How unjust I was! Or rather, how naive" (189).*

The journeys of both the missionary and the mission boy have resulted in self-understanding. In addition, this clarity of vision, a new maturity, allows Denis to discover the final truth: that Father Drumont was always a stranger in Africa: "The Father had gone and will never return. What would he come back here for, anyway? We loved him so little. . . . As if he were not one of us . . . for he was not one of us" (216).†

I noted at the beginning of the discussion of *Le Pauvre Christ de Bomba* that Mongo Beti set the missionary and the mission boy on parallel but separate journeys. They are separate in part because the protagonists differ in age and racial identity: Father Drumont is an aging European; Denis is an African youth. Yet the journeys are parallel because both the man and the boy make two important discoveries — about *self* and *other*. Denis begins to trust in himself when he breaks free from Father Drumont's value system. He also comes to see Father Drumont not as an adopted father, but as the stranger, the colonizer. Father Drumont, on the other hand, finally understands why his dream fails. He realizes that he has been viewing Africans and African society as the projections of his own fantasy. He had not truly known the place where he had spent the past twenty years of his life; he had been no more than a stranger in an alien land.

The subject of the discovery that *self* makes of *other* has led Tzvetan Todorov to undertake a probing analysis of the Spaniards' conquest of America in the early sixteenth century. In this work, Todorov provides important clues that apply to European colonialism in Africa as well. Moreover, in the Spanish conquest the Spanish missionary's role is very important; the cross accompanies the sword. After examining Columbus's discovery, Cortés's conquest, and missionary activity (Las Casas and Sahagun as examples), Todorov draws two important conclusions. First, the Spaniards were able to

---

* Ouais, je pense à la sévérité avec laquelle je jugeais les Tala au cours des quinze jours qu'a duré notre tournée. Je me rappelle que je les considérais même comme des monstres. Comme j'étais injuste! Ou, plutôt, comme j'étais naïf! (245)

† Le R.P.S. est parti et nous ne le reverrons certainement plus jamais. Au fait, qu'est-ce qu'il reviendrait faire ici? Pourquoi reviendrait-il? Nous l'avons si peu aimé . . . Comme s'il n'était pas des nôtres . . . Parce qu'il n'était pas des nôtres (277).

act so brutally toward the Aztecs because they viewed them as objects rather than human beings (*The Conquest*, 103). Second, he concludes that self-knowledge develops through knowledge of the other (254). This conclusion to a detailed examination of the process of colonial conquest applies to our study as well. Father Drumont and Denis are both naïve, unable to interpret correctly either their words and actions or those of the people around them—until they come to understand each other. Ironically, for both the missionary and the mission boy this comprehension begins with acknowledging one another as stranger: as *other*.

Pursuing Todorov's work further, I suggest that the three incidents involving Father Drumont—the destruction of the xylophones, the humiliation of Sanga Boto, and the interrogation of the women of the *sixa*—can be reinterpreted to mirror elements of the Spanish conquest. Turning back to the history of the New World, we recall that Cortés and his soldiers, though vastly outnumbered, conquered the Aztecs in less than two years. In 1517, bearing the cross and the sword, they were the first to introduce the "civilizing mission" to the non-Western world. Todorov reminds the reader that in their attempt to civilize the Aztecs, in their campaign to suppress human sacrifice, cannibalism, polygamy, and homosexuality, and to introduce Christianity, European clothes, domestic animals, and tools to the Indians of the "New World," the Spanish conquerors committed genocide; they destroyed a people (*The Conquest*, 177).

During Cortés's campaign, he and his soldiers did away with the cultural, religious, and social fabric of the Aztecs. Desecrating temples and sanctuaries, they put an end to certain festivals. There is a parallel here with Father Drumont's smashing of the xylophones. In addition, Montezuma, the Aztec leader, was captured and made to suffer public humiliation. The Spaniards report that the leader of the Aztecs, shortly before his death—some say that he was killed by the Spaniards, others say it was by his own people—asked to convert to Christianity. Sanga Boto is captured, publicly humiliated, and is forced to profess his Christian faith. Finally, documentation by Spanish scribes of the period attests that military information was obtained and conversion was carried out by physical violence. The interrogations of Father Drumont for the alleged purpose of getting to the bottom of the *sixa* scandal were punitive and unnecessarily brutal. The fact that men armed with whips forced confessions from unarmed women already weakened by malnutrition and disease gives proof of the cruelty of the missionary.

Three major aspects of Cortés's "pacification" policy reappear in the novel: the destruction of cultural elements, the deposing of a leader, and, finally, conversion by force. Although admittedly modified in Father Drumont's journey to eventual lucidity, they do reveal Father Drumont to be a cog in the colonial wheel. Hence, the missionary must be reinterpreted as a colonialist unable to recognize the violence contained in his religious zeal. I therefore view Drumont with less compassion than Cassirer, who considers the missionary to be a man of ideals (227) and disagree with Melone that he is a crazed fool (36).

Having drawn parallels between colonialism in Africa and the Spanish conquest, I acknowledge that Drumont differs from Cortés; he is neither a military nor a political strategist. Through Cortés's genius for domination, the *conquistadores* remain in the New World; Father Drumont, his eyes opened to the true effects of the colonizing mission, chooses to withdraw. The priest's journey to self-discovery leads to a journey home, a return to Europe where the Christian message that inspired his misguided mission has historical and cultural roots, and where his Christian ancestors are buried. He leaves Denis, the African child turned adult, to wonder whether Christianity truly belongs in Africa (245).

Having attained maturity, Denis, like the initiate in African coming-of-age ceremonies, has crossed the threshold. He has "died" as a child and been "reborn" as an adult. With lucidity, Denis can no longer function as Beti's naïve, innocent, and unreliable narrator. Irony, comedy, parody disappear when Denis assumes a new role. The novel ends with Denis embarking upon another journey, in search of a new job. Does this new quest mean that Denis has abandoned gods, traditional and Christian, for materialism? Beti gives no further hints. The reader is left to speculate.

The Colonial School: *L'Aventure ambiguë*

In his study of narrative perspectives in *Le Pauvre Christ de Bomba*, Fernando Lambert states that Beti's novel evokes Cheikh Hamidou Kane's *L'Aventure ambiguë*; both works plunge the reader into a characteristic religious universe, one Christian, the other Muslim. Lambert notes, however, that Christianity appears wholly foreign to Cameroun, whereas Islam has deep roots in Senegal ("Narrative Perspectives" 78).

Islam was first brought to West Africa in the eleventh century by

North African brotherhoods. Christian missionary activity, accompanying European exploration, began four centuries later.[4] Five centuries of contact with Christianity vs. nine centuries of contact with Islam would not normally qualify the former as wholly foreign and the latter as deeply rooted. As Beti makes very clear, however, the Catholic church, strongly linked to colonization, served utilitarian ends: "Isn't it true that the soldier, the merchant and the missionary are the three faces of the same allegory?" ("Le Pauvre Christ de Bomba expliqué!..." 125).[*] Kane, on the other hand, views Islam, a non-Western religion divorced from European colonialism, as the key element in transmitting spiritual values. He depicts his people as true believers: "But we are among the last men on earth to possess God as He veritably is in His Oneness..." (9)[5†]

Among the Toucouleur of Senegal, Kane's ethnic group, Islamization took place in the eighteenth century; the *torodbe* (religious aristocracy) drove out the animist Peul dynasty in 1776. In the past two centuries, the Toucouleur have felt themselves to be the carriers of Muslim civilization and from the time of their conversion began to launch holy wars on neighboring groups (Behrman 21). Although Islam did not profoundly touch the Senegalese masses until the nineteenth century, Lambert's assessment of the contrasting role of religion in Africa and in the two works is apt. For Beti, Christianity is an arm of colonialism; he rejects it. For Kane, Islam is a powerful spiritual force that must be used in the struggle to resist Western materialism.

From the outset, Samba Diallo's itinerary bears more resemblance to Laye's than to Denis's, for he, like the Malinké child, begins the initiation process within traditional society and then enters the colonial world for Western schooling. Samba Diallo's itinerary begins at the Quranic school, the Foyer Ardent, when he is seven years old. Two years later, he enters the colonial school in his village. Samba later attends the French Lycée in Dakar and, upon completing the French baccalaureat, journeys to Paris to study European philosophy.

Samba's fate differs from that of Laye and Denis. Unlike Laye, aboard a plane bound for Paris, or Denis, planning to work for a Greek merchant, Samba finds no new beginning; his journey ends

---

[*] N'est-ce pas plutôt que le soldat, le marchand et le missionaire sont les trois faces d'une même allégorie?

[†] Mais nous sommes parmi les derniers hommes au monde à posseder Dieu tel qu'il est véritablement dans son Unicité...(20).

in closure. Upon his return home, he losses his life, killed by the fool who believes that Samba refuses to pray at the tomb of his Quranic teacher.

The novel that ends with the murder of the protagonist begins with a violent scene. Samba, no more than nine years old at the time, is beaten by his teacher for stumbling over the Quranic verse he was to have memorized that day: "That day, Thierno had beaten him again. And yet Samba Diallo knew his sacred verse. It was only that he had made a slip of the tongue" (3).* Kane shows the use of corporal punishment in the classroom in this opening scene to establish several key elements. First, by placing the child at the Foyer Ardent (the "Glowing Hearth") in the beginning pages of the novel, he introduces the spiritual quest of his protagonist. Second, the initial scene allows the author to emphasize the importance of the sacred word. Finally, Kane uses Thierno to reveal Samba's religious bent; the child is gifted in reciting the sacred words of the Quran. Indeed, Thierno, the master, wants Samba Diallo to follow his own path and become religious leader and teacher of his people, the Diallobé. He beats the boy because he believes that Samba is capable of attaining perfection in reciting the sacred word.

The relationship between Thierno and Samba is always expressed as one of the teacher and pupil. Once admitted to the Foyer Ardent, however, the pupil, Samba Diallo, no longer belongs to his family for the several years of Quranic schooling. Thus, for the duration of the apprenticeship, Samba, like Denis, will be removed from his biological parents and have a foster father, a spiritual guide, to initiate him.

I have used the verb "initiate" rather than "educate" because of the specific nature of Samba Diallo's early Quranic schooling. "Educate" is comprehensive and implies a wide area of learning, achieved by experience or formal instruction. Samba is taught to memorize verses of the Quran faultlessly. Only after he has mastered the mechanics will he begin to study the meaning of the words. As a Poular speaker, Samba finds the classical Arabic verses are all the more mysterious.[6] Kane is careful to show that Samba as a child is caught up in the mystery: "This sentence — which he did not under-stand, for which he was suffering martyrdom — he loved it for its

---

* Ce jour-là, Thierno l'avait encore battu. Cependant, Samba Diallo savait son verset. Simplement sa langue lui avait fourché (13).

mystery and its somber beauty" (4).[*] As an adult, Samba is aware that his Quranic education was incomplete because he had never learned more than the skill of recitation: "I had interrupted my studies with the teacher of the Diallobé at the very moment when he was about to initiate me at last into the rational understanding of what up to then I had done no more than recite — with wonder, to be sure" (148—49).[†]

Samba Diallo's incomplete Quranic education resembles Laye's experience; Laye's initiation into Malinké tradition was incomplete because the youth left his father's forge before he could learn the mystery of the little black snake. Both Samba and Laye are cut off from the rational comprehension of their culture of origin by their transfer to the French colonial school. They become cultural hybrids largely because both Toucouleur and Malinké traditions call for a maturation process. One gains the wisdom of Kem Tanne only when one has lived long enough in the community to be an elder; Samba and Laye leave the Foyer Ardent and the forge too soon.

Critics have traced the origin of Kane's protagonist, Thierno. In a discussion with Kane's relative, the Mauritanian poet and linguist Oumar Ba, Bernadette Cailler confirmed that Thierno (the Poular word for *marabout*) was indeed Kane's Quranic teacher as well as Ba's own (745). Samba Gadjigo and Kenneth Harrow find links to Toucouleur historical figures. Gadjigo states that Thierno recalls the leader Souleymane Bal, who inspired the eighteenth-century revolt against the animists that established Islam in the region (48). To Harrow, Thierno, in his denial of materialism, is reminiscent of the Toucouleur leader of the Tijani brotherhood, Al Hajj Umar (1794/ 97—1864), who became an important figure in converting the Senegalese population to Islam ("*L'Aventure ambiguë*" 72).

The child Samba is aware that Thierno is a very old man: "old, emaciated, withered and shrunken by mortifications of the flesh" (6).[‡] The boy sees in the withered, worn-out body a man who is deeply committed to God. Yet the child does not seem truly aware that his spiritual guide is preparing to make the ultimate journey, that he is preparing for death. Thierno's increasing frailty is particu-

---

[*] Cette phrase qu'il ne comprenait pas, pour laquelle il souffrait le martyre, il l'aimait pour son mystère et sa sombre beauté (14).

[†] 'J'avais interrompu mes études chez le maître des Diallobé au moment précis où il allait m'initier enfin à la compréhension rationnelle de ce que, jusque-là, je n'avais fait que réciter, avec émerveillement il est vrai (173).

[‡] vieux, maigre, émacié, tout desséché par ses macérations (17)

larly apparent at the moment of prayer. Although the narrator presents several scenes in which Thierno's ailments are evident, Samba is absent from these scenes. By the time the Master is so near death that he is unable to will his body into the position for prayer, Samba is far away in Paris. He returns home after Thierno's death and then meets his own death at the hands of the fool.

Thierno, who has been teaching for more than forty years, is fully aware that time is running out. Were Samba left in his care to become an accomplished *marabout*, it is not clear that the Master would have the time to fulfill his mission and leave as a legacy to the Diallobé the perfect spiritual successor. Thierno's violence toward Samba may originate in frustration and fear that he will not have the time to prepare Samba as his suitable successor. When Samba is taken from the Master, the latter's dream is destroyed.

Appearing in five of the nine chapters of part one, Thierno is a dominant presence in the first half of the novel. He dominates as a spiritual presence who keeps his audience, the Diallobé, in suspense by not imposing his will on them. Although he is opposed to compromising with the colonial power, Thierno only speaks to emphasize his own limitations, stating "We must build solid dwellings for men, and within those dwellings we must save God. That I know. But do not ask me what should be done tomorrow morning, for that I do not know" (10).* His refusal to speak out against the colonial school allows Samba's aunt, the Grande Royale, to wrest Samba from Thierno's control and set him on the next leg of his journey, to the French colonial school.

As spiritual guide to Samba Diallo, Thierno bears certain similarities to the Christian missionary Father Drumont. Most obvious is that he, like Drumont, is the initial protector of a child embarking upon a journey of initiation. Both the priest and the *marabout* become temporary foster fathers for their respective charges. Later, both men abandon them. Returning to Europe, Father Drumont abandons Denis to an unknown fate. Thierno dies, leaving the Diallobé's spiritual life in the hands of a pragmatist who welcomes the colonial school and shares none of Thierno's spiritual concerns. In addition, they share personality traits. Both men exhibit uncontrollable fits of violence when frustrated by the limitations of human beings. They

---

* "Il faut construire des demeures solides pour les hommes et il faut sauver Dieu à l'intérieur de ces demeures. Cela je le sais. Mais ne me demandez pas ce qu'il faut faire demain matin, je ne le sais pas" (21–22).

seek perfection and lash out at human error. Thierno is angry when Samba unwittingly and unwillingly stumbles over a Quranic verse; Father Drumont is furious when the villagers cannot muster the religious fervor and conviction he desires. Finally, both the missionary and the *marabout* are caught in a similar struggle, in a lonely battle against Western materialism. They respond in the same way, both refusing to compromise and yet wavering at decisive moments.

Thierno's inability to make a political decision for the Diallobé contrasts with the Grande Royale's clear sense of purpose. His refusal to enter into dialogue with the West is in direct conflict with her beliefs. If Thierno represents the spiritual path and religious vocation in Samba's life, the Grande Royale offers a pragmatic approach to solving political and cultural dilemmas in a rapidly changing society. Thierno is spiritual guide; the Grande Royale is a catalyst for change.

Sister of the chief and therefore member of the ruling aristocracy, Samba's aunt has power and authority not shared by other women in Diallobé society. She reveals her political acumen in her dealings with the Diallobé rulers and the masses. Convinced that her people want progress but that many nobles are opposed, she calls a meeting of all the Diallobé and breaks with tradition by inviting women as well as men. She then asks for the people's support in her plan to establish a French colonial school. Since women customarily take no part in political discussions and decisions, the men are too confused by their presence to mount opposition to the Grande Royale's decision. Moreover, the women add their voices in support of schools for their children. Thus in one blow the Grande Royale has her victory.

The Grande Royale, whose demeanor is regal and whose face reflects the history of the nation (31), makes two important decisions for her people: she openly supports the new school, and she arranges to have Samba Diallo join it. In addition to encouraging her people toward contact with the West, is she not grooming her young nephew for a political role? The Grande Royale's pragmatism is clearly linked to self-interest. She wants her people preserved and is intent upon the aristocracy maintaining its control. She fears that if the children of the Diallobé elite do not acquire Western training first (the masses second), the aristocracy will lose its political power: "The foreign school is the new form of the war which those who have come here are waging, and we must send our elite there, expecting that all the country will follow them" (33–34).* In her

---

* L'école étrangère est la forme nouvelle de la guerre que nous font ceux qui sont venus et il faut y envoyer notre élite en attendant d'y pousser tout le pays (47).

opposition to Thierno, the Grande Royale adds maternal concern to political motives. Recognizing the youth's attraction to death, she proposes a second reason for removing her nephew from the Foyer Ardent. The Quranic school is an unhealthy psychological environment for a morbid child attracted to death. She clearly wants Samba to function well in this world, not prepare himself for the next.

The Grande Royale's political skill and success in defending the political supremacy of the Toucouleur aristocracy reflects historical reality. In studies of the role of Muslim brotherhoods in Senegalese politics (the Qadriyya, Muridiyya, Layenne, and Tijaniyya), Lucy Behrman and Christian Coulon note an important distinction between the role of *marabouts* among the Toucouleur and the Wolofs. The Wolofs embraced Islam in the form of religious brotherhoods in the late nineteenth century because the French had broken the power of the nobility and the social system was in severe crisis; people were groping for security and a focus in their lives (Behrman 26—27). For Kane's Toucouleur of the Fouta Toro, however, the colonial experience had been less intense; colonialism had strained the social fabric to a lesser degree. Politics and social matters remained under the direction of important clans (Coulon 67). Thus, the *marabouts* almost never had the opportunity to rise to power; they could not replace the nobles as leaders of the ethnic group.[7]

Once Samba leaves Thierno and returns to his family, his father assumes the role of spiritual guide. Samba acknowledges this transfer of roles: "The words of his father had once more restored his serenity, as in former days the words of the teacher had done" (39).[*] The Knight is the appropriate "unofficial" teacher for this part of the journey because he, unlike Thierno, has knowledge of the West. Kane presents Samba's father as a man so well versed in European philosophy that he can conduct a lengthy discussion with his son concerning the writings of Pascal.

In spite of his own Western training (which is never clearly explained), the Knight is unhappy with the chief's decision to send Samba to the colonial school. The fact that the Knight was not consulted in the matter emphasizes the power of the clan rulers (in this instance, the chief, influenced by his sister) in deciding personal

---

[*] La parole de son père l'avait rasséréné une fois encore, comme jadis celle du maître (114).

affairs. A high priority is given to the well-being of the community, sometimes at the expense of the individual. Although he had previously expressed a willingness to compromise with the colonizers (in order to save a people that trusts in God [20]), the Knight views the clan's action as a sign that the royal family is capitulating to the West. In the struggle between Thierno and the Grande Royale, he is aligned with the *marabout*, with the conservative voices.

The Knight's anguish is revealed in a troubling vision:

> A post on our globe was burning with a blinding brilliance, as if a fire had been lighted on an immense hearth. At the heart of this fierce light and heat a swarm of human beings seemed to be giving themselves over to an incomprehensible and fantastic mimicry of worship. Emerging from all sides, from deep valleys of shadow, floods of human creatures of all colors were pouring in; and in the measure of their approach to the hearth, these beings took up, insensibly, the rhythm which encompassed them, while under the effect of the light they lost their original colors, which gave way to the wan tint that filled the air roundabout. (64)*

In this hallucination, Western materialism and technology draw Third World people from their shadows to searing light. In their worship of the new gods of materialism, they lose their sense of identity. Samba's father shuts his eyes on this vision, but his son will eventually be exposed to seduction by the Western world.

The transition from the Foyer Ardent to the French school strengthens the bonds between father and son, although Samba never forgets his inspiring teacher Thierno. Samba reveals great feeling for his father when he offers his recitation of the Quran in honor of the Knight. The recitation is depicted as a family celebration, not exclusively a rite that bonds fathers and sons. It is one of the few times in the work that Samba's mother's presence is indicated. She draws close to her son for the historic occasion, the traditional recitation from memory of the Quran by the *taleb*, the student who has completed his Quranic training.

As Samba is being initiated into the Western educational system

---

* Un point de notre globe brillait d'un éclat aveuglant, comme si un foyer immense y eût été allumé. Au coeur de ce brasier, un grouillement d'humains semblait se livrer à une incompréhensible et fantastique mimique d'adoration. Débouchant de partout, de profondes vallées d'ombres déversaient des flots d'êtres humains de toutes les couleurs, d'êtres qui, à mesure qu'ils approchaient du foyer, épousaient insensiblement le rhythme ambiant et, sous l'effet de la lumière, perdaient leurs couleurs originales pour la blafarde teinte qui recouvrait tout alentour (82).

and his years at the Foyer Ardent become memories, he reflects upon the way in which the Knight's role in society differs from Thierno's. The son is aware that his father functions in the secular world. Although a devout Muslim, Samba's father holds an administrative post in the colonial structure. This situation causes Samba to wonder whether the Knight can be as pious as the master: "When he is in his office, he is less close to God than the teacher is in the fields" (87). * A philosophical discussion with the Knight leads them both to reflect upon the nature of work and its place in a life committed to God. To Samba's concern that the two cannot be reconciled, the Knight answers as a sage: "If a man believes in God, the time he takes from prayer for work is still prayer" (91). † The father confirms for the son that the extremely ascetic life of the master is not the only path to a holy life.

In contrast to Thierno, a man with a clearly prescribed role and "script," the Quran, to transmit to his students, the Knight has a less defined program to present to his son. Samba's guide on the journey towards his initial contact with the West, to the French colonial school on the African continent, is a man who views the path with ambivalence. The Knight communicates his own doubts and fears concerning a Western education to his son at the same time that he nurtures the boy's religious zeal. Father and son have long philosophical discussions; most important for both, however, is that they also pray together.

The Knight also has a more ambiguous role in Diallobé society than Thierno. His role is ambiguous for the following reasons: an aristocratic member of the Diallobé clan, he does not embrace the Grande Royale's pragmatism, nor is he concerned with manipulating temporal power. A profoundly religious man, he shares the *marabout*'s religious commitment and his attachment to Islamic traditions; he does not share Thierno's deep hostility toward the West and, moreover, affirms the need to compromise with the French. [8]

As a member of the elite and a pillar of the traditional community, the Knight approaches contact with the West with hesitation and misgiving. Yet in his discussion with Paul Lacroix, a French administrator, the Knight expresses his faith in a future that embraces both

---

* Quand il est au bureau, il est moins près de Dieu encore que le maître du champs (107).

† "Si un homme croit en Dieu, le temps qu'il prend à sa prière pour travailler est encore prière" (112).

African and European values, a world in which he sees Samba playing a key role: "M. Lacroix, this future—I accept it," he said. "My son is the pledge of that. He will contribute to its building. It is my wish that he contribute, not as a stranger come from distant regions, but as an artisan responsible for the destinies of the citadel" (73).*

Samba is unaccompanied on the third leg of his journey, to Paris, where he enrolls for studies in European philosophy. As a child he needed an intercessor; having internalized the voices of his Quranic teacher and devout father, Samba is now able to travel alone. Although no spiritual guides accompany Samba now, he does not forget them. In times of crisis, Samba turns to Thierno and his father. In the Paris metro, he recalls his teacher's face and, speaking to the apparition, admits his distress: "The shadows are closing in on me. I no longer burn at the heart of people and things" (150).†
Similarly, Samba writes of spiritual anguish to his father. Finally, it is his father's response to Samba's letter, a cry of distress, that calls him back home.

The Knight's letter acknowledges that his worst fears have been confirmed. The earlier ironic vision has become reality. Although Samba has not been seduced by the bright light of Western materialism, he has become exhausted in his struggle against it, a lonely struggle to preserve his religious values and African identity in a sterile and mechanized world from which God seems to have disappeared. The Knight blames himself for having allowed his son to embark upon the journey to the West. Calling Samba home, the father assumes the role once more of spiritual guide to his son and urges Samba to renew his efforts to reach God. The Knight reminds his son that God is not a parent to be blamed for one's misfortunes.

As a philosophy student in Paris, Samba sheds his earlier passivity. No longer a pawn in the hands of the ruling elders, he now defends his philosophical and religious beliefs with eloquence. To his friend Lucienne, a committed Communist, he expresses an unshaken belief in a world of the spirit. At the same time, however, he admits his sense of loss and confusion: "Lucienne, that scene, it is a sham! Behind it, there is something a thousand times more beautiful, a

---

* "Moniseur Lacroix, cet avenir, je l'accepte. Mon fils en est le gage. Il·contribuera à le bâtir. Je veux qu'il y contribue, non plus en étranger venu des lointains, mais en artisan responsable des destinées de la cité" (92).

† "Les ténèbres me gagnent. Je ne brûle plus au coeur des êtres et des choses" (174).

thousand times more true! But I can no longer find that world's pathway" (134).* Samba admits to Lucienne's family that he fears becoming a hybrid, caught between two worlds, a stranger to both: "It may be that we shall be captured at the end of our itinerary, vanquished by our adventure itself. It suddenly occurs to us that, all along our road, we have not ceased to metamorphose ourselves, and we see ourselves as other than what we were. Sometimes the metamorphosis is not even finished. We have turned ourselves into hybrids, and there we are left. Then we hide ourselves, filled with shame" (104).†

Samba uses metaphors of journey—road, adventure, itinerary (*chemin, aventure, itinéraire*)—in expressing his sense of loss and confusion. This loss of direction is further accentuated in two subsequent episodes. Walking the streets of Paris, Samba enters into a surrealist landscape in which people have become transformed into objects (140). Meeting a family of mixed African and Caribbean ancestry living in Paris, he recognizes their situation as more alienating than his own; they have lost their original ties to Africa. When Adele, the young daughter of the family, asks him to help her in her spiritual quest, he withdraws in confusion, responding, "I don't know whether one can ever find that road again, once one has lost it" (149).‡ Having come to the end of his journey to the West, Samba Diallo exclaims with sadness and lucidity: "I am like a broken balafong, like a musical instrument that has gone dead. I have the impression that nothing touches me anymore" (139).§ With these words, the Diallobé prince not only acknowledges his defeat; he expresses a foreshadowing of his imminent assassination at the hands of the fool.

With a stroke reminiscent of nineteenth-century European novels of initiation (Stendhal's *Le Rouge et le noir*, George Eliot's *The Mill on*

---

* "Lucienne, ce décor, c'est due faux! Derrière, il y a mille fois plus beau, mille fois plus vrai! Mais je ne retrouve plus le chemin de ce monde" (157).

† "Il arrive que nous soyons capturés au bout de notre itinéraire, vaincus par notre aventure même. Il nous apparaît soudain que, tout au long de notre cheminement, nous n'avons pas cessé de nous métamorphoser, et que nous voilà devenus autres. Quelquefois, la métamorphose ne s'achève pas, elle nous installe dans l'hybride et nous y laisse. Alors, nous nous cachons, remplis de honte" (124–25).

‡ "Je ne sais pas si on retrouve jamais ce chemin, quand on l'a perdu" (173–74).

§ "Je suis comme un balafon crevé, comme un instrument de musique mort. J'ai l'impression que plus rien ne me touche" (163).

the Floss), Kane kills off the young protagonist. Why? Victor Aire, who calls Samba's death a pseudo-suicide (758), argues that the death of Samba and the epilogue allow Kane to open the novel to two levels of interpretation. On the political and cultural level, Aire believes that Samba's death signifies failure. Having become a hybrid, he is sacrificed to God by the fool who, like Samba, was traumatized by his encounter with the West but who, unlike his victim, did not experience the French colonial education that would have turned him into a hybrid too. On the religious and spiritual level, however, Aire argues that the novel ends in victory. In death Samba finds the harmony that eluded him from the time he left the Foyer Ardent.

Commenting on the death of his protagonist, Kane explains:

> In my view this is not a hopeless ending. The death of Samba Diallo is only the proof that there is a real conflict. You understand, if there had not been the initial civilization in which Samba was rooted, there would have been no problem when he was introduced to Western civilization; he would have thrived in it. On the contrary, he dies because of it. Why? His death leads to reflection. It means: 1) That we do have permanent values, as I previously stated, and we therefore must nurture them or search for them if they are in risk of disappearing. 2) By not recognizing that, we reach the point of negating ourselves and our specific values; this will destroy us. In other words, Western values inculcated indiscriminately can lead to the destruction of the African who is unable to assimilate them. (Eboussi, 214)[*]

The final chapter is an epilogue in which the dying (or dead?) Samba enters into dialogue with a mysterious and comforting voice; the latter leads him towards peace and reconciliation: "Be attentive — for, see, you are reborn to being. There is no more light, there is no more weight, the darkness is no more. Feel how antagonisms do not exist" (164).[†] With death as the ultimate source of the peace and

---

[*] Pour moi cette fin n'est pas désespérée. La mort de Samba Diallo est seulement la preuve qu'il y a un véritable conflit. Vous comprenez, si l'n'y avait pas eu de civilisation première dans laquelle Samba était enraciné, il n'y aurait pas eu de problème lorsqu'on l'a introduit dans le circuit de la civilisation occidentale; il s'y serait épanoui. Au contraire il en meurt. Pourquoi? sa mort oblige à réfléchir. Elle signifie: 1) Que nous avons des valeurs irréductibles comme je l'ai dit plus haut, et qu'il nous fait donc les cultiver, les rechercher si elles sont en train de se perdre. 2) Qu'à défaut de reconnaître cela, on aboutit à une négation de nous-mêmes, de ces valeurs spécifiques et cela nous tuera. Autrement dit les valeurs occidentales inculquées sans discernement peuvent provoquer la destruction de l'homme africain incapable de faire sa synthèse.

[†] "Sois attentif, car voici que tu renais à l'être. Il n'y a plus de lumière, il n'y a plus de poids, l'ombre n'est plus. Sens comme il n'existe pas d'antagonismes" (189).

harmony that Samba found so elusive in life, the fool is the final intercessor. Stabbing Samba, whom he has mistaken for an infidel, he frees him to make the final leg of the journey, to his final resting place, where all conflicts cease.

It is important to view the fool as a catalyst rather than as a guide. In this perspective, structural symmetry appears in the novel, which is carefully constructed upon a two-part division (nine chapters in part one, nine chapters in part two, with the additional chapter ten as an epilogue) that separates Samba's childhood from his young adult years. In part one, then, Thierno is the spiritual guide, and the Grande Royale, the catalyst for change. In part two, the Knight replaces Thierno as spiritual guide; the fool replaces the Grande Royale. Her decision sets in motion the outward journey with the goal of acquiring Western power — "the art of conquering without being in the right" (33).* The fool's apparently spontaneous violent gesture, one thrust of his knife, brings one journey to an end and sets another in motion; the fool frees Samba to enter the world beyond.

In the attempt to uncover traditional narrative elements in the work, it is tempting to embrace this theory of structural symmetry. Repetition is, after all, a key structural device of the oral narrative. As I have noted in Diop's "L'Héritage," it remains a key structural element as well when the traditional oral narrative is transposed through writing to the printed page.

The epilogue has been given careful readings by numerous critics. William Shiver concludes that Kane's use of interior monologue in the novel conveys the hero's conscious transcendence through death (210). His interpretation implies that Kane is approximating Samba's physical and metaphysical experience as he makes the final journey, crossing the threshold to the hereafter.

Chartier, who focuses on the symbolism of fire and water in the text, thereby giving the entire novel a Bachelardian reading, emphasizes reconciliation in the epilogue. Examining the first scene, Samba's beating at the hands of his angry Master, she establishes the link between fire and the sacred word. In that scene, in which the sacred word is described as "the flashing sentence" (4),† "the incandescent text" (6),‡ Samba learns that trial by fire — "l'épreuve du feu

---

* La'art de vaincre sans avoir raison (47).

† la phrase *étincelante* (14)

‡ le verset *incandescent* (19)

purificateur" — is part of the initiation ritual. Later, when Samba crosses the water (having traveled from Africa to Europe), he loses his faith (fire) in Europe and returns home to die. Concluding that these two images provide the unifying element in Kane's work, the critic finds the dialectic between fire and water reconciled in the epilogue, in Samba's final words: "Sea, the limpidity of your wave is awaiting my gaze. I fix my eyes upon you, and you glitter, without limit. I wish for you, through all eternity" (166).[*]

I do not dispute the importance of spiritual reconciliation but emphasize Kane's rejection of reintegration within the community. In this, he departs from the traditional ending of the folk narrative, as does Beti. We recall that Denis returns to his family temporarily after the departure of Father Drumont but, in danger of being conscripted for the road gang, he leaves again. Yet there are examples of contemporary francophone African fiction in which reintegration occurs. In Mouloud Mammeri's novel *Le Sommeil du juste*, for example, the alienated protagonist returns home to share a prison cell with members of his family. As much a hybrid as Samba Diallo, Mammeri's Arezki finds reintegration through *engagement*, commitment to the Algerian independence movement.

The lack of political involvement in *L'Aventure ambiguë* leads Tidjani-Serpos to criticize Kane for using a mystical denouement that solves no societal problems: "*Ambiguous Adventure* is merely the long story of a general malaise in which, on the ideological level, economic and political problems are hidden behind an interminable discourse about African spirituality and Western materialism" (202).[†] Harrow offers an interesting response, convinced that Samba Diallo and the Knight express the attitude of Sufi mystics towards politics: they seek neither wealth nor power in this world ("*L'Aventure ambiguë*" 72). Whether or not Sufism is a contributing factor, I believe that we should applaud Kane's efforts at insisting upon the spiritual dimension of life rather than reproach him for neglecting political and social problems.

Were Kane to have chosen to reintegrate his protagonist into the

---

[*] "Mer, la limpidité de ton flot est attente de mon regard. Je te regarde, et tu reluis, sans limite. Je te veux, pour l'éternité" (191).

[†] *L'Aventure ambiguë* n'est que la longue histoire d'un malaise général dont les causes économiques et politiques sont voilées sur le plan des idées par un interminable discours sur le spiritualisme africain et le matérialisme occidental (202).

community at the end of the work, he presumably would have written a scene that would take place upon Samba's return: an encounter between father and son. Resuming his role as spiritual guide, the father would be able to help his son renew community ties after the journey to the West ended in failure. This additional encounter would also reinforce the mimesis that Kane, with the mystical epilogue, refuses at the end of the work.

In terms of the novel's structure and the novelist's intent, however, chapters 9 and 10 (Samba's death and the mystical epilogue) are appropriate. First, the fool's action brings the protagonist's spiritual journey to a close. Second, the mystical epilogue allows Kane to make important ideological and literary choices.

Perhaps Kane has two motives in choosing the mystical ending. On ideological grounds, he may wish to present the spiritual quest and triumph as the dominant aspect of Samba Diallo's journey. In this way, the novelist becomes, as Harrow suggests, the defender of the Islamic faith ("*L'Aventure ambiguë*" 70), and not—to the dismay of Tidjani-Serpos—a political visionary. At the same time, he may wish to fuse mimetic with allegorical elements, stretching the limits of the genre, while granting his semi-autobiographical protagonist the freedom that "slice of life" realism would not allow. Kane took the first step in this direction with his initial decision to give the characters names that, as Vincent Monteil notes in his introduction to the novel, suggest pieces on a chessboard (9).

By concluding with the mystical and poetic epilogue, the novelist assumes the role of Kem Tanne. As Mohamadou Kane explains: "Kem Tanne does not explain, he interprets. In other words, he does not use one proposition alone to reduce a difficulty; he discloses a meaning which is acceptable to the mind, without closing the door on additional possible meanings" ("Document pédagogique" 37).* The sage does not provide one key or one conclusive answer to human dilemmas. Imbued with traditional wisdom, the novelist, like the venerable sage, keeps the door open to further interpretation.

Whereas Camara Laye in his autobiographical novel of initiation captures a vanishing world—Africa poised at the point of contact with the West—Beti and Kane move forward chronologically and

---

* Kem Tanne n'explique pas, il interprète. Autrement dit, il ne s'emploie pas, par une proposition unique, à rèduire une difficulté; il dévoile un sens acceptable pour l'esprit, sans pour autant fermer la porte à d'autres significations possibles (37).

depict the effects of the French presence — the European church, the European school — in Africa. Focusing on the process of initiation, Beti and Kane, like Camara Laye, place the African on center stage as a thinking, speaking, feeling subject. They also use the journey motif, as Conrad had in the colonialist novel, as a metaphor for self-discovery and self-understanding. The colonized — Laye, Denis, Samba — and the colonizers — Marlow, Father Drumont — all mature during the course of their physical and spiritual journeys. Yet lucidity is tinged with pessimism. Either they do not learn enough traditional teachings to live in harmony with their people (Laye, Samba), or they discover that their idols — Kurtz and Father Drumont — are "hollow men" (Marlow, Denis). The rising tide of nationalism, the growing political consciousness that Beti and Kane barely suggest, leads to optimism, to renewed faith in the future, in some, but not all, subsequent fiction.

Chapter 3

▼▼▼▼▼▼▼

Catalyst for Change

OUSMANE SEMBÈNE, *Les Bouts de bois de Dieu*
KATEB YACINE, *Nedjma*

The African novelist offers episodes drawn from "real life" (and particularly from his own life) as a challenge to the African stereotypes — Conrad's portrait of gleaming dark bodies set against a lush tropical landscape — that appear in colonialist fiction. Thus, Mongo Beti draws upon his own experience at a Christian mission; Cheikh Hamidou Kane depicts his dual Quranic and French education; Camara Laye describes the initiation ceremonies — the night of Konden Diara and circumcision — that are used among the Malinké when adolescents cross the threshold to adulthood.

In a continuing effort to depict African reality, the novelist faces two related questions: How is one to adapt realism, a European literary tradition, to fit African needs? How should one use African history, particularly the confrontation between Europe and Africa in the colonial period, to authenticate the African experience in this century? In this study of the journey motif in francophone African fiction, a third question arises: How does the journey figure in historically based novels?

Both Ousmane Sembène's *Les Bouts de bois de Dieu* and Kateb Yacine's *Nedjma* use historical events to promote individual and collective maturation. In Sembène's work, the Dakar-Niger railway strike of 1947 is presented as a collective experience that profoundly alters the lives of the protagonists. In Kateb's novel, the Algerian uprising of 1945 in Sétif and Guelma equally transforms the lives of the participants. In both works the collective experience is emphasized and the individual is viewed as part of the collective. A new political awareness is presented as both an individual and a group process. Kateb has called his work an "autobiographie au pluriel" (Déjeux, "Kateb Yacine," 216), thereby emphasizing his belief that personal experience is significant within a larger social unit—family, clan, generation, and finally, emerging nation.

I have chosen these two novels because they depart from the earlier emphasis upon the individual journey. Sembène and Kateb transform the individual journey to self-understanding into a collective. In the same vein, they stress the importance of historical events that promote a new sense of communal identity, replacing tribalism with nationalism. This is an important step toward national identity. In their work, then, the journey motif is transformed. Although Birago Diop's narrative "L'Héritage" concerns a collective unit—three brothers—the three journeys are truly one: they are identical in time, space, and resolution. An analysis of *Les Bouts de bois de Dieu* and *Nedjma* will reveal that although Sembène and Kateb emphasize the historical and collective dimensions of colonialism, they differ in the expression of their common concerns. In the attempt to depict African reality, Sembène turns to one form of realism, social realism, whereas Kateb adapts another: poetic realism.

Dakar-Niger Railway Strike: Ousmane Sembène

> I am not constructing a theory of the African novel. Yet I remember that in that Africa of bygone days, in classical Africa, the *griot* was not only the dynamic element of his tribe, clan, village, but also the obvious witness to every event. He was the one who, under the palaver tree, recorded and presented everyone's actions and gestures. The conception of my work stems from this precept: to remain as close as I can to reality and the people. (*L'Harmattan*, "Note to the reader," 1)*

With this statement, Ousmane Sembène affirms his commitment to African oral tradition and to European social realism. Embracing oral tradition, he assumes the role of *griot*: witness, recorder, narrator of events. This is the literary persona that Robert Scholes and Robert Kellogg have called the *histor*, the narrator they link to the bard of Homeric epic (266). Adopting social realism, Sembène depicts an event in *Les Bouts de bois de Dieu*[1] that is anchored in historical reality:

---

* Je ne fais pas la théorie du roman africain. Je me souviens pourtant que jadis dans cette Afrique qui passe pour classique, le griot était, non seulement l'élément dynamique de sa tribu, clan, village, mais aussi le témoin patent de chaque événement. C'est lui qui enregistrait, déposait devant tous sous l'arbre du palabre les faits et les gestes de chacun. La conception de mon travail découle de cet enseignement: rester au plus près du réel et du peuple (*L'Harmattan*, "Avertissement au lecteur" 1).

the Dakar–Niger railway strike of 1947. Situating his protagonists within the historical framework, Sembène emphasizes their social role. In his study of the African novel, Shatto Arthur Gakwandi explains that for the protagonist of social realism, "his aspirations, achievements and disappointments are seen as conditioned by his place in a given society and can be used to raise wider ethical, moral and social issues" (127).

Although this novel, published in 1960, belongs chronologically to the earlier African works discussed—*L'Enfant noir, Le Pauvre Christ de Bomba, L'Aventure ambiguë*—it marks a departure from them. *Les Bouts de bois de Dieu* does not center on one protagonist (admittedly two in Beti's novel), but on many. It is neither an autobiographical work in which reality is tinged with nostalgia by the passage of time, such as *L'Enfant noir*, nor is it a first-person narrative in which reality is restricted by the ingenuousness, the limited perspective of the narrator, as in *Le Pauvre Christ de Bomba*. This novel differs from *L'Aventure ambiguë* in not emphasizing the individualization of the protagonist.

Finally, in terms of both content and technique, this work offers an important contrast to colonialist literature, to *Heart of Darkness* published sixty years earlier. Both concern the impact of colonialism in Africa, Conrad's novella from the European point of view, Sembène's novel from the African perspective. The images of Africa, however, are dramatically different. Conrad's Africa is dark and enclosed; Sembène's is light and open (Blake 401). Moreover, the first-person narration that emphasizes Marlow's alienation from the African landscape, both people and nature, results in a profound sense of pessimism. Sembène's third-person narration, entering into the consciousness of many characters and recording their individual and collective transformation, has the opposite effect; the novel is optimistic.

Les Bouts de bois de Dieu is important for this study because of the specific way in which Sembène uses the journey motif. In this novel, Sembène presents both individual and collective journeys, with emphasis upon the latter. Because there are three coordinated centers of political activity on the railroad line—Bamako in Mali, Thiès and Dakar in Senegal—protagonists are always on the move, particularly Ibrahima Bakayoko, the leader of the strike.[2] Most important, the victory that concludes the novel occurs as a result of a collective journey. With a set of specific political demands—higher wages, increased benefits—a group of women, wives of the railway workers in the Senegalese city of Thiès, march on Dakar. This event opens the door to a new understanding of the role and importance of women within the context of francophone African literature. It was particularly significant in the 1960s, when the novel was first published, because francophone sub-Saharan African women writers did not emerge until the 1980s.

In the discussion of *Les Bouts de bois de Dieu*, I propose to raise the following questions: Do Sembène's protagonists conform to the model of the traditional oral narrative by making the circular journey that results in self-understanding? Do the events that Sembène places within the historical context serve a didactic function similar to the encounters in oral narrative, and thereby lead to lucidity? Finally, I wish to explore Sembène's use of two distinct literary techniques that blend traditional and modern elements. On the one hand, Sembène emerges as the *griot*: witness, recorder, narrator of events, as well as master of the epic tradition. On the other hand, the author appears as cameraman, "filming" his protagonists in motion.

In this novel, Sembène presents a double dialectic: realism vs. epic; the individual hero (Bakayoko) vs. the collective hero (the people). The novelist assumes the task of creating protagonists who conform to reality but reflect elements of the epic tradition. Thus, he depicts the blind Maïmouna as prophetess and as goddess of the night; he imbues the charismatic Bakayoko with the *griot*'s powerful gift of persuasive speech; he emphasizes the wisdom and deep religious conviction of the venerable sage, Fa Keïta. In this way, Sembène, a Marxist committed to social change, shows respect for the traditional belief system. If, as Birago Diop states in his poem "Souffles," "those who are dead have not departed,"[3*] then Sembène's individual hero should be rooted in African legend and history.

Depicting Bakayoko as a visionary leader, Sembène can best justify the actions of this protagonist by linking his exploits to those of the legendary Soundjata, founder of the Empire of Mali.[4] The implied reader can assume that the masses portrayed in the novel, with a cultural heritage that may differ from that of the reader, view Bakayoko as a modern-day Soundjata and are supporting their leader as a political visionary who has roots in their common past. In addition, Bakayoko's mother, Niakoro, establishes her son's historical credentials. During the railroad workers' first political struggle, the

---

* Ceux qui sont morts ne sont pas partis.

defeated strike of 1938, both her husband, Bakayoko's father, and a son, Bakayoko's older brother, lost their lives. Thus, the leader of the strike is linked by strong family ties to martyrs of the struggle. This legendary and historical grounding may not be acceptable to all readers. Mineke Schipper, for example, considers Bakayoko almost too romantically idealized to be realistically acceptable (*Toward a Definition of Realism*, 571).

To distinguish Bakayoko from the people and create suspense in the novel, Sembène employs a classic theatrical device (one which he may have recalled from Molière's *Tartuffe*). He keeps Bakayoko in the wings while a series of characters draws attention to his absence. Although Bakayoko is mentioned as early as the first chapter, he appears at last on page 265 of the 370-page novel. Before his appearance, Bakayoko's importance to the strikers is expressed in several significant ways. First, his absence is felt as a loss: "It's too bad Bakayoko isn't here; if he were, they wouldn't talk like that" (35).[*] Second, his words are respected, transmitted from one person to another, and guarded as wisdom: "Bakayoko told us: It isn't those who are taken by force, put in chains and sold as slaves who are the real slaves; it is those who accept it morally and physically" (36).[†] Finally, those who respect his mastery of the word also need him: "[We] wish that Ibrahim Bakayoko was with us today. He knows how to speak to us and all of us listen to him" (23).[‡]

It is possible that Sembène uses this device, as Schipper suggests, for realistic reasons (*Toward a Definition of Realism*, 573). In his study of the constraints of realism, Philippe Hamon discusses the danger of placing too great an emphasis upon one protagonist: "There is the great risk of causing a 'deflation' of the realist illusion, of reintroducing the romantic, heroic and imaginary as genres" (436).[§] With Bakayoko offstage for much of the novel, Sembène may be attempting a solution to the novelist's dilemma of romantic idealization.

---

[*] "Notre Bakayoko est loin: s'il était là, ceux-là, ceux-là ne parleraient pas comme ça" (44).

[†] Bakayoko a dit: "Ce ne sont pas ceux qui sont pris par force, enchaînés et vendus comme les esclaves qui sont les vrais esclaves, ce sont ceux qui acceptent moralement et physiquement de l'être" (45).

[‡] "Ce qu'il faudrait aujourd'hui c'est que Bakayoko soit parmi nous. Il sait parler et nous l'écoutons tous" (27).

[§] Le risque est grand de provoquer aussi une 'déflation' de l'illusion réaliste, de réintroduire le romanesque, l'héroïque et le merveilleux comme genres (436).

To describe Bakayoko, Sembène uses alternating points of view. For example, his mother, Niakoro, emphasizes her son's frequent voyages from one union headquarters to the other. "And Ibrahim, my son—everyone knows my son. Ever since his father's death he has never been content to stay in one place. He was restless even while I still carried him" (13).* When Bakayoko finally appears, his uncle Bakary describes the apparition who arrives without warning one evening, surprising the old man:

> Bakary *had been studying the man before him* as he spoke. On entering the house, Bakayoko had placed his short upper tunic, of the type called a *froc*, in a corner with his walking stick and pack, and now he was wearing only a pair of white trousers, striped in black. His soft sandals were the kind worn by Peul shepherds, with leather straps that laced high on the ankles. A straw hat with a wide brim to shade his eyes from the sun hung down across his back, supported by the thong knotted beneath his chin. (235, emphasis mine)†

Here Bakary provides ethnographic data, describing Bakayoko's dress as that of a simple peasant, although the articles of clothing belong to different ethnic groups of West Africa and serve to confirm Bakayoko's commitment to transcending ethnicity in the construction of a new Africa.

Later, at a meeting between the strike officials and a French railroad inspector, the latter gives an additional description of Bakayoko.

> *Edouard seized the opportunity to study his neighbor.* The thick lips, marked by little slanting ridges and pressed firmly together, gave the man's face an expression of hardness which was borne out by the narrow, deep-set eyes. A long scar, reaching from the left side of his nose to the underpart of his jaw, seemed only to accentuate the severity of his features. (238, emphasis mine)‡

In the manner of Balzac, Edouard describes physiognomy that reflects a

---

* "Ibrahima par-ci, Ibrahima par-là. Depuis la mort de son père, il ne tient plus en place. C'est vrai qu'il remuait déjà quand il était dans mon ventre" (15).

† Tout en parlant, Bakary *examinait l'homme qu'il avait devant lui*. Bakayoko était vêtu d'un pantalon blanc ravé de noir; en entrant, il avait posé son froc dans un coin avec sa canne et son baluchon. Il était chaussé de sandales de berger peulh dont les lanières de cuir s'entrelaçaient sur ses chevilles, son maka était rejeté sur son dos (265, emphasis mine).

‡ *Edouard regardait son voisin à la dérobée.* Les lèvres épaisses, striées de rides obliques, donnaient au visage, lorsqu'elles se serraient, une impression de dureté que ne démentaient pas les yeux légèrement bridés profondément enfoncés dans les orbites. Une longue balafre, qui partait de l'aile gauche du nez et atteignait la mâchoire inférieure, accentuait la sévérité des traits (268, emphasis mine).

psychological trait, for Bakayoko's one character flaw is his lack of feelings. Edouard's description also creates an aura of mystery. Neither he nor the reader ever learn the origin of the long scar that suggests but never explains a former violent incident.

Unlike Niakoro and Bakary, two close relatives of the strike leader who reappear in various parts of the novel to express the voice of tradition, Edouard, a stranger from a different culture and class, is a "defunctionalized character" (to borrow Hamon's term); he replaces the narrator temporarily by providing the reader with additional information concerning Bakayoko.[5]

Yet the narrator carefully studies the actions of Bakayoko at the community meeting in Dakar held after the women's march and emphasizes Bakayoko's vitality in word and deed. Bakayoko grabs the microphone, galvanizing the crowd; he speaks to them first in Wolof, then translates his words into Bambara, Toucouleur, and French. Preceding the general strike in Dakar that leads to victory, this scene reveals Bakayoko's importance as an orator in a society that values the spoken word. Moreover, this scene places Bakayoko in opposition to both the French colonial administration and to the Serigne d'Dakarou, the Islamic leader. The latter praises the French and warns the people against foreign influence (assistance from unions abroad). Hence, the religious leader makes a speech which, in contrast to Bakayoko's, is most inappropriate and conflicts with the sentiments of the people.

Finally, Bakayoko, speaking with a friend, describes himself.

> "When I am in the cabin of my engine, I take on a sense of absolute identity with everything that is in the train, no matter whether it is passengers or just freight. I experience everything that happens along its whole length. In the stations I observe the people, but once the engine is on its way, I forget everything else. My role then is nothing except to guide that machine to the spot where it is supposed to go. I don't even know any longer whether it is my heart that is beating to the rhythm of the engine, or the engine to the rhythm of my heart. And for me, that is the way it has to be with this strike—we must all take on a sense of identity with it...(284−85)*

---

* "Quand je suis sur la plate-forme de mon Diesel, je fais corps avec toute le rame, qu'il s'agisse de voyageurs ou de marchandises. Je ressens tout ce qui se passe au long du convoi, dans les gares, je vois les gens. Mais dès que la machine est en route, j'oublie tout. Mon rôle n'est plus que de conduire cette machine à l'endroit où elle doit aller. Je ne sais plus si c'est mon coeur qui bat au rythme du moteur ou le moteur au rythme de mon coeur. Pour moi c'est ainsi qu'il en est de cette grève, nous devons faire corps avec elle..." (323)

In this discussion with Alioune, he reveals his thoughts and feelings concerning his role as leader of the strike. In Bakayoko's psyche, the individual disappears in the collective effort.

Although Bakayoko is skilled as an orator, he values the written word, always urging the workers to read books. At the leader's suggestion, Tiémoko borrows Malraux's *La Condition humaine* from Bakayoko's library; the novel gives Tiémoko the idea to put Diara, a traitor, on trial, thereby initiating a new form of discipline.[6] By means of the spoken and the written word, Bakayoko wishes to convey an ideology that includes his faith in the machine, in the modernization of Africa. During the strike, the workers remember Bakayoko's words: "The kind of man we were is dead, and our only hope for a new life lies in the machine, which knows neither a language nor a race" (109).*

Bakayoko uses his mastery of the word to transmit a revolutionary message. He calls for social, political, and economic change. Roger Chemain views Bakayoko as a *maître de la parole* who rejects the rhetorical virtuosity of the traditional *griot* but uses the word as both *la parole enseignante*, to instruct his people in ideology and politics, and as *le verbe créateur*, to create political action, mobilizing the troops (169). Chemain concludes: "With this creative and fertile value of the word, the Marxist protagonist Bakayoko rejoins the ancestral core of West African mythologies" (179).†

Is Bakayoko a catalyst for change? The spiritual guide of his people? A protagonist in search of self-understanding? Sembène creates interest and complexity in the novel by suggesting that Bakayoko fits all three roles. He clearly is a catalyst for change who, like the Grande Royale in *L'Aventure ambiguë*, keeps the community's eyes on the future. Whereas Samba Diallo's aunt sought to learn the skill of conquering without right, "the art of winning without being in the right,"‡ Bakayoko has taught his disciple, Tiémoko: "It is not necessssary to be right to argue, but to win it is necessary both to be right and never to falter" (119).§ He is also a spiritual guide; the faith

---

* "L'homme que nous étions est mort et notre seul salut pour une nouvelle vie est dans la machine, la machine qui, elle, n'a ni langage, ni race" (127).

† Par cette valeur créatrice, fécondante de la parole, le personnage du marxiste Bakayoko rejoint le fond ancestral des mythologies de l'Quest africain (170).

‡ l'art de vaincre sans avoir raison

§ "Pour raisonner, il ne s'agit pas d'avoir raison mais pour vaincre, il faut avoir raison et ne pas trahir" (140).

he preaches is Marxism. Indeed, Case reminds us that Bakayoko bears the first name of a prophet and guide, Ibrahima (280).

Finally, Bakayoko's itinerary does lead to lucidity, to a new understanding of personal relationships. Having placed the interests of the community above his own, thereby rejecting all emotional commitment in his life, Bakayoko first disappoints his followers. Members of the community criticize him for not returning home for the burial of his mother, Niakoro, and not attending the funeral of his close friend, Doudou. Bakary says to him, "Sometimes I wonder if you have a heart" (258).[*]

The turning point in Bakayoko's life occurs following the death of Penda. The organizer of the women's march is killed by the police as the marchers approach Dakar. Upon hearing the news of her death, Bakayoko is genuinely grieved. For the first time, he questions the emotional cost of the struggle: the toll in human lives, the blood shed for the promise of a better future. "'Penda, too. . .' he murmured, and suddenly discouragement stabbed at him like the claws of a hawk plunging on its prey. Was all of the learning he had managed to acquire, all of the effort of a mind he had harnessed so rigidly to the service of this cause — was all of that to vanish now, before the specter of these two corpses?" (289).[†] Bakayoko then makes an effort to draw closer to his wife, a woman he has largely ignored. Sembène suggests that Bakayoko's feelings have deepened because of the strike, and that he has gained maturity. Having fought exclusively for political, economic, and social changes in society, Bakayoko now begins to transform personal relationships, beginning with his marriage.

A parallel can be drawn between Bakayoko's journey to self-understanding and his daughter Ad'jibid'ji's successful solution to an enigma. Appearing first as a precocious child who challenges tradition, including woman's role in society, Ab'jibid'ji wrestles with a riddle that her grandmother Niakoro posed shortly before her death: "What washes water?" She finds the answer following the events of the strike in which the entire community attained maturity as a result of

---

[*] "Je me demande parfois si tu as un coeur" (293).

[†] "Penda aussi. . .," murmura-t-il, et d'un seul coup, peut-être pour la première fois de sa vie, le découragement s'abattit sur lui tel un épervier qui plonge sur sa proie. Tous les livres lus, tous les enseignements glanés çà et là, tous les efforts d'une pensée mise au service d'une volonté bien dressée, tout cela devenait-il vain devant des cadavres? (328)

their victorious struggle. Ad'jibid'ji reaffirms her link to tradition, telling Fa Keïta: "It is the spirit. The water is clear and pure, but the spirit is purer still" (324).* Thus, we may conclude that the experience of the strike has taught the little girl to think and her father to feel.

Since Bakayoko's effect on others, more than theirs upon him, provides much of the momentum of the novel, Martin T. Bestman describes him as a figure "at the center of a magnetic field" (182).[7] Bestman's metaphor of the magnetic field helps the reader see Bakayoko's followers as characters who resemble the leader but lack at least one important attribute. For example, Lahbib, the "brain" behind the union, lacks Bakayoko's oratory skill; Tiémoko lacks both Bakayoko's verbal ability and his sophistication. N'Deye Touti, culturally alienated, lacks Bakayoko's commitment to the struggle. Ramatoulaye's attack upon her brother's ram is instinctive and visceral; she lacks ideological underpinning.

This list can be lengthened to include *almost* all the characters in the novel. There are three exceptions: Penda, Maïmouna, and Fa Keïta. Remaining independent of Bakayoko, the three appear as archetypal figures: Penda as goddess of war, Maïmouna as blind prophetess, and Fa Keïta as sage. Moreover, their courage is tested in events that recall encounters depicted in oral narrative. For Penda and Maïmouna, the event is the women's march to Dakar. In this endeavor, a political demonstration that projects the women toward political action and challenges societal norms, Penda organizes the marchers while Maïmouna inspires and protects them. Fa Keïta is tested in a different way. Incarcerated in a brutal prison camp during the women's march from Thiès to Dakar, he experiences this confinement as a spiritual crisis in which he nearly loses his faith in God and respect for human beings.

Before the women undertake the march, Penda has already proved her commitment by taking charge of the distribution of food rations. Although her reputation as a woman of loose morals alienates several of the women, some of whom call her a *piting* (a prostitute), Penda establishes her authority over them. Most important, the march is her idea; she proposes it at a public meeting held by the strike organizers in Thiès: "I speak in the name of all the women, but I am just the voice they have chosen to tell you what they have decided to do. Yesterday we all laughed together, men and women,

---

* "C'est l'esprit, car l'eau est claire, mais l'esprit est plus limpide encore" (368).

and today we weep together, but for us women this strike still means the possibility of a better life tomorrow. We owe it to ourselves to hold up our heads and not to give in now. So we have decided that tomorrow we will march together to Dakar" (254–55).*

Sembène emphasizes the importance of the march in several ways. It is the longest chapter in the novel and the only one in which the action moves from one city to another (from Thiès to Dakar). This chapter follows Bakayoko's long-awaited return, although the strike leader does not accompany the women on the march. Here Sembène interjects ambiguity. He allows the reader to interpret Bakayoko's absence by offering two possibilities. Either the women do not need the charismatic leader, or they have effectively replaced him with one of their own. Sembène introduces another ambiguity. Granting Penda her role as leader of the march, Sembène subtly undercuts her power by accentuating the importance of Maïmouna in their common effort. The blind woman's songs and her presence inspire the marchers: "All of the women seemed to want to walk behind Maïmouna, as if she trailed a protective wake in which they would be safe" (273).† Moreover, Maïmouna emerges as a protagonist whose clarity of vision surpasses that of sighted people. During the march, she warns Penda against Bakayoko's insensitivity: "He is blinder to his neighbor than I am" (269).‡ Finally, assuming the epic role of blind prophetess, she warns the marchers of an impending storm (305).

As the march progresses, it takes on epic proportions. For example, the marchers leave on a very dark night and face the blazing sun at noon in their trek across a sterile, almost surrealist, landscape. Eventually they get caught in a fierce windstorm. They also endure the physical hardships of extreme heat and water shortages as well as psychological problems: conflict within the group, discouragement, fear.

The political impact of the women marchers arriving in Dakar is

---

* "Je parle au nom de toutes les femmes, mais je ne suis que leur porte-parole. Pour nous cette grève, c'est la possibilité d'une vie meilleure. Hier nous riions ensemble, aujourd'hui nous pleurons avec nos enfants devant nos marmites ou rien ne bouillonne. Nous nous devons de garder la tête haute et ne pas céder. Et demain nous allons marcher jusqu'à N'Dakarou (Dakar)" (288).

† "Les femmes marchaient derrière Maïmouna comme si l'aveugle laissait après elle un silage protecteur" (309).

‡ "Pour son prochain, il est plus aveugle que moi" (304).

crucial in initiating the general strike that results in the railway workers' ultimate victory. On the one hand, the success of the march can be attributed to the strength and courage of the leaders, to Maïmouna's spiritual force joined to Penda's political commitment. On the other hand, it can be considered the triumph of collective social transformation. I favor the second interpretation; the women have matured ideologically and have reached a new level of consciousness by creating a genuine revolutionary movement, in contrast to the men, who remain tied to the formal structure of the railroad workers' union and are unable to free themselves from their dependency upon the charismatic leader (291–92).[8]

The emphasis upon the women's victory to the exclusion of the men, however, ignores the balance that Sembène establishes between individual and collective consciousness on one hand, political commitment and spiritual faith on the other. Just as the women are marching to Dakar, claiming their right to political power by their actions, a group of male strikers, including Fa Keïta, faces torture in a prison camp in Bamako. In contrast to the women, who meet the dangers of open space, of the long journey between Thiès and Dakar, the men test their courage in a threatening closed space, locked behind a double row of barbed wire from which escape is impossible. Bearing in mind the contrast in metaphors — the women's march, the men's incarceration — we discern similarities in the tests of courage of both groups. For example, the women first encounter the darkness and then the blinding heat of day; so do the men. Fa Keïta is thrust into a pitch-black cell in which his eyes, unaccustomed to the darkness, are incapable of seeing. Then he and the fellow prisoners are forced to walk in circles in the prison yard under a blazing sun.

Unlike the triumph of the women marchers, who find strength in unity, the male prisoners discover that they are powerless as individuals and are unable to unite against their oppressors. When the old man rebels, defying the guard by praying in the prison yard, he is beaten and then ignored. His action does not incite an uprising. The prisoners are not liberated until the general strike is declared.

Upon his release from prison, Fa Keïta calls the younger leaders together to admit to them that the experience has shaken his beliefs. In prison, he had wanted to kill his captors and began to doubt the existence of God; in other words, he had journeyed to the edge of despair. His message to the younger generation of union organizers is a warning against violence and hatred: "hatred must not dwell with you" (324).* Fa Keïta's words are repeated by Maïmouna singing the last stanza of "The Legend of Goumba" in the closing paragraph of the book: "But happy is the man who does battle without hatred" (333).†

The repetition of the spiritual message emphasizes the importance of didacticism, of moral instruction, in the novel. The message also links Maïmouna with Fa Keïta, giving both a man and a woman legitimacy as spiritual guides within the community. These two figures — the one who is blind in the external world although she has keen inner vision, the other who is a profoundly religious elder — have significant roles to play in this society that has just made important material gains. Moreover, by turning to oral tradition for the last word, to "The Legend of Goumba," Sembène grants an important historical and legendary dimension — as well as a spiritual one — to a political struggle.

Thus, in terms of the novel's structure, Sembène achieves an important balance between oral tradition and social realism. Indirectly, the novelist is reminding his readers at the end of the work that this strike, grounded in historical reality, is part of a larger context, a Mega-History, the history of African peoples. In fact, the strike of railway workers in 1947 is a foreshadowing of the subsequent struggle for independence.

Sembène has also established an equilibrium in the novel between the individual and the collective hero. Important as catalyst, organizer, and orator, Bakayoko is no more and no less than the charismatic leader. He is not the soul of the struggle, for the spiritual dimension, articulated by Fa Keïta and Maïmouna, is centered in the people. As Sembène said in an interview with Carrie Dailey Moore, "The people make the revolution" (214).‡

Finally, Sembène maintains a balance between traditional and modern elements as well by assuming the dual role of *griot* and cameraman. The former, rooted in tradition, and the latter, created by modern technology, express Sembène's attitude towards artistic expression: "I say that the artist is the heart-beat of the people" (Moore, "Evolution of an African Artist" 215).§

---

* "il ne faut pas que la haine vous habite" (367).

† Mais heureux est celui qui combat sans haine (379).

‡ C'est le peuple qui fait le révolution.

§ Je dis que l'artiste est la pulsation du peuple.

We must bear in mind that Sembène's interpretation of his role as *griot* is not an orthodox one. In the African savannah, the *griot* is a professional storyteller, a member of a traditional caste. The term originated with French anthropologists and is derived from the Wolof word *gewel*. The *griot's* profession calls for a knowledge of the history of his region, the genealogy of kings, a great number of tales and legends. He may accompany his performance with the *kora* (lute), *balafong* (xylophone), and drum. As performing artist, he has historically been dependent upon wealthy and illustrious benefactors and has earned his way by praising others. The *griot's* position within the community is therefore ambiguous. Since he has access to the community's ear and may manipulate public opinion, the *griot* can achieve great power. Considered necessary to the social harmony of the group, he is often feared and scorned: feared for his ability to slander, and scorned for his subordinate role and extortionist technique. It is not surprising that in an earlier era the *griot*, like the actor of Shakespeare's time, existing on the fringes of society, was refused burial in the village cemetery. Tradition called for his burial in the hollow trunk of the giant baobab tree.[9]

It appears, then, that Sembène uses the term *griot* as an expression of artistic mastery and views his role as one of professional storyteller, not praise-singer. In his discussion of Sembène's approach to oral tradition, Mbye Baboucar Cham makes a distinction, useful for our purposes, between *gewel*, professional performer of oral narrative, and *lebkat*, storyteller. Cham explains that in addition to performance skills, the *gewel*, in contrast to the *lebkat*, needs *xamxam*, knowledge, gained by training in history and culture (*Ousmane Sembène* 26). In his view, Sembène considers his role to be an amalgam of both: the modern *griot-conteur*.

It is apparent that Sembène, embracing elements of oral tradition, does more than transpose orality to the printed page or, as in the case of his films, to the screen. For example, the novelist adapts or rejects supernatural elements of Wolof oral narrative to comply with the requirements of realism. Where traditional oral narrative emphasizes the preservation of social order, Sembène's political philosophy challenges that order. Just as Beti's Denis and Kane's Samba Diallo cannot rejoin the community in the way that Momar, Birame, and Moussa are reintegrated in Diop's traditional narrative. "L'Héritage," neither can Sembène's protagonists. Penda's death, like Samba Diallo's, may be best interpreted as the impossibility of reintegration within a rapidly changing society.[10]

Where in the novel does the narrator clearly become the *griot*? Most obviously, the narrator assumes the role of oral historian. Following Penda's speech, in which she proposes the women's march, the *griot*-narrator states: "It was the first time in living memory that a woman had spoken in public in Thies..." (255).* As community historian, he attests to the revolutionary nature of Penda's proposal. The *griot*-narrator is there, like Stendhal and Balzac's narrators, to provide commentary. As Scholes and Kellogg explain, the commentary often labelled "intrusive" is merely the *histor* going about his business (266).

The *griot* appears as well when realist discourse assumes an epic quality. For example, as the women make their difficult journey from Thiès to Dakar, the narrator states: "An inky night flowed through the city, somber and viscid, as if the heavens had decanted a layer of crude oil across the earth. The cries and shouts that pierced the darkness were like fitful flashes of lightning, but the ceaseless sound of the tam-tams seemed to carry with it a promise that dawn would come" (257).† In this passage, the *griot*-narrator transmits visual and auditory images anchored in the reality of the experience, the departure for Dakar, which by means of dramatic intensity and lyrical prose impose an epic overlay on the realist narrative.

As the *griot* represents one aesthetic dimension, conveying the verbal artistry of indigenous Africa, the cameraman represents another, transmitting the visual intensity of the "moving picture." The narrator assumes the role of cameraman for two reasons: first, to compress time and space, thereby linking the three cities of Bamako, Thiès, Dakar into one large community;[11] second, as the camera moves, it seizes characters *in movement*. Ramatoulaye is "filmed" killing her brother's ram as a toreador would be filmed at a bullfight. The courtyard takes on the appearance of an arena.

The camera is first fixed on Ramatoulaye at the moment that she perceives the ram she has vowed to kill: "Ramatoulaye, who rarely hurried, raced into the larger courtyard like an avenging fury. From the veranda of the main house she saw the ram coming out of

---

* De mémoire d'homme c'était la première fois qu'une femme avait pris la parole en public à Thiès...(289).

† Une nuit couleur d'encre s'était étendue sur la ville, sombre, visqueuse, comme si le ciel se fût mis à déverser du pétrole brut sur la terre. Pourtant des cris et des appels perçaient les ténèbres tels des éclairs et le bruit du tam-tam qui n'avait pas cessé semblait annoncer la venue de l'aube (291).

Bineta's cabin chewing contentedly on a piece of red and white striped material" (96).*

Capturing the difference in rhythm and intensity, Ramatoulaye's agitation in contrast to the deliberate actions of the ram, the camera then focuses on Ramatoulaye as she prepares to attack. The camera records the stand-off as the woman and the animal size up one another and then turns to the spectators: "Houdia M'Baye and the children were completely stunned. Wide-eyed and openmouthed, they could only stare helplessly, first at the woman and then at the ram. The frightened cat thrust its head between the crooked legs of little N'Dole" (97).†

In the arena, where the ram attacks first, tension is released as the ensuing melee takes a comic turn. Houdia M'Baye tries to cover the half-naked body of Ramatoulaye, who loses most of her clothes struggling with the ram. Although Ramatoulaye succeeds in killing the animal, she needs the help of Houdia M'Baye, who strikes the first blow. In the final frames, the camera focuses on the wounded heroine, staring at herself.

The visual sequence is interrupted as verbal narrative resumes. The narrator returns to interpret Ramatoulaye's stare. "There was neither pride nor arrogance in her attitude, just a kind of satisfaction, as if what she had done had been only a duty she could not a avoid" (98).‡ The interruption is necessary; the narrator's commentary, albeit intrusive, serves to remind the reader that although Ramatoulaye's revolt originates as a response to her brother's avarice and hypocrisy, it results in a new awareness.[12] This individual rebellion becomes a collective one; the women, led by Ramatoulaye, subsequently attack the police.

With its emphasis upon the participation of women and the collective experience, as well as its profound expression of optimism, *Les Bouts de bois de Dieu* marks a new turn in the African novel. In a work that depicts feats of heroism, the *griot*-narrator becomes the

---

* Ramatoulaye, qui courait rarement, se précipita comme une furie. Sur la véranda, elle aperçut le bélier qui sortait paisiblement de chez Bineta en mâchonnant un bout d'étoffe rouge rayée de blanc (113).

† Houdia M'Baye et les enfants étaient complètement hébétés. Bouches et yeux grands ouverts, ils regardaient tantôt la femme, tantôt le bélier. La chatte avait passé sa tête entre les jambes torses du petit N'Dole (114).

‡ Il n'y avait dans son regard ni fierté ni orgueil, simplement une sorte de satisfaction comme si son acte n'avait été qu'un devoir dicté par la fatalité (115).

praise-singer of the people. As Soundjata is reported to have said when reunited with his *griot*, "There would not be any heroes if deeds were condemned to be forgotten by men, for we act to win the admiration of the living, and the veneration of future generations" (Niane 108).* Maintaining the balance between individual and collective identity on the one hand and traditional and modern aesthetics on the other, Sembène infuses vitality into the African novel, a genre that had borrowed significantly from its European counterpart and was seeking an authentic means of expression. For Ousmane Sembène in Senegal and Kateb Yacine in Algeria (where, in 1954, the Algerian struggle for independence had begun), history—and therefore the recreation of historical events—becomes a key element in the search for an authentic voice in modern African fiction.

Uprisings of Sétif and Guelma: Kateb Yacine

The Maghrebian (North African) novel written in French, like its counterpart in francophone sub-Saharan Africa, is a product of the *fait colonial*, the French presence in a colonized nation. At first a cautious description of daily life, as exemplified by Mouloud Feraoun's *Le Fils du pauvre* (1950), set in the Algerian novelist's rural Kabylia, the novel reflected the Maghrebian writer's search for a new identity, one that would express the colonial experience and reaffirm the traditions of a pre-colonial cultural heritage. The novel quickly became a cry of anguish and resentment. The Algerian novelist Mohammed Dib's *La Grande Maison* (1952), the Tunisian Albert Memmi's *La Statue de sel* (1953), the Moroccan Driss Chraibi's *Le Passé simple* (1954) are part of a corpus that reflects growing Maghrebian alienation in the era marked by the end of World War II and the beginning of the Algerian independence struggle in 1954.

Kateb Yacine, whose surname "kateb" means "writer" in Arabic,[13] is perhaps the most compelling of the writers of the "generation of 1954"[14] because he boldly rejected not only colonial domination but its accepted European literary traditions, choosing to experiment with form and language. As Edouard Glissant remarked in his introduction to the Algerian writer's collection of theatrical pieces, *Le Cercle des représailles*, Kateb's style is one of poetic realism (10).

---

* "Il n'y aurait pas de héros si les actions étaient condamnés à l'oubli des hommes, car nous agissons pour soulever l'admiration de ceux qui vivent, et provoquer la vénération de ceux qui doivent venir."

In contrast to Sembène, a social realist whose work contains elements of the African epic tradition, a writer who strives for clarity and eschews ambiguity as he transmits his ideological message, Kateb explores myth, probes the unconscious, ignores chronology. He forces the reader to struggle with the text in an attempt to achieve the clarity that Sembène grants so willingly. Following the publication of *Nedjma*, the Algerian poet Jean Sénac called the writer a terrorist of the French language: "Far from allowing himself to be colonized by this language, he, in a pathetic embrace, wrenched a strange and new meaning from it" (65).* Kateb himself states:

> So, reader, you have fallen for it! You let me confuse the path! As if the real characters in this novel were dead! Reader, this is how insignificant we are in the face of the void. Choose! Either I serve you a fine slice of life cooked rare as recommended by the critics, or you settle for the imaginary fare of backward countries. Do you prefer surrealist creamed soup? Must we reheat a sketch of a stunted world? Don't you want some philosophical whipped cream?
>
> Whatever the case may be, as the orators say, let's carry on. Let's not change gears. We will be a disoriented bomber. ("Un rêve dans un réve" 31)†

The publication of *Nedjma* (1956) coincided with the advent of the "nouveau roman" in France, as French writers rejected previously established literary norms. For example, the psychological element or phenomenon replaced the individual; therefore, jealousy replaced the jealous protagonist (Lesage 14). Techniques used by Robbe-Grillet can be found in Kateb's work, for the Algerian novelist disregards chronology, substitutes pattern for plot, and explores unorthodox approaches to characterization as well. In a study that appeared in *Esprit* in 1958, Olivier de Magny includes Kateb Yacine with Michel Butor, Nathalie Sarraute, Alain Robbe-Grillet, and other French writers of the "nouveau roman." To place Kateb within the

---

* Loin de se laisser coloniser par cette langue, il lui a arraché dans une pathétique étreinte, un sens insolite et nouveau (65).

† Alors, lecteur, tu marches dans la combine! Tu me laisses brouiller la piste! Comme si les vrais personnages de ce roman étaient morts! C'est là, lecteur, que nous nous faisons tout petits devant le vide. Choisis: ou bien je te servirai une bonne tranche de vie, saignante comme la recommandent les critiques, ou bien tu te contenteras du repas imaginaire des pays arriérés. Préfères-tu une soupe au lait surréaliste? Cette esquisse d'un univers rabougri, faut-il la réchauffer? Ne veux-tu pas quelque crème philosophique bien fouetté?

Quoi qu'il en soit, ainsi que disent les orateurs, poursuivons. Ne changeons jamais de vitesse. Soyons un bombardier désorienté.

context of a French literary tradition is misleading, however, for the Algerian writer's philosophical commitment has always been to Algeria, and his literary effort is an expression of his Algerian identity. Moreover, as subsequent critics have noted, an American connection cannot be ignored, there are specific affinities between the Algerian writer and William Faulkner.[15] Kateb has said that following the success of *Nedjma* (and *Le Polygone étoilé*) he faced the choice of becoming a novelist of the French avant-garde and losing his Algerian public or affirming his links with his own people by turning to popular theatre in dialectical Arabic; he chose the latter course ("La Situation de l'écrivain algérien").

In this work, Kateb emphasizes the fact that his personal experiences in colonial Algeria represent those of his people and his generation and are meaningful within an historical and political context. By focusing on an event that had a lasting effect upon him personally, Kateb differs from Sembène in his approach to the historical event. For Sembène, the Dakar-Niger railway strike is a didactic device that projects a victorious image. Writing with distance and objectivity about a political struggle that ended in 1947 in triumph for the African strikers, Sembène presents it as a positive foreshadowing of French West African independence in 1960. Kateb depicts an historical event, the May 8 uprising, that ended in Algerian defeat and harsh repression by the French and left him traumatized as well. It, too, was a foreshadowing of independence, but Kateb, unlike Sembène, had less distance and objectivity. *Nedjma* was published prior to Algerian independence; the Algerian novelist had no certainty at the time that Algeria would win the struggle.

On May 8, 1945, as the European population of Algeria celebrated the Allied victory in Europe, riots broke out in the Arab quarters of several cities in Algeria; the two most violent demonstrations were in Sétif and nearby Guelma, where police fired on civilians bearing illegal nationalist banners. Days of terror followed; an estimated 6,000 to 9,000 people were killed. The violence that rocked Sétif widened the cleavage between the Arab and European populations. The *Echo d'Alger*, a newspaper expressing European sympathies, announced that "the hour of the gendarme" had come for North Africa (Gordon 54).

A sixteen-year-old student at the French *collège* in Sétif, Kateb participated in the demonstrations. He felt the shock of the riots intimately: several members of his family were killed; his mother became insane; he was expelled from school and arrested. The Sétif riots put an end to the writer's formal education. While Kateb was in prison, the cousin with whom he was in love married someone else: "A mother gone insane, a failed revolution, an impossible love" ("Une Interview").*

Published almost a decade after the traumatic events of May 1945, *Nedjma* is a novel of obsessive love, colonial and incestuous violence, and ambiguous genealogy. It is the story of four men linked by family ties. Two brothers, Lakhdar and Mourad, are cousins of Mustapha and Rachid. All four are in love with the beautiful and enigmatic Nedjma ("star" in Arabic). She, in turn, is either their sister or cousin.

In this work, the reader is first initiated into the world of the Algerian laborer: its poverty, indignity, and violence. The novel opens *in medias res*. Lakhdar has just escaped from the prison in which he was serving a sentence for striking his French boss at a construction site where the four companions worked. Lakhdar's escape sets off further violence between Arabs and Europeans. With the intention of interceding on Lakhdar's behalf, following the dispute between his boss and his brother, Mourad attends a wedding reception for his boss's daughter. At the raucous wedding party, Mourad strikes and kills the drunken bridegroom, who is beating an Arab servant. He is jailed and eventually shares a prison cell with Rachid, arrested later in a street fight with a Frenchman.

The path of the four protagonists leads from the construction yard to prison and back again, a pattern that Kateb considers to be very much part of the Algerian experience: "Algeria being both a construction site and a prison" ("Un Rêve dans un rêve," 31).† Two forms of exile — the life of the itinerant worker and the prisoner — are introduced as autobiographical fragments in the novel.

Throughout *Nedjma* there are references to prisons, infamous and sinister, where the militant, once caught, becomes a powerless victim. Lakhdar and Mustapha are both incarcerated following the May 8 demonstration. Lakhdar is tortured in prison. Mustapha's diary records the cries of other prisoners:[16]

> There were nineteen in the room now.
> The barber Si Khelifa was still shouting.
> The heavy door had opened four times.

---

* La mère cinglée, la révolution assassinée, l'amour impossible.

† L'Algérie étant à la fois chantier et prison.

Tayeb had not come back. They were shooting close by.
Close to the prison. Close to the prison. (76)*

Rachid is later sent to prison as an army deserter. In addition, Lakhdar, Mourad, and Rachid are arrested for aggression against Frenchmen. Thus, three of the four protagonists are jailed once for a crime against the state and once for individual assault.

The prison motif is given additional emphasis by the form of the novel. *Nedjma* is structured upon its *leitmotif*, the six-pointed star. There are six parts to the work, each of which is further subdivided into twelve chapters of varied length. Maurice Nadeau has explained the architecture of *Nedjma* in this way:

> He [Kateb Yacine] has constructed a stellar universe. In its center, he placed a sun: Nedjma, around whom a certain numbers of stars, large and small, gravitate; they too have satellites. If the star is immobile and shines with more or less the same intensity, we know it only through its reflection upon the other stars that surround it and whose fixed movements periodically approach or withdraw from its light. This is also true of their satellites. And because these stars are prisoners of the same movement that at fixed intervals, makes them appear, there is a kind of eternal return, a complete confusion of past, present, and future. ("Kateb Yacine juge l'islamisme," 13)†

Lakhdar, Mourad, Mustapha, Rachid, and Nedjma are prisoners of the same movement, one that Nadeau calls an eternal return. The novel accentuates the circular movement through repetition, beginning with Lakhdar's escape:

> Lakhdar has escaped from his cell.

---

* Ils étaient maintenant dix-neuf dans la salle.
Le coiffeur Si Khelifa hurlait toujours.
La lourde porte s'était ouverte quatre fois.
Tayeb n'était pas revenu. On fusillait tout près.
Tout près de la prison. Tout près de la prison (57).

† Il [Kateb Yacine] a construit un univers stellaire. En son centre, il a disposé un soleil: Nedjma, autour duquel gravitent un certain nombre d'étoiles grandes et petites, pourvues elles-mêmes de satellites. Si le soleil est fixe et brille à peu près toujours avec la même intensité, nous ne la connaissons que par ses reflets sur les astres qui l'entourent et dont le mouvement régulier les approche ou les éloigne périodiquement de sa lumière. Il en va de même, par rapport à eux, de leurs satellites. Et comme ces astres sont prisonniers du même mouvement qui, à intervalles fixes, les rend également présents, il s'ensuit dans une espèce de retour éternel, une confusion complet du passé, du présent et de l'avenir (13).

> At dawn, his shadow appears on the landing; everyone looks up,
>   indifferently.
> Mourad stares at the fugitive. "So what? They'll get you later."
> "They know your name."
> "I don't have any papers."
> "They'll look for you here."
> "Shut up. Don't nag." (11)*

The penultimate scene repeats the initial escape:

> Lakhdar has escaped from his cell.
> At dawn, when his shadow appeared on the landing, everyone
>   looked up indifferently.
> Mourad stares at the fugitive.
> "So what? They'll get you later."
> "They know your name."
> "I don't have any papers."
> "They'll look for you here."
> "Shut up. Don't nag." (343)[17][†]

Stylistically, the two scenes are not identical. By placing the verb *apparaître* in the present and avoiding subordinating conjunctions in the first scene, but changing to the past tense and inserting a subordinate conjunction in the second, the writer signals an important transformation in the text. The use of the past tense in the penultimate scene restablishes a sense of chronology, of time passing, that is absent in the early pages of the novel. Moreover, the uninitiated reader who first learned from Lakhdar's companions that Lakhdar will be recaptured (for the path is predetermined), has become the

---

* Lakhdar s'est echappé de sa cellule.
A l'aurore, sa silhouette apparaít sur le palier;
chacun relève la tête, sans grande emotion.
Mourad dévisage le fugitif.
"Rien d'extraordinaire. Tu seras repris."
"Ils savent ton nom."
"Je n'ai pas de carte d'identité."
"Ils viendront te choper ici."
"Fermez-la. Ne me découragez pas." (11)

† Lakhdar s'est échappé de sa cellule.
A l'aurore, lorsque sa silhouette est apparue sur le palier,
chacun a relevé la tête, sans grande émotion.
Mourad dévisage le fugitif.
"Rien d'extraordinaire. Tu seras repris."
"Ils savent ton nom."
"Je n'ai pas de carte d'identité."
"Ils viendront te choper ici"
"Fermez-la. Ne me découragez pas." (255)

informed reader, initiated to Algerian reality. It is no surprise to reader or protagonist that Lakhdar's escape is temporary and incomplete. As the novel closes, the reader and Lakhdar's companions are equally aware of the spatial and temporal pattern, of the eternal return to closed space, to prison, in colonial Algeria.

Repetition, the double vision of each experience, is a distinctive characteristic of the novel. Rachid tells his story twice: once in a state of delirium while Mourad watches over his sickbed, and once again to a public writer (a *kateb*!) he meets among his fellow hashish smokers. Lakhdar gives his version of the May 8 demonstrations; later, Mustapha recalls the same events. Also, one episode evokes another: Mourad, describing Lakhdar's arrival at the railway station in Bone preceding his visit to Nedjma's villa, recalls that Mustapha arrived under the same conditions two months earlier.

The double vision is most striking midway through the narrative. The twelfth chapter of part 3 begins with Mourad's words: "She came to Constantine without Rachid's knowing how. He was never to know..." (138)* and is followed directly by another chapter which Rachid narrates: "She came to Constantine without my knowing how, I was never to know" (139).† With a change of focalization, passing from the objectivity of the third person to the subjectivity of the first-person narrative, the same scene, Nedjma's arrival in Constantine, is open to yet another interpretation. The repetition of an episode concerning Nedjma emphasizes the obsessive nature of the four protagonists' love for her.

Caught in the circle of violence, the four companions are similarly prisoners of Nedjma, caught in the goddess's spell. She, however, remains elusive. When Lakhdar and Nedjma embrace at her villa, he admits: "Nedjma is the tangible form of the mistress who waits for me, the thorn, the flesh, the seed, but not the soul, not the living unit where I could blend myself without fear of dissolution" (331).‡ Although the four cousins wish to possess her, to make her their captive, they are hers. Reflecting upon her hypnotic power, Nedjma states: "Since they love me, I keep them in my prison...In the long

---

* Elle vint à Constantine sans que Rachid sût comment. Il ne devait jamais le savoir... (104).

† Elle vint à Constantine, je ne sais comment, je ne devais jamais le savior (105).

‡ De l'amante qui m'attend, Nedjma est la forme sensible, l'épine, la chair, le noyau, mais non pas l'âme, non pas l'unité vivante où je pourrais me confondre sans crainte de dissolution (247).

run, it's the prisoner who makes the decision" (89—90).* Mustapha also notes that Nedjma is a prisoner as well, locked in her own world, "reduced to the contemplation of her captive beauty" (248).†

Nedjma is the daughter of a French mother and one of her lovers (Si Mokhtar or Rachid's father) who carried the woman off to a remote grotto where Rachid's father was killed. Nedjma, conceived at this time, was later abandoned by the French woman to be raised by an Arab stepmother, an aunt of Lakhdar and Mourad. As Rachid explains, Nedjma is either his own sister, or more probably, the daughter of Si Mokhtar. She may have unwittingly become involved in an incestuous marriage, for her husband Kamel is one of Si Mokhtar's many illegitimate children. In this society that prohibits incest (marriage between brothers and sisters) but encourages endogamy (marriage between cousins), Nedjma, whose origins are unclear, therefore remains precariously accessible and inaccessible to Rachid and his three companions.

Throughout the novel, Nedjma remains cloaked in shadows. Her participation is minimal; her words, in the form of short conversations and interior monologues, form less than two pages of text in a 256-page work. Nevertheless, her presence as myth and symbol is central to the structure of the work.[18] The myth of Nedjma is transparent. Nedjma—"her ravishers thus condemning the girl to her destiny as a forbidden flower, threatened to the depth and the fragility of her roots" (239)‡—is Algeria, *la patrie perdue*. Pursued by four potential conquerors—Turk, Roman, Arab, and French—Nedjma, as Algeria, embodies the characteristic that the Algerian poet and critic Jean Amrouche first attributed to the Maghreb: "le génie de l'alternance," the elusive spirit of the captive (64).

Kateb, calling this work a plural autobiography, has created four protagonists who assume multiple functions in the text: as narrator, listener, witness, writer. Each in a different way represents a part of Kateb himself. Mustapha is one facet of the writer's autobiography—a schoolboy who reacts against colonialism and who records his impressions as a militant jailed at the time of the Sétif uprising. In addition, Mustapha's father, like Kateb's was a lawyer. Lakhdar (the

---

* "Puisqu'ils m'aiment, je les garde dans ma prison...A la longue, c'est la prisonnière qui décide" (67).

† réduite à la contemplation de sa beauté captive (185).

‡ ses ravisseurs la condamnant ainsi, à ce destin de fleur irrespirable menacé jusqu'à la profondeur et à la fragilité de ses racines (179).

name signifies "green tree, fruitful" in Arabic) is a militant nationalist whose role assumes greater proportions in the tragedy *Le Cadavre encerclé*, when he loses his life, becoming a martyr to the revolution. Mourad appears alternately as witness, victim, and agent of violence. Witness to Rachid's hallucinations, to Lakhdar's arrival in the city of Bone, to Rachid and Si Mokhtar's comings and goings, to Nedjma's childhood (for he grew up in the same house with her), he is then a victim of the colonial situation. He strikes out against it and in so doing commits a crime: he kills the French bridegroom. Mourad is finally a victim of intratribal hostility; he is stabbed by Rachid in prison: "The friend who comes back to me in prison, to wound me with my own knife. Rachid who was my friend, the friend of my brother, who then became our enemy though he was still living in my room, he who followed us, Lakhdar and me, to the yards..." (56).*

Rachid, in contrast to his three companions, is inextricably bound to a more symbolic world. He is haunted by the distant past of tribal Algeria — the revolt of the Numidians against the Romans, the former glory of the ancient cities of Hippone (Bone, now Annaba) and Cirta (Constantine). Born shortly after his father's mysterious death at the hands of an unknown assassin (presumably Si Mokhtar), Rachid is compelled to avenge his father's murder. From the moment of his birth, Rachid is fated to bear the burden of the past. Destiny leads him to follow Si Mokhtar, first as his constant companion in Bone and Constantine, then on a pilgrimage to Mecca, and finally to the ancestral homeland where the old man is slain by a jealous tribesman and Nedjma is reclaimed by the ancestral clan, the Keblouti.

Through Rachid, the novelist introduces precolonial history presented as the theme of past glory. At the same time, he depicts a protagonist who appears locked in the past and seems unable to come to grips with the present. Unlike his cousins, Rachid does not become a militant nationalist marked exclusively by the May 8 uprising.[19] By frequenting Si Mokhtar, Rachid learns from the old man to look to the ancestral tribe for the cornerstone of national identity. Si Mokhtar tells Rachid: "You should remember the destiny of this country we come from; it is not a French province, and has neither bey nor sultan; perhaps you are thinking of Algeria, still

---

* "L'ami qui me rejoint au bagne, pour me blesser avec mon propre couteau, Rachid qui fut mon ami, celui de mon frère, et devint aussitôt notre adversaire sans cesser d'occuper ma chambre, lui qui nous suivit, Lakhdar et moi, au chantier..." (42).

invaded, of its inextricable past, for we are not a nation, not yet, you know that: we are only decimated tribes. It is not a step backward to honor our tribe, the only link that remains to us by which we can unite and restore our people, even if we hope for more than that . . ." (170–71).*

Rachid accompanies Si Mokhtar on two distinctly different journeys: a pilgrimage to Mecca and a journey to the ancestral homeland. Si Mokhtar appears to undertake the pilgrimage on a whim, suddenly deciding to cleanse his debauched soul. Accompanying him in the belief that the old man is indeed his father's assassin, Rachid plans to kill Si Mokhtar once he has learned the truth from him regarding Nedjma's origins. On the one hand, the pilgrimage to Mecca, a thwarted journey that involves stowaways, false identification papers, and an imaginary stolen money box, provides comic relief. Kateb satirizes the pilgrimage, stripping it of religious significance, and pokes fun at Si Mokhtar, depicting him as an endearing buffoon upon whom Rachid is finally unable to seek revenge. On the other hand, the thwarted pilgrimage is a catalyst; it prompts Si Mokhtar to hatch a plan for another journey, the return to Nadhor, the ancestral homeland, with both Rachid and Nedjma.

The aborted journey to Mecca also reveals that Si Mokhtar is an important link to oral tradition. First, he can be interpreted as the intercessor in oral narrative, transmitting wisdom to Rachid. Thus, in Rachid's quest to uncover the mystery surrounding his father's death, a crime that is never solved, he is guided by Si Mokhtar to the discovery of his own heritage. Second, Si Mokhtar can be viewed as the *griot* recounting the legends of the Keblouti to Rachid, tales that Rachid will remember later in his prison cell. Finally, the old man, a buffoon and a lecher, may recall the trickster of African oral narrative. In the comic episode of the false pilgrimage to Mecca, Si Mokhtar, humorous and cunning, reminds us of Djoh'a, the Algerian trickster of popular folklore. Djoh'a becomes more recognizable, however, as "Nuage de Fumée" in Kateb's satirical play *La Poudre d'intelligence.*[20]

---

* "Tu dois songer à la destinée de ce pays d'où nous venons, quo n'est ni une province française, et qui n'a ni bey ni sultan; tu penses peut-être à l'Algérie toujours envahie, à son inextricable passé, car nous ne sommes pas une nation, pas encore, sache-le: nous ne sommes que des tribus décimées. Ce n'est pas revenir en arrière que d'honorer notre tribu, le seul lien qui nous reste pour nous réunir et nous retrouver, même si nous espérons mieux que cela . . ." (128–29).

The true inspiration for Si Mokhtar is Si Tahar ben Lounissi, a well-known personality in Constantine during Kateb's youth. Ben Lounissi probably provided Kateb with the story of his own pilgrimage to Mecca, although the novelist had been on a writing assignment to the Middle East as well (Arnaud, *La littérature maghrébine*, 300). Indeed, Si Mokhtar helps Rachid by acquainting him with the precolonial past and returning with him to the ancestral homeland, just as Kateb's spiritual father guided him by distributing the young poet's first poems and introducing him to Algerian nationalists in Sétif ("La Situation de l'écrivain algérien").

Rachid comes close to happiness during the trip to the ancestral homeland. With pipe in hand, Nedjma at his side, Rachid approaches the cherished "luxe, calme, et volupté" to which he aspires: "After all the three of us were taking the rest we had always longed for during the years of perpetual exile, of separation, of hard labor, or of idleness and debauchery" (178).* Paradise — "les derniers hectares de la tribu" — is the place where Rachid will be able to erase the traces of alienation, of wandering upon foreign soil.

The trip back to the homeland is climaxed by an erotic scene in which Nedjma takes a bath in a clearing, presumably unaware that Rachid as well as a stranger half-hidden in the shrubs are watching her. A hashish smoker, Rachid is paralyzed by the drug and unable to speak to the mysterious intruder and send him away: "it is long since my tongue has stirred, like a building infested with dragons!" (186–7).† When he relates the episode some time later to a stranger in Constantine, Rachid is once more enveloped in the fumes of the hashish smokers.

The two journeys appear on the surface to end in failure. The first one results in Rachid and Si Mokhtar returning home without setting foot in Mecca. The second ends with Si Mokhtar's death, Rachid's expulsion from the Nadhor, Nedjma's return to the tribe. In the course of the first journey, however, Rachid, who was in search of the key to his individual past, the mystery surrounding his father's death, discovers the collective past. Aboard ship, he is initiated by his old companion into oral tradition. Si Mokhtar says,

---

* Il faut dire que nous étions tous les trois, enfin! dans la période de repos que nous avions toujours souhaitée, depuis des années de perpétuel exil, de séparation, de dur labeur, ou d'inaction et de débauche (135).

† "Ll y a longtemps que ma langue remue comme un édifice infesté de dragons!" (142).

"All I know I heard from my father, who heard it from his, and so on" (156).* Rachid's initiation is political as well as historical, for Si Mokhtar explains the tribe's unsuccessful strategy against the French conquerors, their defensive regrouping in a remote area: "The Nadhor inhabitants had remained unsubdued. They didn't attack, just pushed deeper into the forest, pretending to ignore the new conquerors; the decades passed without the French being able to extend their influence. It was then that the tribe was decimated" (166).† Therefore, just as Mustapha and Lakhdar are initiated politically, learning that sporadic violent demonstrations against the French result in further repression and no political gains, Rachid learns from Si Mokhtar that the Keblouti's political strategy of retreat is equally ineffective. Although Rachid's own agenda in embarking upon the second journey with Si Mokhtar is to escape with Nedjma to a remote paradise, the result of his association with Si Mokhtar is a cultural, historical, and political awakening.

The return to the ancestral homeland, an episode of important symbolic value, is difficult to place chronologically and raises the question: is it Rachid's dream or reality? Nevertheless, the death of Si Mokhtar in the Nadhor at the hands of a demented tribesman puts an end to one era and marks the beginning of another; political destiny is now in the hands of Rachid's generation. Although Rachid's fellow tribesman reject him as a member of the branch of Keblouti deserters, the experience of having returned to the ancestral homeland binds the young man to his precolonial heritage. Rachid loses Nedjma in the course of the journey but, helped by Si Mokhtar, spiritual father and intercessor, he gains important knowledge that sets him apart from his three companions. He learns to value the tribe as an important historical phase and at the same time to see beyond it to the construction of the modern state. In this, he represents Kateb Yacine's individual journey to self-understanding, a model that the writer sets forth for a collective voice, for the Algerian nation.

Were Kateb to have chosen a linear narrative, he might have ended the work at this point. By returning to the earlier episodes—

---

* "Tout ce que je sais, je le tiens de mon père, qui le tient de son père, et ainsi de suite" (124)

† Les habitants du Nadhor étaient restés insoumis. Ils n'attaquaient pas, mais s'enfonçaient dans la forêt, affectant d'ignorer les nouveaux conquérants; les décades passaient sans que les Français aient pu étendre leur influence. C'est alors que la tribu fut décimée (125).

Lakhdar's escape from prison and the subsequent separation of the three companions following Mourad's arrest — the Algerian novelist imparts a circular structure to the work, giving added dimension to the two dominant metaphors of the work: Nedjma and prison. In colonial Algeria, where the four companions are obsessed with Nedjma and caught in a circle of violence, time — past, present and future — is represented as a closed circuit: the present and the future are mere repetitions of the past with its indelible mark of conquest. If the circle is representative of the colonial situation, it nonetheless also reflects the legacy of the ancestral past. As Georges Poulet explains:

> There is no form more complete than the circle. No form is more durable either. The circle that Euclid describes and the one which modern mathematics traces not only resemble one another but converge. The clock's face, the wheel of fortune traverse time intact without being altered by the variations they record or produce. Each time the mind wishes to represent time's duration, it must move the same curve around the same center. Whatever the distances to be measured, men of all times have only used one compass. (1)*

We have seen that Kateb's four protagonists are trapped within a circle of violence, all four launched upon a predetermined circular journey that takes them from prison to construction yards and back to prison. The colonial jail, the inevitable enclosure to which they are destined to return, is truly the microcosm of the macrocosm. It symbolizes colonial Algeria, which is indeed prison for the colonized.[21] The circular journey, then, characteristic of African folk narrative, is illustrated by Kateb in a distinct way. Whereas previous francophone African fiction, including Sembène's novel *Les Bout de bois de Dieu*, departs from traditional folk narrative by concluding with rupture rather than reintegration, Kateb's fictional world is closed in upon itself. His fiction ends in repetition, in eternal return.

Not only do Rachid and his companions move on a circular trajectory between construction site and prison, but their movements often appear to lack purpose and itinerary. In the beginning of the

---

* Pas de forme plus achevée que le cercle. Pas de forme plus durable non plus. Le cercle que décrit Euclide, et celui que trace la mathématique moderne, non seulement se ressemblent mais se confondent. Le cadran des horloges, la roue de la fortune traversent intacts le temps, sans être modifiés par les variations qu'ils enregistrent ou déterminent. Chaque fois que l'esprit veut se représenter l'étendue, il fait se mouvoir une même courbe autour d'un même centre. Quel que soit l'écartement des branches, les hommes de toutes les époques ne sont jamais servis que d'un seul compas.

novel, when the three companions leave town without Mourad — he is in prison — they have a clouded sense of space and time: "They meet on the road, turning their backs to the quarry; they stamp on the ground strewn with bare branches; the north wind pushes them over the brush and they plunge into the fog; the absence of any itinerary abolishes the notion of time" (44).* Discussing the absence of itinerary, Louis Tremaine notes that the three figures, enveloped in fog and darkness, are on a trajectory away from something, but *toward* nothing ("Absence of Itinerary," 28). He adds that Rachid, Lakhdar, and Mustapha, fleeing in the middle of the night, are running away from the consequences of acts of violence; yet violence in colonial Algeria is inevitable and inescapable. Most important in Tremaine's discussion is the conclusion that violence is inflicted upon the group as much by insiders — members of the clan — as by outsiders — French colonizers. We recall that Rachid stabs Mourad in prison and the demented tribesman kills Si Mokhtar in the Nadhor. Tremaine explains, "Those who flee may escape a particular eruption of violence, but they cannot escape violence itself, for they carry it within themselves" ("Absence of Itinerary," 31).

In the study of the journey motif, it is important to contrast Rachid and Si Mokhtar's thwarted journeys that propose goals they do not achieve with the seemingly purposeless itineraries of the three figures who take leave of one another on the darkened road. The tension between itinerary and aimless wandering, a spatial dialectic, is linked in Kateb's world to temporal conflict of past, present, and future. When Algeria emerges from the colonial past through victory against the French colonizer, the concept of itinerary will return.

Marc Gontard has written that the two images that open and close the novel — Lakhdar's escape, the three figures disappearing in the night — represent dream and reality. In his view, Lakhdar dreams of escaping from an incarcerating world that offers no escape. Lakhdar's fantasy contrasts with harsh reality, the break-up of the Keblouti clan and the dispersion of its members, as symbolized by the final solitary journeys into the night. In her discussion of the same episodes, Kristine Aurbakken also contrasts Lakhdar's escape, which she considers *repli*, a returning to the clan, with the subsequent separation of the three companions on the road.

---

* Ils se regroupent le long de la route, tournant le dos à la carrièrer; ils piétinent sur le sol jonché de branches nues; le vent du nord les pousse à travers la broussaille, et ils s'enfoncent dans la brume; l'absence d'itinéraire abolit la notion du temps (32–33).

She views the latter as *sortie*, the end of tribal cohesion (199). The critic suggests that *repli* (which Si Mokhtar told Rachid was the traditional ineffective response to the invader and the key to the clan's defeat) is now replaced by a new tactic, *sortie*.

Aurbakken's interpretation grants more importance to the separation of the three companions, viewed as a break with the tribal past, than the absence of itinerary, the aimless wandering, that Tremaine emphasizes. Indeed she suggests that the three companions, having acquired political consciousness, are venturing forth on the road toward national liberation: "From the tribal of the Nadhor to the national road of Sétif, from the 'sun at its zenith' to the 'sun still high' of May 8, 1945, experiencing along the way the revolution of bodies sharpened by the male sun, the remembering conscience has forged a dual path of rupture and passage, from the Ancestor to the Nation; this path where absence had been experienced as the point of departure of the writing act: 'the absence of itinerary abolishes the notion of time'" (Aurbakken's translation 203).*

Although the absence of itinerary concerns us most directly because of its relationship to the journey motif, another element bears an important relationship to it: absence of inventory (lack of written history). In his attempt to reconstitute genealogy, both individual and collective history, Rachid is aware of the absence of written history: "For the history of our tribe is written nowhere, but no thread is ever broken for a man who seeks out his origins" (192).†
In his pursuit of Si Mokhtar (who as guardian of popular wisdom and culture embodies attributes of the West African *griot*), Rachid, as I have noted, establishes links to oral tradition. By recounting to Rachid the history of the Keblouti as told to him by his own father, Si Mokhtar, in effect, accepts the orphaned Rachid as an adopted son. Rachid, in turn, commits to memory all that Si Mokhtar has told him and then confides first in Mourad and then in the public writer. Hence, orality is clearly established in the novel as an important link to personal and collective history.

---

* De la terre tribale du Nadhor à la route nationale de Sétif, du "soleil au zénith" au "soleil encore haut" du 8 mai 1945 en passant par la révolution de corps qui s'aiguise sous le soleil masculin, la conscience remémorante s'est frayé la double voie de la rupture et du passage, de l'Ancêtre à la Nation, cette voie dont l'absence s'etait fait ressentir comme point de départ à l'écriture: "l'absence d'itinéraire abolit la notion du temps."

† Car l'histoire de notre tribu n'est écrite nulle part, mais aucun fil n'est jamais rompu pour qui recherche ses origines (146).

Yet when Rachid tells his story to Mourad he is feverish, suffering from malaria. Later, when he talks to the public writer—who listens, but records nothing in writing—he is enveloped in hashish fumes. The public writer notes his mental confusion: "Rachid could no longer tell what he was thinking from what he was saying" (232).*
Therefore, Rachid's oral narrative remains ambiguous, clouded in mystery. It is not always clear what Rachid recalls, what he invents. As Rachid focuses upon the semi-mythic past, his thoughts spiral inward, and he is caught in a labyrinth between light and darkness: "I could neither resign myself to the light of day, nor recover my star..." (235).† The reader leaves Rachid caught up in the past and admitting to the public writer: "...I am entangled in too many deaths, too many deaths" (247).[22]‡

Mustapha breaks into Rachid's hallucinations; his diary brings the narrative back to daylight. The precise, clipped journalistic style of Mustapha's diary contrasts with Rachid's ephemeral dreams in smoke-filled rooms and with the ghosts Rachid conjures up in the dark solitude of his prisoner's cell. Presenting the early years of Kateb's own life, the diary records the immediate rather than the mythical past and expresses individual rather than collective experience. In his diary, Mustapha reveals his growing alienation as a schoolboy in a colonized nation. Particularly poignant episodes are those that depict the sharp division between the life of his Algerian mother and his French schoolteacher. Yet when Mustapha dwells upon his vision of Nedjma, he too is caught up in the same spell that envelops Rachid. He writes: "Hair of glowing steel, delicate, hot where the sun strikes it, disordered like a hive of hornets!...Nedjma laughing at the breaking wave, tending an orchard, the present vanishes, and I fall asleep, giddy..." (109–110).§ Obsessed with Nedjma, searching for identity, Rachid and Mustapha are bound by common preoccupations. Orality and writing—the former expressed by Rachid, the latter by Mustapha—converge in the cousins' mutual belief in the rebirth of Algeria, a nation emerging from its tribal and colonial past.

---

* Rachid ne distinguait plus ce qu'il pensait de ce qu'il disait (174).

† "Je ne pouvais ni me résigner à la lumière du jour, ni retrouver mon étoile..."(177).

‡ "...je suis mêlé à trop de morts, trop de morts" (184).

§ Cheveux de fer ardent fragile chaud où le soleil converge en désordre, ainsi qu'une poignée de guêpes!...Nedjma, rieuse à la ruèe de la vague, gardienne d'un verger, présent disparu, et je m'endors évaporé...(82).

The study of the journey motif in two historically based novels, Sembène's *Les Bouts de bois de Dieu* and Kateb's *Nedjma*, reveals that both works maintain the balance between individual and collective identity. In addition, Sembène and Kateb capture an identical historical moment, when a new ideal of national identity replaces the concept of clan. Moreover, the discussion of *Nedjma* suggests an affirmative response to the two questions posed with respect to Sembène's novel: Do Kateb's protagonists conform to the model of the traditional oral narrative by making the circular journey that results in self-understanding? Do the events that Kateb places within the historical context serve a didactic function similar to the encounters in oral narrative and thereby lead to lucidity? Rachid's initiation in the company of Si Mokhtar can be considered an example of the former, whereas the experience of the four companions during the May 8 uprising is clearly an example of the latter. In Kateb's work, as in Sembène's, the reader uncovers traces of traditional oral narrative embedded within (not superimposed upon) a modern African novel.

Yet the two novels differ remarkably in their portrayal of women. In *Les Bouts de bois de Dieu*, Ramatoulaye, Penda, and Maïmouna are a new breed of women, breaking traditional social barriers and moving triumphantly toward political power. Penda's public speech calling women to action is in marked contrast to Nedjma's silence. Kateb's novel, however, is the record of male obsession. The four cousins who love Nedjma wish to possess her. As Rachid states, "And who has not imprisoned his mistress, dreamed of the woman who could wait for him jailed in some ideal bath?" (183)*

Kateb's Nedjma is an enigmatic and ambiguous character whom the novelist links to the legendary heroic Berber woman warrior, La Kahena, and to Algerian woman forced to silence and seclusion within the patriarchy. The writer has said that Nedjma's silence in the novel stems from the silence imposed upon Algeria's women ("La Situation de l'écrivain algérien"). With the publication of *Le Polygone étoilé* in 1966, Nedjma emerges from the shadows to become a dynamic political presence, a goddess of action. "Here she is at the height of her legend, after absurd persecutions; here she is free, and yet we had believed her to be dead, for we had lost her during the war, lost, recaptured, and nothing threatens her as much as the

---

* "Et qui n'a pas enfermé son amante, qui n'a pas rêvé de la femme capable de l'attendre dans quelque baignoire ideale?" (138−39)

impetuosity of her own warriors; you see we loved her too much; and when it comes to love we are fierce" (144).*

In the earlier novel, Nedjma remains the prisoner of male obsession, a victim of enclosure. Let us recall, however, that in Kateb's fictional world, the male protagonists discover that the journey outward, as a conquest of physical space, is an illusion; in colonial Algeria, this journey leads only to prison. Nedjma is therefore a prisoner of the imprisoned. Representative of Algerian women, she is forced to silence because of the dual constraints upon her freedom: colonialism and patriarchy.[23]

Although Sembène and Kateb differ in the portrayal of women — Sembène depicting a concrete female protagonist who is an agent of social transformation, in contrast to Kateb, who provides his reader with an abstraction, a prisoner of male fantasy who is a *persona erotica* (Aresu 371) — nevertheless the distance between the two writers decreases when one examines two factors: myth and reality. Sembène portrays the blind Maïmouna as prophetess, as goddess of night, and grants epic dimensions to the women's march to Dakar. In addition, he depicts Bakayoko, the African union leader, as a modern-day Soundjata, a protagonist who bears resemblance to the legendary founder of the Empire of Mali. Thus, Sembène's social realism carries traces of myth and legend.

Kateb, on the other hand, suggests that Nedjma, the abstraction, is capable of being inserted into reality. He does so when he grants her the power of speech. For example, when Nedjma speaks to Lakhdar, who has just been released from prison following the May 8 uprising, she chooses to discuss the political situation:

> "Aren't you going to tell how they arrested you?"
> "Apparently I'm a rioter." (321–22)[†]

In this brief exchange that involves political reality, the May 8 uprising, Nedjma joins her male counterparts, Rachid, Mourad, Lakhdar, and Mustapha, as colonized subject concerned with the early stages of the independence struggle.

---

* La voici arrivée à la hauteur de sa légende, après d'absurdes persécutions, la voici libre et pourtant, on l'avait crue morte car nous l'avions perdue dans la guerre, perdue, reconquise, et rien ne la menace autant que la fougue de ses propres guerriers; c'est que nous l'aimions trop; et qu'en amour, nous sommes féroces (144).

† "Tu ne racontes pas comment ils t'ont arrêté?"
  "Paraît que je suis un émeutier." (240)

　　　Sembène and Kateb blend myth and reality, but in different proportions. Although they differ in their form of realism and thereby adopt divergent stylistic innovations, both novelists express a national identity that is rooted in precolonial history but that transcends a tribal and colonial legacy. In this way, they attain a new sophistication of thought and expression and significantly mark subsequent francophone African fiction.

Chapter 4

▼▼▼▼▼▼▼

Independence Acquired — Hope or Disillusionment?

AHMADOU KOUROUMA, *Les Soleils des indépendances*
MOULOUD MAMMERI, *La Traversée*

Built upon the premise of the superiority of European civilization — a belief held steadfastly by Europeans caught up in the late nineteenth-century "scramble for Africa" — the civilizing mission came to justify conquest and rule in Africa. In exchange for important natural resources, colonial powers provided African peoples with "moral" and material comfort: Christian principles in one realm, modern implements in the other.

Although the French colonial presence in Africa was represented in three geographic areas — North, West, and Equatorial Africa — North Africa in general, and Algeria in particular, became the prime focus of French colonization. In the Maghreb, Algeria was considered an integral part of France, whereas Morocco and Tunisia, as protectorates, were allowed to retain the appearance of sovereign states. By 1945, one million French lived on Algerian soil, many cultivating excellent farmlands with the most modern agricultural techniques. Yet in contrast to the commitment to Algeria, France did very little until the end of World War II to develop sub-Saharan Africa, where a less hospitable climate deterred large-scale colonization.

Challenging the political authority of colonial powers weakened by war, African independence movements that had begun in the 1920s and 1930s gained new momentum in the immediate post—World War II period. France, however, tried to head off the rising tide of nationalism with too few conciliatory measures too late. The 1956 *Loi Cadre* (Framework law) granted limited autonomy to both French West Africa and French Equatorial Africa. In 1958, General

De Gaulle offered African colonies membership in the French community. Only Guinea refused, choosing total independence. Two years later, deeply committed to crushing the Algerian liberation struggle, France granted independence to all her other African colonies.[1]

Reflecting the new social and political realities of the postindependence era, in which the colonizer has been replaced by a political elite, francophone African literature has transformed the theme of disillusionment. Where the colonizer was once the sole object of criticism, now African technocrats, cadres, and government officials are depicted exploiting the masses they had promised to uplift. Concurrently, the style of African writing reveals increased experimentation with form and language, a shift away from the rules imposed by the French colonial school. In this regard, Kateb Yacine, assuming the role of "terrorist" of the French language, and Ousmane Sembéne, emerging as *griot*, are early initiators in the quest for an authentic voice, one that takes into account the importance of the oral tradition.

The study of Ahmadou Kourouma's *Les Soleils des indépendances* (1970) and Mouloud Mammeri's *La Traversée* (1982), will reveal affinities and divergences between the two writers who share a commitment to expose corruption, repression, and hypocrisy in postcolonial Africa and to reaffirm the vitality of oral tradition. Kourouma's Fama and Mammeri's Mourad are both ill equipped for life in postindependence Africa, but for entirely different reasons. Fama, a Malinké prince, lacks the skills, such as literacy, for success in modern Africa. Mourad, an Algerian technocrat, refuses to compromise his revolutionary ideals. In both novels, the journey motif becomes an individual rather than a collective experience. The reader will find Kourouma using oral narrative structures and infusing French prose with Malinké expressions as he assumes the role of *griot* to relate Fama's adventures. In contrast, Mammeri, a realist whose prose is poetical and philosophical, reworks a literacy tradition embraced by André Gide, Isabelle Eberhardt, and Ernest Psichari, French writers for whom travel in the Sahara became a metaphor for spiritual discovery.[2] Kourouma's novel, set in the "traditional" world, reveals important stylistic innovations, whereas Mammeri's work, "modern" in orientation, remains stylistically more conservative.

Prince of a Vanishing Kingdom: Ahmadou Kourouma

The will to reproduce the Champs-Elysées and call it Boulevard Valéry Giscard d'Estaing, then name Avenue Foch the Voie Triomphale; the impulse to develop the café as a place for meetings and discussion — imitating Paris; the similarity between two famous restaurants, the Toit d'Abidjan atop the Hôtel Ivoire and the Tour d'Argent in Paris; the emphatic proliferation of Western table manners for the improved education of Ivoirians; the repetition of the ideology of literacy in almost the same way as in France; the permanency of Westernization in school books conceived and published in the Ivory Coast; the hommage paid Parisian artists, painters, and jewellers on constant cultural and commercial missions to Abidjan; the initiation-exhibition of the bureaucratic elite to Western taste, etc.; isn't that enough to highlight the desired cultural dependency that is even considered the only way to salvation? (7)[*]

This critique of cultural dependency by Ivoirian sociologist Abdou Touré explains Ahmadou Kourouma's choice of protagonist, an individual reduced to marginality in the new era dominated by French culture and technology and undermined by corruption as well. By focusing upon Fama, the disinherited Malinké prince, Kourouma breaks the pattern of writers who portray cultural hybrids in African literature. Illiterate in French — "as illiterate as a donkey's tail" (14)[3†] — unskilled in modern technology, Fama cannot join the ruling elite in the new era of the "suns of independence." He represents the disgruntled displaced masses lured from the village to the city by promises of opportunity, only to encounter an ever-deepening poverty.

Fama lives in a topsy-turvy world; "a world turned upside-down" (61)[‡] becomes a metaphor for the protagonist's condition.[4] In Fama's mind, independence is the root of all evil, responsible for his misfortunes and those of his society as a whole. With the coming of independence to his country, the hereditary Malinké prince of Horodougou has been deprived of all former privilege. Fama first

---

[*] La volonté de reproduire l'avenue des Champs-Eylsées sous le nom de boulevard V. Giscard d'Estaing, puis l'avenue Foch sous celui de Voie Triomphale; l'incitation à développer le café comme lieu de rencontre et du discours — à l'instar de Paris; la similitude de deux restaurants célèbres, à savoir le Toit d'Abidjan sis au sommet de la tour de l'Hôtel Ivoire et la Tour d'Argent à Paris; la diffusion avec insistance des manières de table occidentales pour la bonne education des Ivoiriens; la répétition de l'idéologie de l'alphabétisation presque sur le même mode qu'en France; la permanence de l'occidentalisme dans les manuels scolaires pourtant conçus et fabriqués en Côte d'Ivoire; l'encensement des artistes, peintres et joailliers parisiens en missions culturelles et commerciales constantes à Abidjan; l'initiation-exhibition de l'élite bureaucratique au goût artistique occidentale, etc., n'en voilà-t-il pas assez pour mettre en relief la dépendance culturelle voulue et même considérée comme seule voie du salut? (7).

[†] analphabète comme la queue d'un âne (23)

[‡] le monde renversé (92)

appears in the capital city, far from his village of origin; here the prince without a kingdom is reduced to accepting handouts as praise-singer at Malinké funerals. In addition, Fama is plagued by sterility, believing incorrectly that his wife, Salimata, is responsible for the couple's lack of a heir.

Presenting an illiterate protagonist in a society in which literacy is a prerequisite to joining the ruling elite, Kourouma explores the psychological and sociological effects of marginality in a context that differs from the earlier works of Camara Laye and Cheikh Hamidou Kane. Whereas their protagonists struggle to integrate newly acquired European language and technology with traditional African social and spiritual values, Kourouma portrays the plight of the individual who has been left behind. Indeed, Fama represents Laye and Samba's traditional brother, the African not offered the outward journey.

In *Les Soleils des indépendances*, Kourouma uses elements of oral tradition to alter the relationship between the narrator and the reading public, to stretch the limits of conventional French syntax, and, finally, to transform the journey motif. This triple transformation is apparent in the opening passage of the novel: "One week had passed since Ibrahima Kone, of the Malinké race, had met his end in the capital city, or, to put it in Malinké: he had been defeated by a mere cold" (3).*

Rosemary Schikora notes several oral elements in this first sentence: the formulaic opening ("one week had passed" — (*il y avait une semaine*), the euphemistic verb ("had met his end" —*avait fini*), the references to the capital and Ibrahima Kone that go unexplained but are understood by those who share the narrator's cultural context, the use of the pronoun "we" to bridge the gap between narrator and audience, and finally the proverbial expression, borrowed from the Malinké language ("he had been defeated by a mere cold" — *il n'avait pas soutenu un petit rhume*) ("African Fiction in French" 72). By substituting "had met his end" for "died" (*avait fini* for *est mort*) the narrator establishes a linguistic pattern, the simulation of Malinké speech. Kourouma assumes the narrative voice of the *griot* and, although limited by the written word on the printed page, he attempts to recreate both the spontaneity of oral performance and the characteristic interchange between performer and audience.

---

* Il y avait une semaine qu'avait fini dans la capitale Kone Ibrahima, de race malinké, ou disons-le en malinké; il n'avait pas soutenu un petit rhume (7).

The theme of the introductory passage is central to the work. The novel opens with the funeral of one Malinké, an event that will be repeated two more times before the novel closes with the death of the protagonist, Fama. The demise of the obscure Kone Ibrahima is significant in terms of the journey motif, because his death is represented in the text as a circular journey, one that leads to an eternal return. According to Malinké belief, the human spirit experiences an endlessly recurrent cycle of life and death. Ibrahima's spirit is therefore bound to come back to life again: "[it] walked back to the Malinké homeland, there to bring joy to a mother through *reincarnation* as a Malinké infant" (4).[5]* Thus, Kourouma informs the reader at the outset that the narration will unfold within the framework of Malinké tradition. In addition, narrative time accommodates the storyteller who transforms it as he sees fit. Ibrahima's spirit travels to his village and back, a distance of 2,000 kilometers, in the blink of an eye.[6]

In this setting Fama is introduced as a comic, pitiful intrusion, claiming the ambiguous status of prince and vulture: "He, Fama, born to gold, food in plenty, honour and women! Born to prefer one gold to another, to choose between many dishes, to bed his favourite of a hundred wives! What was he now? A scavenger..." (5).† Arriving late at the funeral, Fama interrupts the ceremony when he is angered by a *griot* who publicly shames him by drawing attention to Fama's tardiness and linking his family to a far less illustrious one. Just as the opening sentence established the oral dimension of the novel with great economy, the first scene deftly places the protagonist in his social context. Throughout the novel, he will be psychologically disoriented, angrily blaming others for his own misfortunes, and he will also be in constant physical movement, in the city, in the village, or travelling between the two.

In "le monde renversé," Fama's topsy-turvy world, the journey motif undergoes several transformations. Fama does not journey outward, encounter a series of adventures, and return to the point of departure to face reintegration (the destiny of the travelling hero in oral narrative) or rupture (the fate of the protagonist in the modern

---

* Elle a marché jusqu'au terroir malinké où elle ferait le bonheur d'une mère en *se réincarnant* dans un bébé malinké (emphasis mine) (8).

† Lui, Fama, né dans l'or, le manger, l'honneur et les femmes! Eduqué pour préférer l'or à l'or, pour choisir le manger parmi d'autres, et coucher sa favorite parmi cent épouses! Qu'était-il devenu? Un charognard...(10).

African novel). The journey motif assumes a unique configuration, emphasizing the contrast between city and village as Fama journeys back and forth between them. From aimless wandering in the capital, interrupted by prayers and funerals, quite reminiscent of Kateb's four protagonists who lack itinerary, Fama journeys to the village and back twice. He undertakes the first journey to attend his cousin Lacina's funeral and the second to return home to die in his village. The second journey is interrupted twice. First, Fama is imprisoned in the capital. Later, he is mortally wounded at the frontier between the Bois d'Ebènes (Côte d'Ivoire) and Nikinai (Guinea) as he tries to reach Togobala. Fama's travels within the capital present the journey motif in embryonic form; they foreshadow Fama's journeys to Togobala.

Another transformation involves the concept of threatening space. Let us recall Kunene's words concerning the fear of traveling that appears in oral narratives: "Out there is a jungle. The hero who turns his back on the courtyards and cattle-folds and grazing fields of his home is entering this jungle with all its beasts and monsters" (189). In Fama's world, however, the capital — his home of twenty years — not the bush, represents danger. With no identity card, no party affiliation, no means of employment, and no power of the pen, Fama is as vulnerable in the capital to postindependence "beasts and monsters" as the orphan of oral narratives had been when braving the challenge of bush or jungle. The danger of life in the city is well illustrated when hungry beggars attack Fama's wife, Salimata, because she unexpectedly runs out of the soup she sells in the market.

It is understandable that Fama idealizes the village, where in an earlier era he would have been patriarch, while casting aspersion on his "twenty stupid years in the city" (66),* years of defeat. In contrast to the security, familiarity, and power he would have enjoyed in the village of Togobala before the colonial era, the capital city represents disorientation, danger, and powerlessness for him. More-over, geographically and politically, Fama is a foreigner in the capital city. The village of Togobala is situated in the savannah, in the dry grasslands of the interior, far from the capital (Abidjan), a city in the southern equatorial zone noted for its lush tropical climate, its beaches, and its lagoons. In addition, Togobala lies across the border, in Nikinai.

---

* vingt ans de sottises dans la capitale (99)

There is, however, a discrepancy between Fama's memories of his birthplace and the actual village, which has fallen into extreme poverty and is almost abandoned.

> Eight huts still standing, just that, their walls cracked from roof to ground, their fire-blackened thatch at least five years old. A lot there to plaster and roof before the rains really started. The stable across the way was empty, and the great hut where horses had been tethered had by now forgotten even the smell of horse-piss. Between the two stood the small hut for goats, that now contained all in all: three billy-goats, two nanny-goats and a kid, scrawny and smelly, intended as offerings to Balla's fetishes. As for human beings, there weren't many able-bodied workers. Four men, two of them old, and nine women, seven of them old women who had somehow managed to avoid dying. (73)*

This description of a deteriorating, depopulating, ill-nourished world is similar to Sembène's portrayal of the city of Thiès in *Les Bouts de bois de Dieu*, for both its tone and its emphasis are upon visual images that denote poverty.

> Thiès: a vast, uncertain plain where all the rot of the city had gathered — stakes and crossties, locomotive wheels, rusty shafts, knocked-in jerricans, old mattress springs, bruised and lacerated sheets of steel. And then, a little farther on, on the goat path that leads to the Bambara quarter, piles of old tin cans, heaps of excrement, little mountains of broken pottery and cooking tools, dismantled railway cars, skeletons of motors buried in the dust, and the tiny remains of cats, of rats, of chickens, disputed by the birds. (270)†

---

* Huit cases debout, debout seulement, avec des murs fendillés du toit au sol, le chaume noir et vieux de cinq ans. Beaucoup à pétrir et à couvrir avant le gros de l'hivernage. L'étable d'en face vide; la grande case commune, où étaient mis à l'attache les chevaux, ne se souvenait même plus de l'odeur du pissat. Entre les deux, la petite case des cabrins qui contenait pour tout et tout: trois bouquetins, deux chèvres et un chevreau faméliques et puants destinés à être égorgés aux fétiches de Balla. En fait d'humains, peu de bras travailleurs. Quatre hommes dont deux vieillards, neuf femmes dont sept vieillottes refusant de mourir (110).

† Thiès: un immense terrain vague ou s'amoncellent tous les residus de la ville, des pieux, des traverses, des roues de locomotives, des fûts rouillés, des bidons défoncés, des ressorts de sommiers, des plaques de tôle cabossées et lacérées puis un peu plus loin, sur le sentier de chèvres qui mène vers Bambara, des monceaux de vieilles boîtes de conserves, das amas d'ordures, des monticules de poteries cassées, d'utensiles de ménage, des chassis de wagons démantibulés, des blocs-moteurs ensevelis sous la poussière, des carcasses de chats, de rats, de poulets dont les charognards se disputent les rares lambeaux (35).

Sembène examines a junk pile, revealing its various components: springs, cans, wheels, and the like. Kourouma compiles an inventory that highlights paucity: eight huts, six animals, thirteen villagers. Whereas Thiès is a cemetary for industrial society's rotting and rusting debris, Togobala is a ghost town. In Kourouma's novel, Togobala's emptiness is juxtaposed with Abidjan's dense population and activity. This is evident in the market where Salimata sells her wares. Here the accumulation of sounds adds to the animation: "The morning was alive and humming with activity: on the wharf, workers who had just landed were hurrying off, boatmen and fishermen were already busy, women hawked their wares. Frightened by the uproar, clouds of bats and weaver-birds rose screeching from the palms and mango-trees clustered about the white buildings" (31).[*] By simulating the filming and recording of sights and sounds in city and village, Kourouma, like Sembène, becomes the cameraman creating a social documentary. Moreover, as witness and narrator of events, he emerges as a *griot* as well. Where Sembène depicts feats of heroism and becomes the praise-singer of the people, Kourouma pulls together the various elements that form the portrait of a tragic figure. K. R. Ireland compares Fama, the disinherited Malinkè prince, to Hamlet, the melancholy prince of Denmark, but he states that although Hamlet has the capacity to set things right, Fama has neither the will nor the ability to do so (79). Once Fama is stripped of his illusions and learns that corruption is not confined to the city, but permeates the countryside as well, then he can choose only one form of escape: death.

Kourouma's final transformation of the journey motif is to link it inextricably to death. Within the structure of the novel, each part concerns a death and the ritual of burial: Ibrahima Kone, Lacina, the sorcerer Balla, and, finally, Fama. Kourouma transforms the motif so that, unlike the itinerary of lucidity in Birago Diop's tale "L'Héritage," the quest of three brothers for the wisdom to live better, Fama's trajectory leads to reconciliation with death. Fama attains lucidity when he finally admits that in all aspects — biological, political, economic, social — his life is plagued by sterility. His mar-

---

[*] Partout grouillait et criait l'animation du matin, sur le quai les travailleurs débarquant se hâtaient, les piroguiers et les pêcheurs s'affairaient et les marchandes vendaient à la criée. Epouvantées par les vacarmes, des nuées criardes de chauves-souris et de tisserins s'échappaient des manguiers, des fromagers et des palmiers qui serraient les blancs immeubles (48).

riage is barren. The ruling political party will not admit him. He is economically unproductive: he lives from Salimata's earnings as soup vendor in the market. In other words, the prince has become a social outcast, a begging "vulture" at social gatherings such as funerals.[7]

Finally, Fama's fate is to be the last of his line. In this vein, Fama's constant reference to "damn all the bastards!" (9) — *bâtard des bâtardises* (16) — when speaking of the present reveals his alienation from a world in which his family's past glory has been forgotten. Salimata and Fama are both victims of the present, living in poverty in a poor African neighborhood, presumably Treichville in Abidjan. Unable to produce an heir, they cannot envisage a future. With no successor, the barren couple is cut off from the promise of modernization and westernization; in fact, their situation portends increased alienation for the Malinke prince whose upbringing, comportment, and world view render him anchronistic and obsolete in the new era. For this reason, Fama speaks of "a life that was dying out amidst poverty and barrenness, Independence and the one-party system!" (18).*

His wife Salimata adjusts better than he does to modern life in the city. Her morning chores take her to the market, where she sells her wares and buys provisions, and then home to prepare a meal for herself and Fama. This busy schedule contrasts with Fama's empty one. Unemployed, his boredom is relieved only by daily prayers, aimless wandering, and occasional funerals.

Salimata appears primarily in the first part of the novel where she is presented in four distinct ways. First, she functions as metaphor; the barren wife is yet another example of the sterility that permeates Fama's life. Second, by ensuring food on the table, she maintains the reality principle. In the topsy-turvy world, she has become the family provider. Third, she transforms the journey motif into a spatial-temporal experience. As Salimata's mind shifts back and forth between present and past, she involuntarily recalls her past experiences of excision, rape, and subsequent trauma. The ordeal leaves her afraid of all men except her impotent husband, Fama. Finally, Salimata assumes the role of archetypal victim, treated cruelly in two sociopolitical spheres — traditional and modern Africa — as well as in

---

* "une vie qui se mourait, se consumait dans la pauvreté, la stérilité et le parti unique!" (29).

two geographical locations — village and city. The attack on her by beggars at the marketplace in the city mirrors the rape she has experienced earlier in the village (either by a jealous genie or by the sorceror Tiémoko). Thus, Salimata is depicted as the victim of cruel gods — "she was fated to be barren until she died" (52) *— and as victim of cruel men, sorcerers in the village, beggars in the city.

In this binary world, Fama and Salimata differ in their attitudes toward the past. Whereas Salimata relives a persistent nightmare of excision and rape, Fama dreams of past glory. Kourouma juxtaposes one sleepless night with another: in part one, Salimata, unable to sleep, evokes memories of excision. In part two, Fama spends a sleepless night recalling the history of his family dynasty.

Although part two of *Les Soleils des indépendances* repeats the opening scene by introducing the death of a Malinké — Cousin Lacina follows Ibrahima Kone to his final resting place — it departs from part one by abandoning the earlier focus on a dual consciousness; Salimata all but disappears as the story of Fama's journey to Togobala and back unfolds. Upon the death of Cousin Lacina, Fama returns alone to Togobala to become ruler of his kingdom.

As the novel progresses, Fama's spatial-temporal range surpasses that of his wife. For example, when Fama travels to and from the village, he leaves Salimata behind in the city. Futhermore, whereas Salimata's journeys in time take her back only as far as the excision ceremony of her youth, Fama recalls the distant mythic past (the arrival of Souleymane, founder of the tribe); the period of colonization (the reign of the Malinké leader, Samory, when war and trade flourished); the immediate past (transition from colonialism to "les soleils des indépendances"). Finally, only Fama recounts dream and prophecy, both of which foreshadow his own end.

Fama's recollection of the prophecy made to his ancestor, Bakary, is presented at a critical point in the narrative. It occurs midway through the novel, in a temporal and psychological limbo between past and future. Bakary prophesies the end of his dynasty some time after his reign: "It will end when the sun never sets, when bastards and sons of slaves bind all the provinces together with threads, ribbons and wind, and rule over them; when everything is cowardly and shameless..." (68). † Fama interprets the prophecy as confir-

---

* elle avait le destin de mourir stérile (80).

† Il se fera un jour où le soleil ne se couchera pas, où des fils d'esclaves, des bâtards lieront toutes les provinces avec des fils, des bandes et du vent, et commanderont, où tout sera pleutre, éhonté..." (102)

mation that he will be the last of the Doumbouya chiefs: "He was the only true descendant left, a sterile man living on alms in a city where the sun never sets (electric lights shone in the capital city all night long), where bastards and sons of slaves rule in triumph, having bound the provinces together with wires (the telephone!), ribbons (roads!), and wind (speeches and the wireless!)" (68).[*]

Dreams, however, function in two ways. First, they bring the protagonist closer to death. Fama is arrested for not alerting a politician of a dream that warns of impending danger. Arrested for this "over-sight," the imprisoned Fama ages considerably, becomes disoriented, and loses the will to live. Set free by presidential pardon, he recalls that death had been his sole companion in prison (193); his only wish upon release from prison is to return to Togobala to die. This experience echoes Fa Keïta's incarceration in Sembène's *Les Bouts de bois de Dieu*, but whereas Fa Keïta struggles to maintain his spiritual values, Fama fears that he will lose his life in prison and not be able to fulfill his mission — to return to the village to die.

Second, dreams provide temporary escape. In dream and hallucination, for example, Fama can flee reality by mounting the white steed that first belonged to Souleymane, founder of the dynasty. Approaching Togobala for the first time in twenty years, he recalls his childhood. The image of the horse appears, symbol of nobility and mobility: "His youth! His youth! He came upon it everywhere, saw it galloping on the white charger far away on the horizon..." (70).[8†] In prison, Fama dreams he is riding the animal: "Astride a white charger, Fama was flying or rather floating, his white robe fluttering in the wind, his stirrups and spurs of gold, escorted by a throng of gold-bedecked courtiers. A true Dumbuya! Authentic! The prince of all Horodugu, the only one, the great, the greatest of all" (118–19).[‡]

Thus, dreams provide the illusion of power and glory that have

---

[*] Comme authentique descendant il ne restait que lui, un homme stérile vivant d'aumônes dans une ville où le soleil ne se couche pas (les lampes électriques éclairant toute la nuit dans la capitale) où les fils d'esclaves et les bâtards commandent, triomphent, en liant les provinces par des fils (le téléphone!), des bandes (les routes!) et le vent (les discours et la radio!) (102).

[†] Son enfance! son enfance! Dans tout il la surprenait, la suivant là-bas très loin à l'horizon sur le coursier blanc...(104).

[‡] A califourchon sur un coursier blanc, Fama volait, plutôt naviguait, boubou blanc au vent, l'étrier et l'éperon d'or, une escorte dévouée parée d'or l'honorait, le flattait. Vrai Doumboya! Authentique! Le prince de tout le Horodougou, le seul, le grand, le plus grand de tous (178).

been denied by reality. In Fama's imagination, he becomes Souleymane, the founder of the dynasty, not the last of the lineage. At the same time, dreams free Fama from his prisoner's cell, allowing him to ride freely. They also grant him the respect of his people — a respect that eludes him in real life. The vision of the white horse appears for the last time as Fama lies close to death. "Fama on a white charger gallops, trots, leaps and prances. He is radiant and fulfilled" (135).* Fama's escape through imagination is escapist, but it is also strategic. An aid to survival in prison, the vision of the white horse is a key element in his final journey toward death.

The study of the journey motif in previous works has revealed the importance of intercessors. Just as Kem Tanne provides the key to the puzzling inheritance of Momar, Birame, and Moussa in folk narrative, intercessors play an important role in the African novel. For example, Samba Diallo is guided on his ambiguous journey first by Thierno, his Quranic teacher, and then by his father, the Knight. Similarly, Si Mokhtar, accompanying Rachid in his quest to solve the mystery surrounding his father's death, teaches him during the course of the journey to explore Algeria's precolonial past.

In *Les Soleils des indépendances*, the sorceror Balla, the *griot* Diamourou, and Fama's friend Bakary all appear in the role of intercessor. Fama, however, refuses to heed their advice. Although Balla advises him not to return to the capital, he does so and is subsequently arrested. Upon Fama's release from prison, Bakary warns him to stay in the capital. Fama nevertheless leaves for the village and is mortally wounded by a sacred crocodile at the border crossing. After Fama has dismissed Balla's advice, the narrator interjects, speaking directly to him. The *griot*-narrator becomes another voice warning the protagonist of the danger of turning a deaf ear to an intercessor's counsel: "Ignorant as you were of the things of old, as blind and deaf in the invisible world of shades and spirits as Balla was in our world, you should have heeded the old fetish-priest" (101).† Later, in prison, Fama recalls Balla's words but explains why he cannot heed his advice: "Balla's words went unheeded, because they bounced off the eardrums of a man lured on by his fate, the fate

---

* Fama sur un coursier blanc qui galope, trotte, sautille et caracole. Il est comblé, il est superbe (204).

† "Ignorant comme tu étais des vieilles choses et assui aveugle et sourd dans le monde invisible des mânes et des génies que Balla l'était dans notre monde, tu te devais d'écouter le vieux féticheur" (152).

ordained for the last of the Dumbuya" (117).* Fame considers himself
to be a pawn of destiny.[9] Wedded to fatalism, the Malinké prince
does not believe that he can escape his fate. It has been foretold that
he is to be the last of his lineage.

As he approaches the end of the journey, Fama achieves lucidity,
the painful knowledge that he and his world are obsolete partly
because the ancient Malinké warrior caste has no place: "The colonial
period outlawed and killed war, but favoured trade; Independence
ruined trade, and there was no sign of war. So the Malinké species,
tribes, land and civilization was dying: crippled, deaf, blind...and
sterile" (13).† In addition, Fama is the victim of a corrupt elite that
has lost touch with the people: "These young men back from beyond
the seas don't think like Africans any more" (114).‡ Breaking with
the established pattern of the cultural hybrid, Kourouma satirizes
both the victim, Fama, and the society in which he is socially and
economically marginal.

Kourouma skillfully alters the relationship between narrator and
reader by borrowing the oral performer's bag of tricks. Like Birago
Diop's *Contes d'Amadou Koumba*, Kourouma makes use of dialogue,
repetition, songs, proverbs, and questions to engage the audience.[10]
The narrator involves the reader from the first pages of the novel.[11]
Placing the reader before a supernatural event like Ibrahima Kone's
two-thousand-kilometer journey in the blink of an eye, the narrator
turns to the reader to exclaim, "You seem sceptical" (3).§ Rhetorical
questions also encourage the reader's response: "A blind man — what
could he see? Nothing. An old man with swollen aching legs — when
would they arrive there with him along? Perhaps at sunset. A Kaffir
whose forehead never touched the ground — what would he do there?
Nothing and nothing" (78–79).‖ In this same vein, comic — often

---

* Les paroles de Balla n'ont pas été écoutées, parce qu'elles ricochaient sur le fond des
oreilles d'un homme sollicité par son destin, le destin prescrit au dernier Doumbouya
(176).

† La colonisation a banni et tué la guerre mais favorisé le négoce, les Indépendances
ont cassé le négoce et la guerre ne venait pas. Et l'espèce malinké, les tribus, la terre, la
civilisation se meurent, percluses, sourdes et aveugles...et stériles (21).

‡ Ces jeunes gens débarqués de l'au-delà des mers ne pensent plus comme des nègres
(172).

§ Vous paraissez sceptique! (7).

‖ Un aveugle, que pouvait-il y voir? Rien. Un vieillard aux jambes gonflées de
douleurs, quand pouvait-on arriver avec lui? Peut-être au soleil couchant. Un Cafre
dont le front ne frôle jamais le sol, qu'allait-il y faire? Rien de rien (118).

salacious — comparisons evoke the reader's laughter. Thus, a political party delegate sent to Togobala is "unmanageable as a mad donkey's erection" (4).*

Kourouma uses proverbs to reinforce the Malinké cultural component of the novel, encouraging the reader to enter into the narrator's cultural context.[12] For example, when describing the difficult (but comical) situation confronting Fama, who brings a second wife, Mariam, to his first wife's household, Kourouma states, "Don't gather birds together if you fear the sound of wings" (106).† By comparing the noise of bird wings flapping to co-wives quarrelling, Kourouma treats a sociological reality of Malinké culture, polygamy, within a West African rural context.[13] Similarly, Kourouma's use of proverbs rooted in nature serves to accentuate Fama's association with village life, which corresponds to his preference for Togobala over the capital. In addition, the proverb indicates the progression of the action. Fama had resisted the temptation of polygamy for many years. Had he recalled and continued to heed the proverb, he would have avoided the subsequent quarrels in his home, for, as the proverb clearly explains, fighting between co-wives is inevitable.

Kourouma introduces Malinké songs to further emphasize the oral quality of the novel (105, 192). He chooses to present the French translation rather than either the original Malinké song or a bilingual text. In one instance, he introduces a proverb that is sung by Malinkés in time of trouble:

> Ho, sorrow! Ho, sorrow! Ho, sorrow!
> If you find a mouse on a cat-skin
> Ho, sorrow! Ho, sorrow! Ho, sorrow!
> Everyone knows that death is sorrow. (129)‡

Fama recalls this proverb as he is traveling from the capital to Togobala for the last time. As Fama journeys closer to death, the proverb reinforces the trajectory and foreshadows his demise. Like the mouse in the song, Fama will meet a violent death.

Kourouma also uses another element of oral tradition, the tale embedded in the narrative. For example, Balla the sorceror recounts

---

* indomptable, comme le sexe d'un âne enrage (141).

† On ne rassemble pas des oiseaux quand on craint le bruit des ailes (159).

‡ Ho malheur! Ho malheur! Ho malheur!
Si l'on trouve une souris sur une peau de chat
Ho malheur! Ho malheur! Ho malheur!
Tout le monde sait que la mort est un grand malheur. (194)

his defeat of the *bufle-génie*, the buffalo-spirit. Balla's narrative entertains and instructs. It is a highly colorful tale of pursuit in which Balla and the spirit go through a rapid series of metamorphoses. Granting Balla, the animist, the role of storyteller, Kourouma uses his digressive tale to emphasize the importance of the supernatural within the context of Malinké animism. At the same time, the embedded story as digression accentuates the open-ended quality of Kourouma's narrative. Although Fama's death is foreshadowed, the digressions that mark the narrative in the form of tales, anecdotes, proverbs, and songs serve to create a kaleidoscope effect.[14] This technique simulates the spontaneity of oral performance, in which the storyteller may lengthen or shorten a given tale by his choice of episodes or digressions.

In a variety of ways, Kourouma alters the relationship between narrator and reader and between the written and the spoken word.[15] By assuming the role of *griot*, he depicts a traditonal protagonist whose contact with European culture is minimal, and, in the process of doing so, he succeeds in creating an unforgettable character and revolutionizing francophone African prose.

Saharan Odyssey: Mouloud Mammeri

With independence in 1962, Algeria inherited the Sahara. To some extent, this region has represented a new world, for Algerian cadres are primarily northerners. In the North–South interaction, the North supplies its modern technology to the South, to a desert rich in petroleum. In the process of modernization, the Sahara has been transformed, but not without hardship. Oil derricks mar a former pristine horizon and nomadic Tuaregs face cultural extinction. For the desert people, the intruder has changed costume, for the French colonial officer has been replaced in the postcolonial era by the Algerian technocrat.

The crossing of the Sahara is a theme that holds interest today as it did in the past. As Jean-Robert Henry has noted, modern civilization, with its emphasis on progress, needs to hold on to a vision of a world where the sense of the atemporal and eternal exists: "What more appropriate illustration, sensitive to the steadfastness of nature and nonmodern man than the desert?" (29).* Wedded to this idea of a return to the desert is the notion of a return to the wandering life of

---

* Quelle plus belle illustration concrète, sensible de l'immutabilité de la nature et des hommes non modernes que le désert?

the nomad. Sedentary man is drawn by his imagination to recreate a life of freedom, one of limitless space.

The publication of Mouloud Mammeri's novel *La Traversée*, in 1982, attests to the continued interest on the part of North African writers to find literary inspiration in the theme of the desert.[16] For Mammeri, the encounter with the Sahara implies a recognition of two worlds: one, the oasis where water assures that gardens bloom and enables people to implant their civilization; the other, an unending expanse of barren stretches where unbridled nature resists man's domination.

As a realist, Mammeri emphasizes the social and political factors of this region facing rapid transition. His work is therefore in marked contrast to nineteenth-century French artists, to the writer Fromentin and the painter Delacroix, both of whom were drawn to the Sahara, to its nomads and oasis dwellers, in search of exoticism. Mammeri, however, echoes the tradition of early twentieth-century French writers such as André Gide and Ernest Psichari, who used the Sahara as background to a personal journey, Gide focusing on sexual liberty and Psichari on mysticism.[17]

Although Albert Camus's Algerian landscapes are mainly Mediterranean — Algiers in *L'Etranger*; Oran in *La Peste* — several short stories that appear in *L'Exil et le royaume* (1957) — "La Femme adultère," "Le Rénégat," and "L'Hôte" — are set either in the Sahara or at its periphery. The protagonists: a French tourist "La Femme adultère," a missionary in "Le Rénégat," and a colonial schoolteacher in "L'Hôte" are Europeans isolated in an alien environment; the Sahara accentuates their solitude.[18] English Showalter notes that in Camus's universe the desert represents "the mirror of humanity's existential aloneness in a barren, meaningless creation" (30). Mammeri's protagonist, Mourad, comes to experience this existential solitude when he, like Camus's protagonists, ventures into the Sahara.

La Traversée marked Mammeri's return to the novel after a decade during which he devoted his energies to studying and popularizing Berber oral tradition. It is therefore not surprising to find traces of Mammeri's commitment to his Berber heritage in the work. For example, Mammeri presents an Algerian protagonist of Berber descent, a man born in the mountains of Kabylia. In contrast to Kourouma's Fama — "illiterate as a donkey's tail"* — Mammeri's Mourad is highly literate. He is a writer by profession. A disillusioned

---

* analphabète comme la queue d'un âne

journalist living in Algiers in the late 1970s, Mourad experiences difficulty in independent Algeria because the nation for which he fought now censors his writing. An allegorical piece entitled "La Traversée du désert" expresses his discontent with modern Algeria and brings him under sharp criticism from his editor.

In the guise of allegory, "La Traversée du désert" represents Mourad's view of Algeria's historical experience. The journalist depicts a caravan of refugees fleeing across the desert, led by their "heroes," whose task it is to ensure the group's safety. These heroes are courageous but overly idealistic: "Alone and exalted, they spent their days slashing at obstacles that always returned and their nights counting stars" (32).[*] In this article, Mourad informs his readers that Algeria's heroes died needlessly, victims of their own impetuosity and their need to sacrifice themselves: "The heroes took useless risks; they played with time the way some play knuckle-bones; they did not reckon with obstacles" (33).[†] So rash that they are incompetent, the heroes who do not succumb on the journey cannot survive in the oasis, their final destination. At journey's end, they either die or abandon the oasis, which is depicted as a place of perversion and corruption. Ultimately, the ranks of these heroes are replaced by imitators, *les épigones*. The latter, supported by ideologues, betray the cause: "The ideologues went everywhere repeating that the heroes had died for the epigones, the true Moses, the true saviours. It was thanks to them that the caravan had crossed the desert; they caused the harvests to ripen, the springs to flow, the manna to fall from the trees, and the sun to rise" (37).[‡]

An article reflecting thwarted idealism and frustration, "La Traversée du désert" is eloquent and subversive. The allegory is not at all obscure; Mourad's readers can easily discern the Algerian War in the episode of the desert crossing. Furthermore, his criticism is double-edged. Mourad casts blame on the leaders who sacrifice themselves unnecessarily, and on the people who follow blindly. If

---

[*] Seuls et exaltés, ils occupaient les jours à taillader des obstacles toujours renaissants et les nuits à compter les étoiles.

[†] Les héros prenaient des risques inutiles, ils jouaient avec les heures comme on joue avec des osselets, ils ne supputaient pas les obstacles.

[‡] Les idèologues allèrent partout répétant que c'etait pour les épigones que les héros étaient morts, que les épigones étaient les vrais Moïses salvateurs, que c'était grâce à eux que la caravane avait traversé le désert, eux qui faisaient mûrir les moissons, sourdre les sources, tomber la manne et se lever le soleil.

the martyrs show too much courage, the people do not show enough: "The hero is destined to die young and alone. The sheep's fate is also to perish, but crippled with old age, panting with fear, and if possible, en masse. Heroes jump into death, exploding like stray meteors; sheep hang on to life to the very last drop of blood" (32).*

The piece points to a major problem in the society, namely a lack of genuine leadership. Yet it offers no remedy. Mourad, himself, has reached an impasse. The journalist calls for change because he clearly perceives a betrayal of values, although he himself has no alternative program to present. Mourad has become the angry young man grown somewhat older, a middle-aged version of Arezki, hero of Mammeri's *Le Sommeil du juste*. Also, at forty, Mourad has neither wife nor family. From the dominant viewpoint in his society, he has no more than a tenuous commitment to the future. In this sense, he resembles Fama. Neither of them has an heir; both are the last of their lineage.

The editor's hostile reception to the article provokes Mourad's abrupt resignation from the newspaper, a dramatic gesture of refusal to participate in the system any longer. Self-imposed exile accompanies the resignation as Mourad decides to "abandon the oasis" and move to Paris. His decision is ironic in the sense that he is a former militant who had fought against the French, and is now willing to seek refuge in the French capital. He does, however, postpone his departure to comply with a request from his editor and complete one last assignment for *Alger-Révolution*. This projected article necessitates a trip to the desert, for unlike "La Traversée du désert," it will be factual, not symbolic, an eyewitness account not an imaginary allegory.

"La Traversée du désert" is a catalyst; it serves as a springboard for Mourad's first journey to the Sahara. Mourad is accompanied on this voyage by a team of journalists: two French, two Algerian. None of them are native to this region. Preconceived ideas as well as tensions within the group distort their voyage. Among the men, Serge, a French ex-Communist who is opposed to tradition, fails to appreciate Saharan culture. He states: "We don't bother with relics; we sweep them away" (138).† Boualem, a Muslim religious fanatic, remains obsessed with the mission of spying on his French com-

---

* Le destin des héros est de mourir jeunes et seuls. Celui des moutons est aussi de mourir, mais perclus de vieillesse, sués et, si possible, en masse. Les héros sautent d'un coup dans la mort, ils y explosent comme des météores dévoyés, les moutons s'accrochent à la vie jusqu'à la dernière goutte de sang.

† "On ne compte pas avec des reliques, on les balaie."

panions, the infidels, in order to safeguard his nation's treasure, petroleum. Among the women, Amalia, a French journalist on mission to study the petroleum industry, appears more interested in seducing her male traveling companions than in completing her assignment. Souad, an Algerian journalist and the group's secretary, spends more time recording Amalia's exploits than collecting her notes for a future article.

For Mourad, the journey to the Sahara results in personal discovery and transformation that have political, psychological, and spiritual implications in his life.[19] As Mourad journeys through the desert, stopping at oasis towns, he undergoes a triple initiation. He learns to appreciate the people, the nomads, and the sedentary villagers. In addition, he gains insight into the power as well as the danger of the trackless sands. Finally, the desert crossing represents a journey to self-understanding and ultimately a preparation for his eventual death, the final crossing.

Mammeri presents his readers with a novel that begins in disillusionment and ends in death. Upon returning from the Sahara, the Algerian journalist suffers from acute bouts of fever exacerbated by heavy drinking. Instead of boarding the plane for Paris, Mourad returns to his native village in Kabylia, where he succumbs to the fever.

The novelist places in opposition two journeys: one, "La Traversée du désert"; the other, the assignment to cross the Sahara. The first is a linear trajectory of a caravan that crosses the desert, whereas the second is a circular voyage from Algiers to the desert and back. In point of fact, the second journey contains a subtext, for Mammeri introduces a third voyage, the protagonist's journey to self-understanding. It leads Mourad, like Samba Diallo and Fama before him, to a rendezvous with death.

The theme of the journey as a means to self-understanding, as an internal as well as external experience, is one that Mammeri developed in all of his previous works. In the tradition of the heroes of oral narrative, Mokrane (*La Colline oubliée*), Arezki (*Le Sommeil du juste*), and Bachir (*L'Opium et le bâton*) embark upon the journey that leads them away from the mountain villages of their birth. At first untutored and ill prepared, they return home wiser and more mature. In the colonial world depicted in Mammeri's earlier works, they also become politically aware of their position as second-class citizens. From *La Colline oubliée* (1952) to *L'Opium et le bâton* (1965), Mammeri's protagonists become acculturated as they enter more fully into the modern world. Whereas Mokrane and his fellow villagers of the first novel have little knowledge of a world beyond the mountains, the protagonist of the third work, Doctor Bachir Lazrak, is barley attached to his native Kabylia. In postcolonial Algeria, however, Mourad is neither Mokrane, the *naïf* setting out to discover the world, nor Bachir, a westernized colonial subject. At the opposite end of the spectrum from Kourouma's Fama, he is sophisticated, well educated, articulate, politically astute.

Central to this Saharan experience is Mourad's sentiment of solidarity with the Tuaregs who, like himself, are Berber, although their nomadic traditions are virtually unknown to his people, the Kabyles of the north. Linked to his respect for the people is Mourad's awareness of the changes that have come to the desert. The Sahara no longer represents a refuge for nomadic tribesmen, for it has become a giant oil field. The modernization and industrialization of Algeria have largely destroyed the old way of life. The novelist's description of Hassi-Messaoud attests to the transformation: "Air conditioned, paved roads, concrete, flowers blooming on imported soil" (68).* Tension between the irretrievable past and the impoverished present is presented by the contrast between memories of graceful camels and sights of awkward lumbering trucks: "In Amenas means in Tuareg the gathering place of camel drivers. That was a mere mockery. In place of the camel drivers of yesteryear you could see on the desolate plateau only the broken down frames of large ochre-colored trucks that teetered in the dust like enormous blind beetles" (69).† For Mourad, the disappearance of camel caravans from oasis towns recalls the loss experienced in another geographical context. When Mourad returns to Tasga, his Kabyle village, he finds the old men, like Saharan camels, anachronistic vestiges of yesteryear. More-over, when the elders do not greet Mourad as was customary in the past, he becomes painfully aware of the fragility of their world:

> One of these evenings the wind would blow too strong — and the Tasga central square would be swept clean of their anachronistic carcasses, and nothing would remain of anything that had formed the fabric of their lives, their joys, their losses, their dreams, their laughter. The wind would even carry away the words they loved,

---

* Air conditionné, goudron, béton, fleurs poussées sur de la terre rapportée.

† In Amenas veut dire en touareg le lieu des méharis. Ce n'était plus qu'une dérision. A la place des meharis d'antan on ne voyait plus sur le plateau désolé, que les masses poussives des grands camions ocre, qui brinquebalaient dans la poussière comme d'énormes hannetons aveugles.

those that had cradled them all their life, and soon it would be, in fact it was already the case—it was as if they had never existed. (54)*

Linked by ethnicity, although separated geographically, Kabyles and Tuaregs experience the same plight; in postcolonial Algeria, their cultural life is threatened. Their resistance to Arabization places them in opposition to government policy. In addition, their traditions are menaced by technological transformations—the trucks that replace camels—as well as cultural changes—transistor radios that provide them with Arabic and European music. As Kabyles leave mountain villages to seek greater economic opportunity in Algiers and in France, Tuaregs are enticed by the economic opportunities of fixed wages in the modern industrial sector, particularly in the petroleum industry. Economic and social transformations are clearly threatening their traditional way of life. If Mourad's companions (French or Algerian) do not react to the journey the way he does, their response is attributable in part to the fact that, unlike Mourad, they are not representatives of people facing radical cultural transformation and, perhaps, cultural extinction.

As a journalist, therefore a professional observer, Mourad records both positive and negative aspects of life in the Sahara. When he leaves the paved road and travels on camels rather than in jeeps, he meets proud, courageous people, discovers a beautiful landscape, and finds desert traditions in the form of *ahellils*, oasis festivals.[20] Yet he also perceives the persecution of the desert people and the poverty, as well as the junk and rubble that modern technology has strewn about in the sand.

Several times, Mourad and his journalist companions encounter the government authorities' hostile attitude toward the Tuareg nomads. One Algerian bureaucrat explains: "The Tuaregs have their camels, their violins, their desert, and their talismans, and they are happy. Let them be. But we say no! We say that we have to tear them away from their violins" (84).†

---

* Un de ces soirs il allait venter trop fort—et la place de Tasga serait balayée de leurs carcasses anachroniques, et de tout ce qui avait fait le tissu de leurs jours, de leurs joies, de leurs manques, de leurs rêves et de leurs rires il ne resterait rien, le vent emporterait jusqu'aux mots aimés, qui les avaient bercés toute leur vie, et bientôt ce serait, c'était déjà, comme s'ils n'avaient jamais existé.

† "Les Touaregs ont leurs chameaux, leurs violons, leur désert et leurs amulettes et ils sont heureux, alors qu'on les y laisse. Nous disons non! Nous disons qu'il faut arracher les Touaregs à leurs violons."

In their effort to separate the Tuaregs from their violins and to force a different and alien system of values upon them, the authorities claim to be forging a sense of national unity by imposing the stamp of Arab and Muslim upon people who boast a different historical and cultural legacy. Since this approach resembles the repression of cultural identity that is occurring in Mammeri's native Kabylia, the reader is tempted to replace Tuareg with Kabyle and extend the phrase "we must tear the Tuaregs away from their violins"* metaphorically to the Berbers of Kabylia as well.

Mourad's journey through the desert, filled with poignant episodes, confirms that the desert populace is aware of its plight. First, a French schoolteacher tries to teach Eluard's poem "Liberté" to the nomad school children. They burst into tears, in full knowledge that they have indeed been deprived of their liberty. Then, Mourad meets Ahitaghel, a Tuareg boy who explains that he wants to be a chauffeur so he can remain free to travel the roads as his ancestors had done. Finally, the journalist encounters Ba Salem, a celebrated entertainer at the *ahellils*. Stricken with the *amdouda*, the wish to die, Ba Salem withdraws from life; his death marks the end of a way of life and foreshadows Mourad's fate.

Mammeri had already raised the problem of societies facing cultural extinction in *Le Banquet*, a tragedy set among the Aztecs, and in the accompanying essay, "La Mort absurde des Aztèques." Written in 1971, these works mark the centenary of the French army's victory against Kabyle resistance and express Mammeri's belief that the defeat of the Aztecs by Cortés foreshadowed later global victories of Western materialism and technology. The Spanish conquest in sixteenth-century Mexico not only inaugurated the Occident's triumph that ultimately came to the far reaches of the Sahara but also fostered the West's refusal to respect alterity. Mammeri writes in "La Mort absurde des Aztèques": "Western thought is essentially unifying and reductive. It invented the unique and devastating god, the jealous god. It has room only for a single truth. In its view the crime of the other is its otherness; the other is always intolerable" (16).† Having adopted Western technology, post-colonial Algeria, in Mammeri's view, has assumed its bias towards

---

* Il faut arracher les Touregs à leurs violons.

† La pensée occidentale est par essence unifiante et réductrice. Elle a inventé le dieu unique et dévastateur, le dieu jaloux. Il n'y a de place en elle que pour une seule vérité. Pour elle le crime de l'autre c'est son altérité; l'autre est toujours intolérable.

difference as well. In the name of bringing about a unified society, the modern state often ignores, and even suppresses, ethnic diversity within the country.

In his portrayal of Mourad, Mammeri initially depicts him as an *évolué*, a Westernized African who distances himself from his traditional compatriots, studying them with the objectivity of the social scientist. (In this role, the fictional character resembles the author, who himself was an anthropologist and a novelist.) At the same time, Mourad assumes the role of "écrivain-touriste," the writer inspired by his travels. Arriving a century after Fromentin and Delacroix, he records the death throes of a civilization rather than the vibrant culture that greeted his French predecessors. However, the Saharan odyssey transforms Mourad from scientific observer to participant. Once he comes to recognize his affinity with the Berber Tuaregs, he can no longer maintain his objectivity. All threats to Saharan culture from technology, materialism, and postcolonial government policy rekindle his fears, reminding him of the precarious situation of his own Kabyle Berber culture. Thus, Mourad's journey from Algiers to Tamanrasset and back is an inner journey that evolves into a personal quest for new faith.

Once Mourad recognizes this inner quest, the two journeys that had been placed in opposition at the beginning of the novel — the journalist's allegory and the Saharan journey — begin to converge. Neither Mourad nor the "heroes" he depicts in "La Traversée du désert" successfully complete the "crossing" from revolution to a new life "in the oasis." Unlike his impetuous heroes, however, Mourad gains lucidity. At the end of his stay in the Sahara, his awareness that the Berbers of the south are menaced by the same forces — repression and modernization — that afflict the Berbers of the north, enables him to recognize that he is truly the representative of a dying civilization: "For now I am convinced that although the atavistic desert came late into my life, it had been in my veins forever" (179).*
The lucidity that results from his physical and spiritual journey culminates in his final decision to return to Kabylia, "my hands bare, wearing the ancestral burnoose" (180).† Yet despite his desperate and belated attempt to return to his ancestral homeland, Mourad leaves the Sahara having learned the painful truth that he has nowhere to

---

* Car maintenant je suis sûr que, si le désert atavique n'est entré que tard dans ma vie, il était inscrit dans mes veines depuis toujours.

† les mains nues, couvert du bournous ancestral.

go. The desert offers him a glimpse of truth, not illusion, but it grants him only temporary refuge.

Adrift, he cannot turn to faith for solace, for he shares neither the Islamic fervor of Boualem nor the Christian mysticism of Foucauld. Yet Boualem, the religious zealot, and Mourad both leave the desert stripped of all illusions. Boualem does not find the religious purity he has been seeking among the desert people; Mourad does not encounter either the resistance (to materialism, to political repression) or the cultural vitality that he was seeking. The Tuareg festivals he observes cultivate nostalgia for a lost culture, but they do not generate faith in the future. As Jean-Claude Vatin explains, "Mourad is the visitor to the desert sands in search of dead souls" ("Pour une sociologie politique," 823).*

In keeping with the theme of the desert crossing as a journey to self-understanding, Mammeri borrows two structural elements from traditional oral narrative: the intercessor and the trial of initiation. The intercessor is Ba Salem, a renowned singer at the *ahellils*, the desert festivals. Ba Salem is an anachronism, a poet in an increasingly rational and technological world. Following the death of his wife, Ba Salem gives Mourad a lesson in renunciation, in withdrawing from the world. When Mourad, defeated physically and spiritually, chooses to return to Kabylia rather than fly to Paris, he is following Ba Salem's path of renunciation, for he is allowing himself to die.

Having established the journey motif as a unifying element with symbolic dimensions, Mammeri tests Mourad by forcing him to confront the danger of death in the desert. When he leaves camp to take a walk, Mourad loses his way, only to be rescued some time later by a Tuareg guide. This episode, which Mammeri drew essentially from his own experience,[21] recalls earlier fiction, both Antoine de Saint-Exupéry's adventure of a French aviator in *Terre des Hommes* (1939) and Malek Haddad's experience of an Algerian truck driver in *Je t'offrirai une gazelle* (1959). Although Saint-Exupéry's lost aviator is rescued by a nomad and Haddad's truck driver succumbs in the Sahara, both novels emphasize the psychological strains accompanying overwhelming thirst in the desert. Lost voyagers are aware of their impotence in the dry sands. To survive, they must be rescued. Saint-Exupéry's pilot and Haddad's driver come to understand the fragility of the links of communication — a radio message, a flare.

---

* Mourad est le visiteur des sables, à la quête d'âmes mortes.

Indirectly, the Sahara finally claims Mourad's life, for he later dies in Kabylia of the fever contracted in the desert. Nevertheless, Mourad, like Saint-Exupéry's pilot, is rescued in the Sahara by a nomad. The incident allows Mammeri to accord a metaphysical dimension to the Saharan journey. Mourad himself acknowledges the fragility of life in this arid, silent landscape: "He looked around him trying to get his bearings; everywhere he found the same heap of jagged rocks, positioned upright under the moon" (115).* At this moment, he is experiencing the existential solitude that Camus describes in *L'Exil et le royaume*. Surely by testing Mourad in the desert, in which he is much more a stranger than in the mountains of his native Kabylia, Mammeri heightens the solitary condition of the existential hero.

The passage also recalls scenes from Mammeri's earlier novels in which a solitarily protagonist also confronts the immense power of nature. In Mammeri's first novel, *La Colline oubliée*, for example, Mokrane loses his way in the mountains and dies while trying to cross a snow-capped ridge on his way back to his village. Fording a turbulent river in an attempt to elude the police, Arezki in *Le Sommeil du juste* nearly drowns in the swift current. And Bachir in *L'Opium et le bâton*, convalescing alone in a mountain cave following an ambush in which he almost lost his life, emerges to discover the beauty of his surroundings. In each instance, the protagonist experiences a spiritual transformation. However, for both Mokrane (*La Colline oubliée*) and Mourad (*La Traversée*), the experience precedes death and tempts the reader to ask: does death represent nature's hostility, or is it the promise of peace?

In this novel, Mammeri establishes specific links between Mourad, the journalist, and Mokrane, the Kabyle villager of the first novel. Native sons of Tasga, the village depicted in *La Colline oubliée*, they are laid to rest in the same cemetery. Moreover, as he lies feverish and hallucinating. Mourad relives scenes of his youth in Tasga, recalling characters and incidents of the first novel. For example, he speaks of Taasast, the secret room in Mokrane's house where the young villagers gathered. It came to symbolize a lost paradise to which they as adults could never return.

Shortly before his death Mourad has an imaginary conversation

---

* Il regarda autour de lui pour essayer de se répérer; c'était dans tous les sens le même amoncellement de roches aiguës, plantées droit sous la lune.

with Amalia, the French journalist on the Saharan expedition. He responds to her question:

"A deserter, what is that?"
"It is someone who lives in the desert," said Mourad.
"Or dies there?"
"It's the same thing." (127)*

This play on words suggests that by *déserteur* Mourad refers both to the desert nomads who are now facing extinction and to the urban-dwelling Algerian technocrats who have abandoned the ideals of the Algerian revolution. Mourad belongs to neither group, but the term applies to him as well; he is a *déserteur* in the sense that he has been profoundly transformed by his experience in the desert.

Mammeri's protagonist is vanquished by the desert. Mourad is conquered spiritually by the imaginary Sahara, the interior desert, because he is unable to compromise. As the critic Jacques Madelain explains, the interior desert may be self-imposed or imposed by outside forces (76). For Mammeri's hero the interior desert is imposed by external pressure, by disillusionment caused by political repression in independent Algeria. Mourad is defeated physically as well because the desert is, as W. H. Auden wrote, the Omega of temporal existence: powerful, limitless, indifferent to man (71).

La Traversée continues the literary tradition that began in the nineteenth century when French writers found inspiration in the Sahara. The novel also reaffirms an attitude toward nature expressed in Mammeri's earlier novels: renewing ties with nature, one comes to terms with oneself. In *La Traversée*, the desert replaces the mountain as an ambivalent symbol, a source of danger and refuge. The desert is, after all, an impressive reminder of human vulnerability and nature's splendor.

If we compare Kourouma's Fama with Mammeri's Mourad, it becomes apparent that both protagonists are traveling heroes who, when stripped of their illusions, choose the same form of escape: death. In the course of his travels to and from his village, Fama learns that corruption permeates the countryside in the new era of independence. Mourad, loses his illusions because the Sahara offers little respite from the corruption, hypocrisy, poverty, and repression

---

* "Un déserteur, qu'est-ce que c'est?"
"C'est quelqu'un qui vit au désert," dit Mourad.
"Ou qui y meurt?"
"C'est la même chose."

of the city. For both protagonists, the journey to lucidity results in the recognition of marginality.

Returning to the question posed by the title of this chapter, "Independence Acquired—Hope or Disillusionment?" we find that Kourouma and Mammeri share the sentiment of profound disillusionment. *Les Soleils des indépendances* and *La Traversée* are pessimistic works. Exposing the corruption, greed, and cruelty in a one-party state, Kourouma chooses to portray a tragic hero whose world view and comportment make him anachronistic. Satirizing the new intelligentsia, Algerian technocrats who have replaced French colonial administrators, Mammeri exposes cultural insensitivity and crass materialism in the postcolonial era. In their critique of postcolonial African societies, however, neither Kourouma nor Mammeri suggests that Africa return to colonialism. On the contrary, they both attempt to awaken the public to hypocrisy and the loss of ideals.[22]

An important distinction between the two novelists concerns their relationship to oral tradition. Kourouma depicts a traditional Malinké who is illiterate in French. In keeping with oral tradition, the novelist assumes the role of *griot*, borrowing techniques such as proverbs, repetition, and questions to the audience that imitate oral performance and bring the reader closer to the narrator. Although the bilingual journalist, Mourad, speaks Tamazight, the oral Berber language of Kabylia, he has crossed over from orality to literacy. Neither Mourad's speech nor his writing reveals specific African vocabulary or syntax that marks *Les Soleils des indépendances*. Mammeri, moreover, cannot authentically make use of the tradition of the *griot*, for despite its folklore (song, tales, and poetry), the Berbers of Kabylia do not share the tradition of the *griot*, the professional storyteller/praise-singer/oral historian of West Africa.

Hence, although Kourouma and Mammeri depict similar social and political realities, the two novelists reflect two distinct positions with respect to language. One one hand, Mammeri adopts the colonial language and adapts classical realism to depict the world of the Westernized African, member of an urban elite. On the other hand, Kourouma modifies the colonial language to conform to the cultural and linguistic reality of his protagonist, a traditional rural African. The linguistic choices made by Kourouma and Mammeri illustrate the division between rural and urban, modern and traditional, orality and literacy, and attest to the multiplicity of voices in francophone African fiction today.

Chapter 5

▼▼▼▼▼▼▼

Women's Voice

MARIAMA BÂ, *Une si longue lettre*
ASSIA DJEBAR, *L'Amour, la fantasia; Ombre sultane*

The study of the journey motif in the works of representative male writers reveals a dialectic: successful vs. thwarted journeys. For example, both Sembène and Kateb use historical events as catalysts for individual and collective maturation. Sembène depicts the successful Dakar–Niger railway strike of 1947; Kateb focuses upon the failed Algerian uprisings in Sétif and Guelma in 1945. In Sembène's novel, the women's march to Dakar—a collective demonstration that challenges sociopolitical norms and projects African women toward political action—becomes the decisive factor in initiating a general strike that results in the railway workers' ultimate victory. Thus, Sembène not only writes women into fiction but presents them as a catalyst for change.

When *Les Bouts de bois de Dieu* was published, however, Senegalese women writers had not yet emerged. Although women had been present in sub-Saharan francophone African literature, they were portrayed exclusively by male writers. In the Maghreb, however, Djamila Débêche, Marguérite Taos-Amrouche, and Assia Djebar were published with their male counterparts as early as the mid-1950s. These women writers, however, did not represent the majority of their sisters. They had obtained advanced schooling in the French colonial system.

Two factors contributed to the dominance of male francophone African writers. Throughout Africa, the colonial educational system made greater efforts to educate boys than girls on the assumption that schools should prepare an educated male elite to serve the colonial administration. In addition, traditional African societies viewed European education, particularly higher education, as superfluous training for young girls, who would become dutiful wives

133
▼

and attentive mothers. Portraits of African women in the early francophone African fiction support this position. In *L'Enfant noir*, the role of Laye's mother is to preserve and transmit ancestral traditions, animist and Muslim, and above all to teach her children to respect the family, clan, and village. Sembène's portrait of Bakayoko's mother, Niakoro, in *Les Bouts de bois de Dieu*, affirms this role and characterizes the strike leader's wife as a submissive, docile, passive individual. Bound to the hearth, Assitan would neither accompany Bakayoko on his numerous journeys nor question the clearly established gender rules.

As women writers gained mastery of the tools of self-expression and were able to assume and perfect the craft of writing, critics at first tended to dismiss their efforts. Carole Boyce Davies notes in her introduction to *Ngambika* that critics in the 1950s and 1960s approached all African literature from the point of view of male experience (3).

In recent years, several factors have contributed to focus attention on the African woman writer of French expression. First, writers such as Assia Djebar and Mariama Bâ have achieved a sustained level of competency that could not be ignored. Second, the pool of African women writers has grown larger—African women writing in French and English have gained greater access to higher education in the postcolonial era. In addition, the literary canon has opened up to new writers and new ideas. For example, as the literary canon changed, oral narrative, never exclusively restricted to men, gained in importance. The work of Ruth Finnegan and Harold Scheub reveals the importance of women as performers. Finnegan notes that elderly women in particular are most apt at the art (376).[1]

Moving from orality to writing, women writers insert elements of oral tradition into their work and acknowledge their debt to storytellers, male and female. In fact, both men and women writers pay tribute to the oral narratives that inspired them. In addition to Birago Diop's recognition of the *griot* Amadou Koumba, Mouloud Feraoun's first work, *Le Fils du pauvre*, praises his aunt. Her creative imagination, filled with tales that she, unlike her Western-educated nephew, believed to be true, encouraged his creativity. Initiating him to the oral tradition, Khalti introduced her nephew to "un pays de chimères" (51), a land of illusion. Three decades later Assia Djebar, whose French education gave her access to public space and power, sought to reestablish links with women like Feraoun's aunt, individuals who had been largely ignored by both the French colonizer and the Algerian patriarch.

The works of men and women francophone African writers differ in two important respects. First, male writers emphasize the constraints of colonialism, and with few exceptions — Driss Chraibi's *Le Passé simple*, Rachid Boudjedra's *La Répudiation* — do not study the effects of patriarchy. Second, the journey outward, the freedom to discover new places, is gender based. Traditional restrictions — particularly the enclosure imposed by Islamic societies — keep women from journeying as far away as men and most often prohibit any outward journey at all.

A Berber proverb succinctly expresses the spatial limitation placed on women's freedom of movement: "Man is the outer lamp; woman is the inner lamp." Since women have usually been barred from the opportunity to make the journey outward, the fiction of African women writers focuses upon the journey inward. I have noted that Annis Pratt argues that women's escape through imagination is strategic, a withdrawal into the unconscious for the purpose of personal transformation (177). This chapter introduces and examines the effects of enclosure on African women's writing as well as presents the struggle against the consequences of colonialism and the pressure of patriarchal domination. Bâ's work, *Une si longue lettre*, reveals the positive aspects of enclosure, that is, of private space used as refuge; Djebar's novels, *L'Amour, la fantasia* and *Ombre sultane*, emphasize the importance of the freedom to enter public space.

Enclosure/Disclosure: Mariama Bâ

In her first novel, Bâ chooses the letter as a vehicle for recounting episodes of her heroine's past. Following her husband's death, Ramatoulaye begins a long letter to her childhood friend, Aïssatou, in which she describes her attempts at coping with life after Modou, her husband of twenty-five years, takes a second wife. Choosing a young woman the age of his oldest daughter, Modou then abandons Ramatoulaye and their twelve children.

Bâ received the Noma prize for *Une si longue lettre*, acclaimed by the judges for its significant testimony and true imaginative depth (Zell 199). Given its strong attack on polygamy, however, the novel was studied by the majority of critics primarily as a sociological statement.[2] Critics who focus on the sociopolitical and cultural dimensions of polygamy in the work agree that Ramatoulaye, the heroine, is a victim of a society that endorses and encourages polygamy. They disagree as to whether she uses her energies to heroically overcome obstacles or to bitterly reproach the patriarchal structure. Yet both interpretations acknowledge the stress upon the individual facing a traditional society undergoing rapid transformation. Never-theless, by focusing upon the sociopolitical content, the significant testimony of the work, critics tend to pay less attention to discourse, to the imaginative power of Bâ's novel.

Without neglecting the sociopolitical implications of the work, I will focus upon Ramatoulaye's journey to self-understanding rather than upon the evils of polygamy. My study of the protagonist's narrative discourse challenges the conclusion of Geneviève Slomski, who claims that Bâ's heroine fails in her attempt at self-understanding. She attributes the failed revolt to the narrative structure of the novel; the one-sided correspondence puts forth a highly subjective view that bars any objective critique: "Therefore, we observe that in Bâ's text the narrator's discourse functions both as a portrait and a mask; it conceals as much as it reveals" (135).

While providing important insights into Bâ's fiction through careful textual analysis, the critic dismisses Aïssatou, the narratee. My analysis, in contrast, emphasizes the narratee's role in the novel. In my view, Ramatoulaye chooses to address her long letter (twenty-eight chapters) to Aïssatou because she is both an intimate friend and an important role model. The reader learns that Aïssatou faced the issue of polygamy in her own marriage, refusing it before the crisis occurred in Ramatoulaye's home. Aïssatou's revolt and subsequent "escape" to America makes her Ramatoulaye's ideal reader. Her success in the "new world" is convincing testimony; the journey outward is possible.

Studying the novel in terms of the journey motif, the reader discovers an important transformation from the outer to the inner journey. In Bâ's fictional world, Senegalese men are most often offered the opportunity to make the journey outward, returning home with gained maturity, whereas Senegalese women are usually barred from this experience. Modou has been to France to study; Ramatoulaye has not. Given this context, Aïssatou's journey to the United States is a radical statement of revolt.

Although the novel begins with the death of a patriarch — a structural element that appears in Diop's narrative "L'Héritage" and that echoes the opening pages of Kourouma's *Les Soleils des indépendances* — the death and funeral of Ramatoulaye's estranged hus-band result in enclosure rather than in an outward journey for the protagonist. Following the demise of Modou, Ramatoulaye and her co-wife are committed by Islamic tradition to spend four months of mourning in seclusion. Ramatoulaye uses this period to travel in time rather than space. She recalls the past in an attempt to understand herself better and to cope with the present. By examining thoughts, memories, and the collective experience of family and nation emerging from colonialism, Ramatoulaye sets out to gain a heightened sense of maturity. Barred from the journey to the unknown—the path taken by Marlow, Laye, Samba, Mourad—she withdraws into the past in her quest for lucidity. In other words, unable to embark upon the journey that results in knowledge gained through enriching experience, Ramatoulaye turns to the inner journey that provides knowledge through self-examination and maturity through personal transformation. At journey's end, having explored the past and come to terms with the present, Ramatoulaye can envisage the future.

The reader's task in this work is to evaluate Ramatoulaye's inner journey, bearing in mind a binary construct: the portrait and the mask. Does the novel conceal as much as it reveals? To refine the question: Does enclosure (brought about by the Islamic tradition of respectful mourning) lead to disclosure or, ironically, to concealment and therefore to the self-delusion of a protagonist who proposes an inner journey for the explicit purpose of lucidity and self-understanding?

The novel indeed begins with a direct statement of purpose:[3]

> Dear Aïssatou,
> I have received your letter. By way of reply, I am beginning this diary, my prop in my distress. Our long association has taught me that confiding in others allays pain. (10)*

Having just received a letter from Aïssatou (which we later learn announces Aïssatou's forthcoming visit to Dakar), Ramatoulaye informs her of Modou's death. At the same time, she expresses the need for this correspondence as support in time of crisis. This very long letter, ultimately a diary, will allow Ramatoulaye to disclose her intimate thoughts and justify her responses to life through the act of writing to her ideal reader, her closest friend.

Thus, the death of Modou, not his second marriage and ultimate abandonment of Ramatoulaye and their children, is the catalyst for the letter. The significant subtext in the work, revealed in the opening paragraphs, is the importance of female bonding, presented as a

---

* Aïssatou,
J'ai reçu ton mot. En guise de réponse, j'ouvre ce cahier, point d'appui dans mon désarroi: notre longue pratique m'a enseigne' que la confidence noie la douleur. (7)

legacy of traditional Africa. Ramatoulaye recounts the friendship between their grandmothers and mothers and finally recalls their shared childhood: "We wore out our wrappers and sandals on the same stony road to the koranic school" (1).* Hence, at the beginning of her letter Ramatoulaye acknowledges that Aïssatou is her ideal reader because of common experiences: a shared Islamic past, a long sustained friendship, and a painful experience of polygamy—"Yesterday you were divorced. Today I am a widow" (1).† Later, she will reflect upon Aïssatou's decision, her choice to embark upon the journey outward to a new world and a new life.

Enclosure as an important structuring element of the novel must take into account the Islamic context; the latter influences both narrative content and structure. For example, in most sociocultural contexts, Ramatoulaye would have contacted Aïssatou upon the death of Modou, by letter, telegram, or telephone. The mourning period, an obligation of Islam, provides Ramatoulaye with the time frame in which to write the long letter. Opening the notebook that becomes a 131-page novel, she explains: "My heart concurs with the demands of religion. Reared since childhood on their strict precepts, I expect not to fail. The walls that limit my horizon for four months and ten days do not bother me. I have enough memories in me to ruminate upon" (8).‡

Islam as well provides the vehicle for disclosure. *Mirasse*, an Islamic precept, calls for the disclosure of all possessions of the deceased for the purpose of inheritance. Ramatoulaye states, "The *mirasse* commanded by the Koran requires that a dead person be stripped of his most intimate secrets; thus is exposed to others what was carefully concealed" (9).§ Her religion thus encourages revelations of a deceased person's past so as to praise the individual. Ramatoulaye reinterprets this practice to allow for the disclosure of

---

* Nous, nous avons usé pagnes et sandales sur le même chemin caillouteux de l'école coranique (7).

† Hier tu as divorcé. Aujourd'hui, je suis veuve (8).

‡ Mon coeur s'accorde aux exigences religieuses. Nourrie, dés l'enfance, à leurs sources rigides, je crois que je ne faillirai pas. Les murs qui limitent mon horizon pendant quatre mois et dix jours ne me gênent guère. J'ai en moi assez de souvenirs à ruminer (18).

§ "Le Mirasse" ordonné par le coran nécessite le dépouillement d'un individu mort de ses secrets les plus intimes. Il livre ainsi à autrui ce qui fut soigneusement dissimulé (19).

Modou's financial and emotional treachery. Ramatoulaye explains that upon Modou's death she learned that he had taken a loan to pay for his second wife's home by putting a lien on his first wife's property (a residence that Modou and Ramatoulaye had in fact paid for jointly). Subsequently, Ramatoulaye broadens the definition of disclosure to unveil Modou's emotional breach of faith in their marriage.

Ramatoulaye's reaction to the process of *mirasse* is crucial in her journey toward lucidity and in our understanding of the protagonist.[4] By disclosing Modou's transgressions to the readers (Aïssatou, you, me), Ramatoulaye, the betrayed individual, allows us to seek evidence of a healing process. We can then ascertain whether the victim remains victimized, blocked by Modou's betrayal of their married life, or whether she proves capable of transcending the experience by word and deed, discourse and actions.

For the purpose of analysis, the novel can be separated into three sections. Announcing Modou's death and introducing the concept of *mirasse*, the first part (letters 1−4) puts forth the two structuring devices: enclosure and disclosure. The second part (letters 5−17) depicts Ramatoulaye's journey through time. By means of analepses — reaches into the past or flashbacks — the protagonist gathers information that prepares her for the present. In the third and final part of the novel (letters 18−24), Ramatoulaye, having spent forty days in mourning, forgives Modou. In the final section, however, Ramatoulaye as a widow faces a series of moral and emotional challenges that test her judgment and values. These trials complete the protagonist's maturation process.

Hélène Cixous, a leading exponent of the women's movement in France, has written, "Woman must put herself into the text — as into the world and into history — by her own movement" ("The Laugh of the Medusa," 875). Once Ramatoulaye concludes the description of the rituals surrounding Modou's burial, ethnographic details as well as her open criticism of the crass materialism that spoils tradition, she encounters the difficulty of "putting herself into the text." Ramatoulaye begins with two false starts: first, a *cri de coeur*, in which she proclaims herself a victim; then, a letter to Modou, not to Aïssatou, in which she remembers with great sentimentality their first meeting. Although Ramatoulaye praises Modou's progressive views, his words as she recalls them contradict her portrait; they reveal a young man locked into gender stereotypes. For example, calling Ramatoulaye his "négresse protectrice," Modou languishes in

Paris, missing "the swinging hips of black women walking along the pavements" (14).* Hence, Ramatoulaye's acts of telling and showing contradict one another.

This analepsis, a thirty-year reach into the past, poses the problem of the narrator's reliability. Shlomith Rimmon-Kenan, who considers personal involvement to be a main source of unreliability, defines a reliable narrator as one who provides the reader with "an authoritative account of the fictional truth" (100). I believe that intense personal involvement in her own story leads Ramatoulaye, an autodiegetic or first-person narrator, to insert the story of Aïssatou's marriage into the novel. By writing *about* Aïssatou in addition to writing to her, Ramatoulaye restores the objectivity that will grant reliability to her narrative. Aïssatou serves not only as ideal reader and role model but as reality "anchor" as well.[5] Thus, by using the structural device of doubling, of parallel events or similar experiences that reinforce the sense of parallel lives, Ramatoulaye regains an authoritative voice.

The doubling begins in the first letter, when Ramatoulaye remembers their shared childhood. Later, Ramatoulaye recalls that both young girls were inspired by the extraordinary vision of their European school director. Looking back on these formative years, Ramatoulaye views her school mistress as the one who freed them from tradition. She writes in the first-person plural, thereby emphasizing the school director's effect upon both of them: "To lift us out of the bog of tradition, superstition and custom, to make us appreciate a multitude of civilizations without renouncing our own, to raise our vision of the world, cultivate our personalities, strengthen our qualities, to make up for our inadequacies, to develop universal moral values in us: these were the aims of our admirable headmistress" (15–16).† The director's message is clearly subversive. Urging her students to break with tradition and to affirm their personality, she calls for revolt rather than submission. Ramatoulaye's act of rebellion is to reject the suitor chosen for her by her mother and marry Modou Fall, a man of her own choosing. Similarly,

---

* le dandinement des négresses le long du trottoir (25).

† Nous sortir de l'enlisement des traditions, superstitions et moeurs; nous faire apprécier de multiples civilisations sans reniement de la nôtre; élever notre vision du monde, cultiver notre personnalité, renforcer nos qualités, mater nos défauts; faire fructifier en nous les valeurs de la morale universelle; voilà la tâche que s'etait assignée l'admirable directrice (27–28).

Aïssatou, the daughter of a blacksmith, defies the traditional caste system by marrying a son of royalty. Their rebellion bears later consequences; their choices ironically prepare the way for polygamy. Ramatoulaye chooses a man whose propensity towards infidelity is immediately recognized by her mother. Aïssatou, who marries above her station, incurs the vengeance of a scheming mother-in-law who succeeds in bringing a second wife into her son's household.

Although the doubling creates the dimension of parallel lives in the novel, the narrator reveals that Ramatoulaye and Aïssatou are not at all mirror images of one another. Most important, when their husbands enter into polygamous marriages for different reasons — one to please a scheming mother, the other to find the excitement of lost youth, Aïssatou rebels, Ramatoulaye acquiesces. Aïssatou responds to Mawdo's announcement of his second marriage with an angry letter in which she states her refusal to remain within the marriage: "I will not yield to it. I cannot accept what you are offering me today in place of the happiness we once had. You want to draw a line between heartfelt love and physical love. I say that there can be no union of bodies without the heart's acceptance, however little that may be" (31).*

Ramatoulaye, who quotes Aïssatou's entire letter, nevertheless cannot bring herself to follow her friend in revolt. Despite her admiration for Aïssatou's refusal of polygamy, Ramatoulaye turns the other cheek. The second section of the novel then discloses not only Modou's treachery but Ramatoulaye's failed revolt. But husband and wife lose touch with their earlier progressive selves. Modou becomes a caricature of an old fool trying to regain his youth: "Modou would leave himself winded trying to imprison youth in its decline, which abandoned him on all sides..." (48).† Ramatoulaye, lacking courage, agrees to a polygamous union out of fear of loneliness. Only after Modou truly abandons her and she is forced to take on the role of single parent does Ramatoulaye resume the rhetoric of revolt. The reader may conclude that Ramatoulaye writes the "long letter" to Aïssatou upon Modou's death because she was unable to write the "short letter," as Aïssatou had done, and thereby reject polygamy.

---

* "Je ne m'y soumettrai point. Au bonheur qui fut nôtre, je ne peux substituer celui que tu me proposes aujourd'hui. Tu veux dissocier l'Amour tout court et l'amour physique. Je te rétorque que la communion charnelle ne peut être sans l'acceptation du coeur, si minime soite-elle" (50).

† Modou s'essouflait à emprisonner une jeunesse déclinante qui le fuyait de partout... (72).

The second section can be characterized as failed revolt, but it prepares the protagonist for the series of trials or challenges that result in her final transformation. This preparation takes the form of comforting past memories on the one hand and acts of independence on the other. The memories of her youth and early adulthood are a source of happiness. Recalling the years when she was first married to Modou, Ramatoulaye turns to nature for inspiration. She depicts the beach at Ngor: "On the fine sand, washed by the waves and swollen with water, naively painted canoes awaited their turn to be launched into the waters. In their hollows small pools of blue water would glisten, full of light from the sky and sun" (21).*

Metaphorically, the boats, waiting to be launched on the vast ocean, correspond to the two idealistic couples whose lives are, at that time, filled with boundless dreams. The reader can situate this optimistic phase chronologically: it occurs in the mid-1960s, when the Senegalese nation was first emerging from colonialism. As Ramatoulaye faces adult responsibilities in her personal life, Senegal assumes the responsibilities of nationhood. Hence, the narrator establishes a direct link between the personal and the historical-political phase.

Placing the two cases of polygamy within this historical context, the narrator invites the reader to question whether Ramatoulaye's experience of abandonment and disillusionment serves as metaphor for the abandonment of ideals and subsequent disillusionment in postindependence West Africa. For example, Aïssatou's husband, Mawdo, pleads his case for polygamy by turning to tradition. Similarly, the excuse of tradition allowed patriarchal authority to retain its grip in Senegal: the political and economic power of the feudal chiefs (particularly the authority of the Mouride and Tidjani brotherhoods) was not challenged in newly independent Senegal.

Ramatoulaye's husband, however, cannot excuse his actions by hiding behind the traditional banner. Unlike Mawdo, whose mother plotted the polygamous union, Modou initiates the situation himself; he chooses to exercise a privilege that enlightened Senegalese reject. Should the reader draw a parallel between Modou's choice of a polygamous union and Senegal's embrace of one-party rule? By creating an imbalance of power, both open the way for potential

---

* Sur le sable fin, rincé par la vague et gorgé d'eau, des pirogues, peintes naïvement, attendaient leur tour d'être lancées sur les eaux. Dans leur coque, luisaient de petites flaques bleues pleines de ciel et de soleil (35).

abuses. I am not suggesting that Bâ's novel is an attack on the political structure rather than the narrative of an inner journey to maturity. These hypotheses nevertheless invite additional interpretation, thereby attributing greater complexity to the text.

The midsection of the novel depicts a protagonist who appears to have lost her earlier rebellious stance and is therefore unable to revolt against her husband's abuse of power. Specific signs toward the end of the section suggest that despite her initial acquiescence Ramatoulaye will recapture both the spirit and the language of revolt. For example, Ramatoulaye recounts her experience of braving the curious stares of a public who wonders why she is alone at the cinema: "People stared at the middle-aged lady without a partner. I would feign indifference, while anger hammered against my nerves and the tears I held back welled up behind my eyes. From the surprised looks, I gauged the slender liberty granted to women" (51).* Hence Ramatoulaye finds the courage to venture alone into public space but at the same time masks her anger towards a hostile public. Later, Aïssatou's gift of a new car allows Ramatoulaye to travel more freely in the city. The Fiat proves to be a challenge to Ramatoulaye, who conquers her fear of driving in order to obtain her driver's license. These experiences affirm Ramatoulaye's presence in public space. Occurring after Modou's departure but before his death, they attest to the protagonist's essentially independent spirit and foreshadow her final transformation.

The fortieth day of mourning marks the beginning of the third and final section of the novel. At this point, the widow forgives her late husband. In addition, suitors begin to ask for her hand: first Ramatoulaye's brother-in-law and then a former suitor propose marriage. Presented with a co-wife several years before, Ramatoulaye is now asked to become one. Refusing her brother-in-law (whose offer is motivated by the desire for her inheritance), Ramatoulaye finally expresses her anger: "My voice has known thirty years of silence, thirty years of harassment. It bursts out, violent, sometimes sarcastic, sometimes contemptuous" (57–58).† Having once greeted the announcement of Modou's second marriage with a smile and feigned

---

* On dévisageait la femme mûre sans compagnon. Je feignais l'indifférence, alors que la colère martelait mes nerfs et que mes larmes retenues embuaient mes yeux. Je mesurais, aux regards étonnés, la minceur de la liberté accordée à la femme (76).

† Ma voix connaît trente années de silence, trente années de brimades. Elle éclate, violente, tantôt sarcastique, tantôt méprisante (85).

indifference, Ramatoulaye now removes the mask of the passive and acquiescent woman and finds the words to affirm her identity. She expresses the conviction that marriage must be a choice between partners, not an arrangement between families: "You forget that I have a heart, a mind, that I am not an object to be passed from hand to hand. You don't know what marriage means to me: it is an act of faith and of love, the total surrender of oneself to the person one has chosen and who has chosen you (I emphasized the word 'chosen.')" (58).*

Later, rejecting the second suitor, Daouda Dieng, whose motivation is affection, not avarice, Ramatoulaye offers him friendship instead of marriage. Ramatoulaye refuses Daouda Dieng's proposal in a letter that explains that she cannot enter into a polygamous marriage because she has suffered the consequences of one: "Abandoned yesterday because of a woman, I cannot lightly bring myself between you and your family" (68).† Hence, Ramatoulaye finally writes a letter rejecting polygamy, although neither the tone nor the circumstances recall Aïssatou's angry words to Mawdo.

Having learned to express her anger openly as she rejects polygamy, Ramatoulaye faces her final trials. Forced to cope with family crises as a single parent, she rises to each occasion: a son's motorcycle accident, then the pregnancy of an unmarried daughter.

As she writes her last letter to Aïssatou, Ramatoulaye eagerly awaits her friend's visit.[6] The dual process of introspection and writing, of enclosure and disclosure, has led Ramatoulaye to cease questioning Modou's initial rejection. No longer a victim, she now expresses new hope in her future. "It is from the dirty and nauseating humus that the green plant sprouts into life, and I can feel new buds springing up in me" (89).‡ Hence, the epistolary novel that began with Modou's death ends in an expression of rebirth.

Unlike Aïssatou, who chose the outward journey and left Senegal in order to begin a new life, Ramatoulaye does not leave her community. She avoids the risk of uprootedness in exile, the challenge

---

* "Tu oublies que j'ai un coeur, une raison, que je ne suis pas un object que l'on passe de main en main. Tu ignores ce que se marier signifie pour moi: c'est un acte de foi et d'amour, un don total de soi à l'être que l'on a choisi et qui vous a choisi. (J'insistais sur le mot choisi.)" (85)

† "Abnandonnée hier, par le fait d'une femme, je ne peux allègrement m'introduire entre toi et ta famille" (100).

‡ C'est de l'humus sale et nauséabond que jaillit la plante verte et je sens pointer en moi, des bourgeons neufs (131).

that her friend assumes, and reaches a new beginning via a different route.

Despite the fact that Bâ's heroine does not embark upon the outward voyage, her experiences reflect the initiation of the hero or heroine of oral narrative. Substituting a temporal for a spatial journey, Bâ's novel recalls Diop's tale "L'Heritage," which centers upon an outward trajectory for the purpose of obtaining wisdom. Both narratives begin with the death of a patriarch, although the father of Momar, Birame, and Moussa has led an exemplary life, in contrast to Ramatoulaye's husband. Moreover, Samba dies at a ripe old age, unlike Modou, struck down in the prime of life. Indeed, the reader is tempted to question whether Modou's fatal and untimely heart attack is retribution for the man's abandonment of his first wife and their twelve children.

In the two narratives, the protagonists set out to find an answer to a disturbing problem: Why had Samba left his sons a puzzling inheritance? Why had Modou abandoned his wife of twenty-five years? Samba's legacy to his sons is the work ethic. At the end of their journey, his three children learn to put away their inheritance and work the land, thereby imitating the exemplary life of their father. Yet the sons' encounter with Kem Tanne, the intercessor, teaches them a more profound truth as well: as they go on in life, they must seek the truth that lies beneath surface reality. Moreover, not only do Momar, Birame, and Moussa gain wisdom, they also learn the value and importance of intercessors.

Ramatoulaye's journey leads to lucidity, and it also occurs on two levels. She discovers that Modou abandoned her because of his weakness and vanity, and she learns a deeper truth: to believe in herself. By removing the mask, the smile of acquiescence, Ramatoulaye recovers her earlier vitality and optimism. Moreover, the successful conclusion of the first journey prepares the protagonist for a second one, a new quest for happiness.

As Samba's three sons are reintegrated into society, so is Ramatoulaye. At the end of the novel, she awaits Aïssatou in the traditional manner, seated on a straw mat. Rather than break with her society, Ramatoulaye works within it to construct and preserve her identity as an individual as well as a member of her community. Bâ's heroine thus reveals a newly found sense of identity that stems from a blending of traditional and modern elements.

Although Diop's narrative "L'Héritage" concerns three sons bereft of a parent, it is not a stock orphan tale. Samba's sons set out to solve the mystery of their puzzling inheritance, not to accomplish an impossible task imposed by a jealous stepmother, the characteristic plot of most orphan tales. For example, Bernard Dadié's "Le Pagne noir" recounts the adventures of Aïwa, sent by her stepmother to whiten a black cloth. As she travels in search of water in which to wash the object, the orphan courageously confronts danger and frustration. Finally, the ghost of Aïwa's mother descends from heaven to replace the black cloth with a white one which the stepmother immediately recognizes as the winding sheet used to bury the mother. Not only does the orphan accomplish the task, she teaches the wicked stepmother a lesson.

One discerns affinities between the narratives of Bâ and Dadié, both of which depict a vulnerable female protagonist. Ramatoulaye, like Aïwa, ventures forth unprotected in a hostile world. She has lost the protection of her husband (a variant of the orphan's loss of a parent) and is forced by a patriarchal society to grapple with a series of difficult tasks. One of her final tests is to reject her two suitors. By refusing a second marriage to which she is not committed by love, Ramatoulaye confronts and overcomes her fear of loneliness. The orphan's trials have been compared to initiation rites (Domowitz 351); Ramatoulaye's tests initiate her to a new stage of life: the role of a single person.

A stock character of the orphan tale, the wicked stepmother or the ogress represents danger and evil in Ramatoulaye's world as well. On one hand, Dame Belle-Mère schemes to have her daughter, Binetou, marry Modou. On the other hand, Mawdo's mother coerces her son to marry his niece, Nabou. Whereas Dame Belle-Mère seeks money, Aïssatou's mother-in-law is motivated by vengeance. Both women challenge Ramatoulaye's conviction that love and choice form the cornerstone of marriage.

In Dadié's orphan tale, Aïwa, despite her hardships, never removes her mask, a smile: "She still wears the smile we find on the lips of young girls" (22).* Finally rewarded for her stoicism and obedience, Aïwa is able to accomplish the impossible task with the help of her mother, a spirit of the dead.[7] Ramatoulaye, on the other hand, discards her smile, the mask of acquiescence, and asserts her individuality and independence. As she assumes a dynamic identity, Ramatoulaye reaffirms the rebellious spirit of her youth. Challenging

---

* Elle sourit encore du sourire qu'on retrouve sur les lèvres des jeunes filles.

the matriarchy and the patriarchy — for both demand submission and obedience — Ramatoulaye looks within herself to find the courage to break free.

Ramatoulaye's intercessor, then, is neither a spirit from the other world — Aïwa's mother — nor a venerable sage — Kem Tanne — but rather Aïssatou. Faithful friend and confidante, she offers Ramatoulaye two gifts, a car and a letter, and thereby provides her with the tools of transformation. The little Fiat allows Ramatoulaye to lay claim to public space by travelling freely in it, thus encouraging her to affirm a new identity. The letter, Aïssatou's declaration of separation from her husband Mawdo, initiates Ramatoulaye to the act of writing as a process as well as a product of liberation.

In contrast to the winding sheet of the dead mother, a white cloth that puts an end to the orphan's quest in Dadié's narrative, the white sheets of Ramatoulaye's notebook represent a new beginning. Represented as a therapeutic activity in the early pages of the novel, writing subsequently results in liberation as well as in healing. Moreover, in Bâ's novel, the act of writing as a process of disclosure that promotes discovery and self-affirmation clearly reinforces female bonding. Hence, the two structuring devices — enclosure and disclosure, the one facilitating the journey inwards, the other recording it — serve another important function: they strengthen communication between Ramatoulaye and Aïssatou. These bonds between narrator and narratee have made it possible for Ramatoulaye to put herself into the text. At the end of her journey, Bâ's heroine has learned to use the written word as a creative tool of self-expression and as a weighty weapon against the patriarchy.

Fleeing the Harem: Assia Djebar

Removing the veils metaphorically to explore individual and collective female identity, Assia Djebar, like Mariama Bâ, depicts the struggle against patriarchy. Djebar too was born into a Muslim culture in which the appropriation of space is gender based: "Man is the outer lamp; woman is the inner lamp." Her work also reveals the importance of enclosure. Whereas Bâ emphasizes its positive aspect, private space as refuge, Djebar distinguishes between comforting haven, conducive to female bonding, and threatening confinement, where woman is victim. Rather than substitute an inner for an outer journey, as Bâ does in *Une si longue lettre*, Djebar emphasizes the importance of the outer journey, but redefines the term. She views the journey not as a voyage to the unknown — Marlow's trip up the Congo

River — but as the experience of circulating freely in public space.

Contrasting and yet complementary images appear in Djebar's recent fiction: two women bathing at the *hammam* (*Ombre sultane*); a small child clutching her father's hand as she walks to school (*L'Amour, la fantasia*); Delacroix's celebrated painting of four women in a harem in Algiers (*Femmes d'Alger dans leur appartement*). Whereas the first scene reflects the importance of female bonding and of closed space as refuge, the second represents the beginning of an outward journey, of initiation to freedom of movement in public space. Finally, Delacroix's painting depicts enclosure as prohibition, as denial of both access to public space as well as the liberty to circulate freely beyond the sealed chambers of the harem.

In Djebar's concluding essay, a postface to her collection of short stories that bears the same title as the Delacroix painting, the writer studies the effects of enclosure as she examines the painting, exploring the relationship between subjects, painter, and public. Djebar discusses the significance of the *regard volé*, the fixed stare of the painter Delacroix who, as a male and a European, is an intruder in the harem. Granted permission to view these cloistered women briefly in 1832, shortly after the French conquest, Delacroix composed the painting from memory in 1834 (completing a second version in 1849). He depicted the women as Oriental dolls in a dimly lit, richly textured interior. To the painter and, by extension, to his public, these Algerian women are objects, decorative and mute prisoners of opulence. Djebar writes: "Submissive prisoners of a closed space lighted with a kind of dream light emanating from nowhere — light of a greenhouse or an aquarium — the genius of Delacroix is to make them at the same time both present and distant — enigmatic to the greatest degree" (170).*

Of the four women in the painting, two whisper together, seated behind a *narguilé*, or water pipe; the third gazes ahead, her body propped up against a set of cushions; the fourth, a black servant whose back is to the viewer, lifts a heavy curtain. All four appear lost in reverie, enclosed in a private world that the painter's gaze has not disturbed. To Djebar, these woman are victims of the patriarchy.[8] They have been denied freedom of movement and free-

---

* Prisonnières résignées d'un lieu clos qui s'éclaire d'une sorte de lumière de rêve venue de nulle part — lumière de serre ou d'aquarium — le génie de Delacroix nous les rend à la fois présentes et lointaines, énigmatiques au plus haut point.

dom of expression. She believes that their facial expressions convey bitterness and hopelessness — *une amertume désesperée.*

By studying the painting, Djebar, whose writings had previously focused on Algeria in the immediate prewar period and the era of the independence, introduces an historical perspective into her writings: the French conquest of Algeria in 1830. Linking these women of Algeria's past to those of the present, she puts forth a feminist interpretation. The necessity to liberate the *odalisques*, representatives of patriarchal oppression, becomes the symbolic quest of Djebar's individual and collective narrative, occurring in both her autobiographical selections and her accounts of women in war. An examination of Delacroix's painting reveals that the two women seated behind the *narguilé* are whispering together. A challenge for Djebar is to reconstruct that conversation. To restore speech to Algerian women, the writer must lend her ear to the whispers in the harem. Although this specific enclosure, the harem, no longer exists as a physical reality in Algeria today, Djebar reminds us that its psychological walls are still present; her writing is in praise of Algerian women who have found the courage to construct a life beyond the sealed-off chambers ruled by the patriarch.

Published in 1985 and 1987 respectively, *L'Amour, la fantasia* and *Ombre sultane* illustrate the theoretical concerns of the essay. Introducing a temporal-spatial journey, both novels present an autodiegetic narrator who, like Bâ's heroine, turns to the past to understand herself better. *L'Amour, la fantasia* emphasizes the temporal journey, setting autobiographical fragments against episodes of the conquest of 1830 and the Algerian revolution of 1954. *Ombre sultane* accentuates the spatial journey, as two Algerian women, one traditional, the other emancipated, lay claim to public and private space.

The day that Assia Djebar's father, a teacher in the French colonial educational system, first escorted his daughter to school — "a little Arab girl going to school for the first time, one autumn morning, walking hand in hand with her father" (3)[9]* — he set her on a bilingual and bicultural journey, albeit an ambiguous one, that freed her from female enclosure. This opening scene in Djebar's fifth novel, *L'Amour, la fantasia*, an autobiographical incident recalled four decades after the event, set in motion the conquest of space and

---

* Fillette arabe allant pour la première fois à l'école, un matin d'automne, main dans la main du père (11).

language necessary for the writer's development as an artist and an intellectual. Although liberated from the female enclosure, the child reached adulthood haunted by the weight of exile. Djebar came to believe that her French education and freedom of movement in public space had excluded her from all aspects of the traditional woman's world, thus separating her from the majority of her Algerian sisters—"the outdoors and the risk, instead of the prison of my peers" (184).* This novel reveals the process and represents the product of the artist's attempt to reestablish links with the maternal world of her past. Djebar does so by assuming the role of translator and scribe. Taking *kalaam*, "word" in Arabic, she transforms it into *écriture*, "writing" in French. Thus, the act of writing, a therapeutic activity for Bâ's protagonist, Ramatoulaye, takes on the same meaning for Djebar's narrator; the process of disclosure promotes discovery, self-affirmation, healing, and female bonding.

Djebar insists that just as space has been sexualized in traditional Algeria—inner space, the home, reserved for women; outer space, the workplace and government, reserved for men—so too has history. The written account of the conquest of Algeria that she uncovers from the archives is French and male; the oral account that she assembles from interviews with participants is Arabic and female. Most important, in this endeavor *écriture* and *kalaam*—the written word in French, the spoken word in Arabic—are unknown and unintelligible each to the other. Djebar uses her language skills, translating, transcribing, interpreting, to bridge the gap between the two.

L'Amour, la fantasia is composed of two narratives that reflect two distinct journeys, one autobiographical, the other historical. The first, reflecting the tradition of the *Künstlerroman*, records the development of the artist; the second traces the history of Algeria from the conquest of 1830 to liberation in 1962. The small hand that gripped her father's as they walked to school together one autumn day in the early 1940s was subsequently offered a pen. Examining her artistic evolution, which she views as a progressive *dévoilement* or removing of the veils, Djebar links *écriture* to space, the freedom of self-expression to the liberty to circulate freely, and in so doing, to lay claim to public space:[10]

---

* le dehors et le risque au lieu de la prison de mes semblables (208).

Just as the pentathlon runner of old needed the starter, so, as soon as I learned the foreign script, my body began to move as if by instinct.

As if the French language suddenly had eyes, and lent them to me to see into liberty; as if the French language blinded the peeping-toms of my clan and, at this price, I could move freely, run headlong down every street, annex the outdoors for my cloistered companions, for the matriarchs of my family who endured a living death. (181)*

She thus defines her relationship to the French language in terms of individual liberation. Djebar could not have become a writer had she not access to the colonizer's language and schools, to *écriture* and public space. Yet these advantages, necessary to one's development as a creative writer, were inaccessible to the majority of her Algerian sisters. Djebar's role then is to place her skills, a result of her unique experience, in the service of the community, thereby "annexing" public space for all Algerian women.

Djebar notes, "Writing does not silence the voice, but awakens it, above all to resurrect so many vanished sisters." (204)† In search of women's contributions to Algerian history, Djebar studies both oral and written history. She turns first to the archives of colonial history, carefully examining French colonial documentation of the period in her attempt to find "les soeurs disparues," Algerian women who, from the beginning of the French conquest of 1830, participated in the struggle against colonialism. Studying French military officers' and soldiers' correspondence in the nineteenth century, letters written to the families back home, as well as official documents, Djebar finds evidence of women's participation in history, thus giving credibility to the struggle of the "soeurs disparues."

In the French archives, Djebar discovers thirty-two accounts of the military campaigns in the 1830s: official reports, correspondence among officers, letters that officers and soldiers sent home to their families. Among these records, in the description of the battle of

---

* Mon corps seul, comme le coureur du pentathlon a besoin du starter pour démarrer, mon corps s'est trouvé en mouvement dès la pratique de l'écriture étrangère.

Comme si soudain la langue française avait des yeux, et qu'elle me les ait donnés pour voir dans la liberté, comme si la langue française aveuglait les males voyeurs de mon clan et qu'à ce prix, je puisse circuler, dégringoler toutes les rues, annexer le dehors pour mes compagnes cloîtrées, pour mes aïeules mortes bien avant le tombeau (204).

† Ecrire ne tue pas la voix mais la réveille, surtout pour ressusciter tant de soeurs disparues (229).

Staoueli in July 1830 as recounted by Baron Barchou, she finds the following trace of Algerian women:

> One of these women lay dead beside the corpse of a French soldier whose heart she had torn out! Another had been fleeing with a child in her arms when a shot wounded her; she seized a stone and crushed the infant's head to prevent it falling alive into our hands; the soldiers finished her off with their bayonets. (18)[*]

Thus, Djebar proves that the "soeurs disparues" were active participants in resistance against the French. The contrast between the two women in this highly visual scene of violence is striking. One is reminded of Orientalist paintings of the period, works by Delacroix, Vernet, Chasseriau. Whereas the first woman warrior appears savage — ripping out a soldier's heart! — the second, a mother who chooses to sacrifice her child rather than surrender the infant alive, is a noble, tragic, stoic figure.

Neither passive bystanders nor secluded *odalisques* of a harem, these women foreshadow later militants of the liberation struggle. Their presence, a reality with a historical point of reference, serves as metaphor for Algeria. Studying the letters of military officers and soldiers, Djebar writes: "Between the lines these letters speak of Algeria as a woman whom it is impossible to tame." (57)[†] Taken by force and subjugated to the will of the conqueror, the Algerian nation nevertheless remains subversive. Jean Amrouche had termed Algeria's stance "le génie de l'alternance," an ability to assume the external appearance of acquiescence while maintaining deep-seated defiance and revolt.

As she studies the historical documents further, Djebar becomes a "spéologue de la mort" (86), reconstituting the horror of two separate incidents of *enfumade*, of asphyxiation by fire in an enclosure that had become a death trap. In 1845, two French officers, Pelissier and Saint-Arnaud, ordered their men to set caves on fire, asphyxiating the tribes that used them as refuge; the chronicle of war and conquest becomes a chronicle of genocide. Pelissier, uncovering the mass tomb, followed his actions with a macabre written testimony, thereby

---

[*] "L'une d'elles gisait à côté d'un cadavre français dont elle avait arraché le coeur! Une autre s'enfuyait tenant un enfant dans ses bras: blessée d'un coup de feu, elle écrasa avec une pierre la tête de l'enfant, pour l'empêcher de tomber vivant dans nos mains; les soldats l'achevèrent elle-même à coups de baïonnette" (28−29).

[†] Ces lettres parlent, dans le fond, d'une Algérie-femme impossible à apprivoiser (69).

unleashing a polemic in Paris. Saint-Arnaud, on the other hand, never returned to the site of the *enfumade* of the Sbeah tribe and sent a confidential report to French military headquarters in Algiers, where it was promptly destroyed. Whereas the first incident was recorded in writing and entered French colonial archives, the second was relegated to oral history, known only to the descendants of the victims. Thus even the legacy of *enfumade* reflects the division between *écriture* and *kalaam*.

In contrast to *écriture*, to male French narrative of the conquest, Djebar presents *kalaam*, peasant women's narratives of the Algerian revolution. By giving written expression to orality, to Algerian oral history as recounted by women who participated in the resistance during the war of liberation, she gives voice to the *porteuses de feu*, the surviving heroines of the Algerian revolution. The chapters "Voix" and "Voix de veuve" allow women who do not have a command of the French language to describe their experiences, events that occurred two decades earlier. On the one hand, they tell of experiences such as hiding in the woods, being captured, jailed, and tortured. On the other hand, they express their feelings of fear, pain, and triumph as they relive these memories. Most important, oral narrative communicates women's true experiences. As oral history bears witness to the courage of women in war, it also reveals their transgression of spatial boundaries in a period of political turmoil. Whereas some women join the men in the rural combat zone, others open their homes to guerrilla fighters. Captured by the French, they face enclosure — confinement in prison and torture.

To retain the flavor of oral narrative when transposed to the printed page, Djebar, like Ahmadou Kourouma, makes frequent use of popular expressions. Cherifa will say, "France came and burnt us out" (117),* using one term (*Francia* in dialectical Arabic) to indicate both the French nation and its people. Another characteristic of oral narrative that Djebar seeks to preserve is the terse style. Although the moment described may be very dramatic and emotionally charged, the tone in which it is conveyed is often unemotional. After spending many months in prison, Cherifa is visited by her father. She states, "When my father saw me, he wept" (140).† Djebar explains, "I noticed that the more the women had suffered, the more they spoke

---

* "La France est venue et elle nous a brûles" (133).
† "En me voyant mon vieux père a pleure" (159).

about it in a very concise, almost dry manner" (Mortimer, "Entretien," 202).*

Whereas popular expressions close the gap between *écriture* and *kalaam*, understatement and terseness create further distance between the two. For example, Cherifa's narrative appears all the more stark, concise, filled with understatement, when juxtaposed with Captain Montagnac's nineteenth-century French prose, richly embellished, tinged with exoticism. The French officer writes to his uncle:

> This little fray offered a charming spectacle. Clouds of horsemen, light as birds, criss-crossing, flitting in every direction, and from time to time the majestic voice of the canon rising above the shouts of triumph and the rifle-shots — all this combined to present a delightful panorama and an exhilirating scene...(54)†

Hence, the French officer attempts to deny the reality of dangerous battle with his use of reassuring adjectives — *charmant, délicieux* — as well as by his rather romantic and inappropriate comparison of soldiers facing death to birds flying across the landscape. Whether relating their own stories or those of their ancestors, women narrators, in contrast, remain wedded to reality. Grandmothers whispering in the dark to their grandchildren assume the role of oral historian as well as family genealogist. In this way Djebar learns of the exploits of her ancestors: Mohammed Ben Aissa El Berkani and Malek Sahraoui El Berkani. The former fought with Emir Abdelkader against the French in the 1840s; the latter lost his life in a rebellion against the French in 1871.[11]

As *écriture* and *kalaam* — written and oral history — complement one another and together provide valid perspective on colonial history, the binary structure of the novel — Algerian history alternating with memories of childhood and adolescence under colonialism — achieves the balance between individual and collective female identity. Tracing her own intellectual journey (the portrait of the artist as a young woman), Djebar focuses specific attention upon incidents that involve the act of writing. As such, they reveal attempts by herself and others to move beyond the confined space imposed upon women. For example, Djebar recalls that her rebellious cousins,

---

* Jai remarqué que plus les femmes avaient souffert, plus elles en parlaient sous une forme concise, a la limite presque sèchement.

† Ce petit combat offrait un coup d'oeil charmant. Ces nuées de cavaliers, légers comme des oiseaux, se croisent, voltigent sur tous les points, ces hourras, ces coups de fusil dominés, de temps à autre, par la voix majestueuse du canon, tout cela présentait un panorama délicieux et une scéne énivrante..." (67).

though cloistered, defy their father and challenge convention by secretly corresponding with male "pen pals" in the Middle East. Thus, her cousins embark upon imaginary journeys to distant lands in their struggle against patriarchal restrictions. Djebar notes, "Sending those endless epistles out into the unknown brought them a breath of fresh air and a temporary escape from their confinement" (44–45).* Whereas Bâ reveals that enclosure results in disclosure because Ramatoulaye uses confinement as refuge in which to examine her life and then reaffirm the discourse of revolt, Djebar shows that the cloistering of adolescents encourages imaginary journeys, escape that provides only temporary and quite illusory happiness.

Recalling other incidents that depict writing as a tool of transformation, Djebar cites her father's defiance of tradition when, away on a voyage, he writes a postcard to his wife rather than send the family the customary formal greeting. Writing his wife's name on the envelope, he affirms her individuality in opposition to the Muslim custom of perpetuating women's anonymity.[12] Djebar also remembers her first adolescent love letters; they, like her father's postcard, were written in French. The language of the colonizer, *la langue adverse*,[13] becomes a language of intimacy as new and subversive customs appear within the home as well. Finally, Djebar writes of her growing need to express herself. She asks, "Is not writing a way of telling what 'I' am?" (58)† and asserts, "The word is a torch" (62).‡

Although the act of writing liberates the individual, writing in the colonizer's language implies the ambiguity associated with a French education. On the one hand, Djebar acknowledges education as a liberating force, but on the other hand, she concludes that it encourages alienation. As a young girl, she is free to enter public space; she is neither veiled nor cloistered. At the same time, the writer is separated from the maternal world, a situation that compels Djebar to exclaim, "Suddenly, I begin to have qualms: isn't it my 'duty' to stay behind with my peers in the gynaeceum?...Why me? Why do I alone, of all my tribe, have this opportunity?" (213)§

---

* Ecrire vers l'inconnu devenait pour elles une manière de respirer un nouvel oxygène. Elles trouvaient là une issue provisoire à leur claustration (56).

† "Ecrire, n'est-ce pas 'me' dire?" (72)

‡ le mot est torche (75).

§ "Soudain, une réticence, un scrupule me taraude; mon devior n'est-il pas de rester 'en arrière,' dans le gynécée, avec mes semblables?...Pourquoi moi? Pourquoi à moi seule, dans la tribu, cette chance?" (239)

Djebar's efforts to preserve oral narrative by recording, transcribing, translating, and later filming may be considered not only attempts to bridge the gap between *écriture* and *kalaam*, but efforts to bring together the male and female sphere. She has explained, "If the first step is to bring back the past through writing in French, the second is to listen to the women who evoke the past through their voices, the maternal language. Then we must carry this recollection from the maternal to the paternal tongue" (Mortimer, "Entretien," 201).[*] Some critics may argue that it is false to characterize the French language as paternal, since Algerian men have continued to speak Arabic in their family and social groups. Djebar, however, views the French language as a source of power and dominance to which certain men (such as her father) had access during the colonial period and to which most women did not.

By alternating historical accounts of the French conquest, oral history of the Algerian revolution, and autobiographical fragments, Djebar sets her individual journey against two distinct and yet complementary backdrops: the conquest of 1830 and the Algerian Revolution of 1954. The former introduced the colonial era; the latter brought it to a close. In this way, the narrator establishes links with Algeria's past, more specifically with women of the past whose heroism has been forgotten.

Djebar presents the reader with interwoven narratives that represent three distinct voices and temporal frames. Reflections on bilingualism as well as lyrical passages in praise of Algerian women add two more voices, conveying greater complexity to the novel. Hence, Djebar creates a polyphonic work that resembles a five-part symphony, an allusion to Beethoven's *Fantasia*. At the same time, she seeks to imitate a North African *fantasia*, the spectacle of charging cavalry: "We pass from the realm of the intimate, from childhood memory to epic or tragic memory — women in relation to war — and I end on a kind of poetic flight" (Mortimer, "Entretien," 203).[†]

Reminding the reader that the *fantasia* is always accompanied by *tzarl-rit* — the *youyous* or shrill cries off women's voices, *le cri dans la*

---

[*] Si le premier volet est de ramener le passé à travers l'écriture en français, le deuxième est d'écouter les femmes qui évoquent le passe par la voix, par la langue maternelle. Ensuite, il faut ramener cette évocation à travers la langue maternelle vers la langue paternelle.

[†] On passe de l'intime, du souvenir d'enfance, au souvenir épique ou tragique — les femmes par rapport à la guerre — et je termine sur une espèce d'envolée poétique.

fantasia — Djebar uses the symphonic and *fantasia*-like structure to blend her voice with those of traditional Maghrebian women. Giving written form to Algerian women's heroic deeds, Djebar as translator and scribe succeeds in forging new links with traditional women of the world she left behind.

In *Ombre sultane*, Djebar continues to create bonds with her maternal world. Alternating the narratives of two women, one traditional, the other emancipated, the novelist again presents a binary structure. Whereas *L'Amour, la fantasia* sets an autobiographical narrative against the backdrop of Algerian history, allowing the narrator to examine her relationship to Algeria's past, this novel juxtaposes a first- and second-person narrative that permits the autodiegetic narrator to discover bonds that link two women.

Using open and closed space metaphorically, Djebar depicts Hajila, a traditional woman, embarking upon an outward journey, and Isma, an emancipated woman, undertaking an inward journey. In the course of the novel, Hajila obtains new freedom by acquiring the right to circulate in the city. Isma comes to terms with the present by returning to the enclosures of her past — the Moorish patios of her childhood days, the bedroom of her married years.

In terms of the journey motif, affinities appear between this novel and *Une si longue lettre*. In both works, the narrator undertakes an inner or temporal journey to childhood, adolescence, and then the early years of marriage. In each novel the "other" embarks upon an outer journey: Aïssatou travels abroad to America, Hajila explores her native city. Moreover, doubling or parallel lives reappear as a structuring device. Isma, like Ramatoulaye, studies two itineraries, her own and Hajila's, in her quest for self-understanding.

Isma, who resembles the emancipated heroines of Djebar's earlier works as well as the writer, and Hajila, cloistered and veiled, share a common experience: they have been married to the same man. After leaving her husband because of conflict that stems from her independence, Isma secretly chooses Hajila, docile and submissive, as his second wife. She then records Hajila's initial acceptance and subsequent refusal of the constraints of the marriage.

As narrator, Isma observes the traditional woman's actions as she assumes control of her life. Hajila does so by secretly leaving the enclosure, her apartment. Hajila's escape occurs after she witnesses an unveiled Algerian woman in a park playing joyfully with her child. In an attempt to capture that same happiness, Hajila sets out to explore the city. Removing her *haïk* and traversing spatial boundaries,

Hajila, in defiance of tradition, discovers a new relationship to the world and is rewarded with access to a "Garden of Eden":[14] "Flowering hedges, winding white gravel paths, benches inviting you to sit among shrubberies, flights of steps with climbing roses rioting over their balustrades: a fit setting for a bride. This is how other people live in foreign countries, according to the television!" (32).*

Establishing a new rapport with her physical surroundings, Hajila brings the discovery home. "Naked" in the streets, Hajila returns to her apartment and stands naked—and transformed—before the bathroom mirror. The discovery of her physical surroundings allows her to contemplate her own body: "You study your body in the mirror, your mind filled with images from outdoors, the light from outdoors, the garden-like-on-the-television. The others are still walking about there; you conjure them up in the water reflected in the mirror, so that they can accompany this woman who is truly naked, this new Hajila who stares back at you coldly" (35).† No longer a stranger in her city, Hajila is no longer a stranger to herself. She now shares with Isma—and the woman in the park—the experience of the light and sunshine of the outdoors. The appropriation of public space denied veiled, cloistered women becomes the key to Hajila's development. Once she has secretly removed her veil and discovered her surroundings, Hajila cannot resume her former passive role.

In her way, Hajila follows the path of Samba's sons initiated by means of the outer journey. Momar, Birame, and Moussa discover that Samba's legacy is the work ethic and are taught by Kem Tanne to probe surface reality; Hajila learns to appropriate public space. One transformation leads to another; Hajila prepares to leave the enclosure. Djebar's message is clear. Access to public space is the first step toward emancipation; there can be no journey to self-understanding without the experience of entering public space, in other words, without some form of the outward journey.

With the freedom to circulate in new space comes Hajila's discovery of language. Her words, however, are recorded by Isma

---

* Des haies fleuries, des allées qui serpentent, avec du gravier blanc, des bancs qui attendent sous des bosquets, des escaliers avec des rampes recouvertes de rosiers: un paysage de fête, dressé en l'honneur d'une mariée à exposer. C'est ainsi que la télévision montre la vie des autres à l'étranger! (41).

† Tu contemples ton corps dans la glace, l'esprit inondé des images du dehors, de la lumière du dehors, du jardin-comme-à-la télévision. Les autres continuent à défiler là-bas; tu les ressuscites dans l'eau du miroir pour qu'ils fassent cortège à la femme vraiment nue, à Hajila nouvelle qui froidement te dévisage (43).

(whose name means "listen" in Arabic). Isma captures each scene and interprets each step of Hajila's revolt and transformation. Beginning "This morning, Hajila, as you stand in the kitchen which is to be the setting for the drama, you are suddenly, for no reason, overcome by grief" (7),* Isma speaks of—and for—Hajila in the second person singular. Isma, who is in fact the narrative voice of the earlier novel, once again becomes translator and scribe for women who can neither speak nor write in French. The narrator alternates the "second wife's" story with her own just as she previously combined autobiographical episodes with the oral narratives of the *porteuses de feu*. Moreover, as the narrator of *L'Amour, la fantasia* uses historical reference in order to situate herself and, in effect, put herself into the text, Isma turns to Hajila's revolt, the traditional woman's appropriation of space, as support for her own quest for self-understanding. Despite the fact that Hajila is neither intimate friend nor narratee, she serves a function similar to Aïssatou. As Aïssatou's journey is crucial to Ramatoulaye's evolution, similarly Hajila's escape and transformation are necessary to Isma's confidence; they restore her faith in the possibility of successful personal and collective transformation.

Moreover, Isma and Hajila also attest to failed communication in their respective marriages. Hajila's arranged marriage was viewed enthusiastically by her mother in the hope that her husband would provide the impoverished family with material comfort. Hajila, however, falls victim to her husband's initial indifference and subsequent brutality. Six months pass before the marriage is consummated; then her husband forces himself upon her with unexpected violence. Later, upon learning that she ventures forth to explore the city, he beats her, shouting, "I'll break your legs and then you'll never go out again, you'll be nailed to a bed..." (87).†

The beginning of their marriage is markedly different for the two women, one who circulates freely in the streets, the other who is confined to her apartment. In counterpoint to Hajila's expression of suffering, Isma recalls memories of fleeting happiness in a marriage that was not arranged by her family. She experiences intimate conversation: "I let the sounds enclose me; my lover's voice breaches the barriers of the night" (66).‡ Hajila, however, encounters silence and

---

* Hajila, une douleur sans raison t'a saisie, ce matin, dans la cuisine qui sera le lieu du mélodrame (15).

† "Te briser les pattes, pour que tu ne sortes plus, pour que tu restes rivée à un lit" (96).

‡ Je laisse les sons me cerner; la voix de l'aimé ouvre les traverses de la nuit (75).

indifference. Isma remembers physical intimacy; her sexual awakening contrasts with Hajila's rape.

Although Isma refers to her husband as *l'aimé*, beloved, she and Hajila both respect tradition; they never call him by his given name. *L'homme, il, lui* reinforce the omnipresence and omnipotence of the patriarchal order that eventually destroys Isma's happiness and condones Hajila's sequestration and humiliation.

Examining the past in an attempt to understand the present, Isma enters the maternal world, returning to the patios of her childhood, enclosures of the veiled and sequestered. These enclosures, space where only women gather, suggest the sealed-off chambers of the harem. Isma recalls that sequestered women often veiled their sentiments as well as their bodies: "The concert of docile women, so ready to revolt, those dithyrambs of harsh words hurled in the face of fate, that threnody of woe, all remained related to the interior of the house, as veiled as the bodies of each woman without" (78).*

Expressions of anger at patriarchal domination, when filtered through memory, confirm Isma's bonds with the maternal sphere. She recalls an anonymous voice: "'How long must I endure this life of drudgery, cursed that I am? Every morning, every day at noon, every evening, my arms are worn out rolling out the couscous! At night, no respite for us wretched women! We still have to suffer them, our masters, and in what an attitude!'—the voice quivers, interupted by a bitter laugh—'with our bare legs stuck up in the air!'" (102).† Although liberated from the harem because her father chose to send her school, Isma is still governed by its rules. When she inadvertently lifts her skirts in public, her naked legs do not arouse the sexual desires of a "master"; they anger her father. Assuming the role of traditional patriarch, he punishes his daughter by sequestering her. Recalled years later, this apparently banal incident bridges the gap between two worlds, allowing Isma to recognize that she and her traditional sisters are all constrained by the patriarchal order. It confirms as well that the dialogue between husband and wife is

---

* Ce choeur de soumissions prête à la révolte, ces strophes de mots heurtés lancés frontalement contre le sort, en somme la parole drapée du malheur restait réleguée, aussi voileé que le corps de chacune au-dehors (87).

† "Jusqu'à quand, ô maudite, cette vie de labeur? Chaque matin, chaque midi et chaque soir, mes bras s'activent aus-dessus du couscoussier! La nuit, nul répit pour nous les malheureuses! Il faut que nous les subissions encore, eux, nos maîtres, et dans quelle posture"—la voix sursaute, l'accent se déchire en rire amer—, "jambes dénudées face au ciel!" (112).

destined to suffer the same fate as the earlier one between father and daughter. Both fail as a consequence of the patriarchy that permeates and dominates Algerian social structure.

As the dialogue between men and women founders — a result of the imbalance of power — Isma turns to the community of women. Through her efforts, two women, victims but not rivals of the same man, meet and establish the beginning of a friendship. Speaking *with* Hajila rather than writing *for* her, Isma initiates an important new dialogue. Significantly, conversation begins at the *hammam*, where the women perform the ritual of bathing together in the hot vapors. The *hammam* is presented as an enclosure that promotes comfort and healing, a refuge from patriarchal society: "*Hammam*, the only temporary reprieve from the harem. The Turkish bath offers a secret consolation to sequestered woman (such as organ music offered in former times to forced religious recluses). This surrogate maternal cocoon providing an escape from the hot-house of cloistration..." (152).*

At the *hammam*, Isma participates in liberating the *odalisque*. Giving Hajila the remaining key to the apartment, Isma provides Hajila with the means of transformation. Hajila can subvert her husband's authority; she can choose to enter and leave her apartment at will. Isma's gift recalls Aïssatou's present to Ramatoulaye. The key, like the auto, not only allows the protagonist to circulate freely in the city; it reveals the commitment of one woman who has broken free to another who is in the process of doing so. Thus, Isma assumes Aïssatou's role as intercessor. Having first intervened in Hajila's life by proposing her to be the ex-husband's new wife, Isma intervenes again after Hajila's revolt. Once Hajila has entered public space, Isma encourages her to continue the outward journey and maintain her new identity.

Echoing Bâ, Djebar calls upon women to support and protect one another in the struggle against the patriarchy. As the Senegalese novelist criticizes women such as Dame Belle-Mère and Nabou's mother, both of whom uphold traditions that enslave and imprison their daughters, so does Djebar. She condemns Hajila's mother, Touma, for sacrificing her daughter: "The matriarchs swaddle their

---

* Hammam, seule rémission du harem....Le bain turc secrète pour les séquestrées (comme autrefois le chant de l'orgue pour les nonnes forcées) une consolation à cette reclusion. Dissoudre la touffeur de la claustration grâce à ce succédané du cocon maternel...(163).

little girls in their own insidious anguish, before they even reach puberty. Mother and daughter, O, harem restored!" (145).* Criticizing the practice of marrying daughters to raise their social and economic standing, she further chastises women like Lla Hadja, whose wicked tongue maligns unfortunate women she refuses to recognize as sisters. In her attack on the patriarchy, Djebar makes a fervent appeal for an end to the rivalry that defeats women by keeping them apart, unaware of their potential strength through female bonding.

Djebar studies the etymology of the Arabic word *derra*. It signifies co-wife in a polygamous union; it also means "wound." She questions the appropriateness of the term: Djebar writes: "Is not the second wife, who appears on the other side of the bed, similar to the first one, almost a part of her, the very one who was frigid and against whom the husband raises avenging arms?" (91).† What if the so-called rivals were to create secure bonds between themselves? What if they were to support and protect one another as sisters?

As the narrator of *L'Amour, la fantasia* delves into Algerian history in search of heroic sisters, Isma turns to literature to find evidence of female bonding. She recalls that in the tales of the *Arabian Nights* the princess Schéhérazade, married to the bloodthirsty sultan who would have her killed at dawn, succeeds in saving her life by telling inventive tales. Schéhérazade, however, first calls upon the help of her sister, Dinarzade, who is to sleep in the nuptial chamber and awaken Schéhérazade each morning before dawn: "To throw light on the role of Dinarzade, as the night progresses! Her voice under the bed coaxes the story-teller up above, to find unfailing inspiration for her tales, and so keep at bay the nightmares that daybreak would bring" (95).‡ Schéhérazade uses her wits, her fertile imagination, to save her life; Djebar reminds the reader that she needs the complicity of her sister as well.

When Isma first observes Hajila walking unveiled in the city she writes, "Here we are both breaking out of the harem, but coming from opposite ends: you exposed from now on to the sunlight

---

* Les matrones emmaillotent leurs fillettes pas encore pubères de leur angoisse insidieuse. Mère et fille, ô harem renouvelé (155).

† La seconde épouse qui apparaît de l'autre côté de la couche n'est-elle pas semblable à la première, quasiment une partie d'elle, celle-là même qui n'a pu jouir et vers laquelle l'époux dresse ses bras vengeurs? (100)

‡ Eclairer Dinarzade de la nuit! Sa voix sous le lit aiguillonne, pour que là-haut l'intarissable conteuse puisse chasser les cauchemars de l'aube (104).

whereas I attempted to plunge back into the night" (2).[15]* Acknowledging separate itineraries in the early pages of the novel — Hajila's outer journey towards the sunshine in contrast to her own inner journey to the darker recesses of her past memories — Isma comes to question whether she and Hajila are truly different. Watching Hajila defy overt oppression and recalling her own struggle against patriarchal domination that was admittedly more subtle and indirect, Isma concludes that she and Hajila share common ground. Both "traditional" and "emancipated" women need public space, freedom to discover the world, as well as private space, refuge such as the *hammam* in which to withdraw from it. Moreover, Isma and Hajila, like their mythic counterparts Schéhérazade and Dinarzade, require the support of one another to escape from vestiges of the harem, from the long night of patriarchy: "At the end of the long night, the odalisque is in flight" (159).†

A study of the novels of Bâ and Djebar reveals that both novelists juxtapose outer and inner journeys. In *Une si longue lettre* and *Ombre sultane* the narrator (Ramatoulaye/Isma) undertakes an inner or temporal journey to childhood, adolescence, and the early years of marriage; the "other" embarks upon an outer or spatial journey. Thus, Aïssatou travels abroad to America; Hajila explores her native city. Although the two novelists acknowledge the importance of outer and inner journeys in the process of personal transformation, Djebar emphasizes the former, Bâ the latter. Moreover, Djebar and Bâ both view female enclosure — the widow's home (*Une si longue lettre*) and the *hammam* (*Ombre sultane*) — as requisites to contemplation and female bonding and as refuge in a patriarchal society. Finally, the technique of doubling or parallel lives serves the same purpose in both works as well. Ramatoulaye writes *to* and *about* Aïssatou; Isma, who begins by writing *about* Hajila, narrating her adventure, concludes by speaking *with* her, entering into dialogue that is important to both of them. Therefore, by examining two itineraries, their own and that of another, Ramatoulaye and Isma come to know themselves.

In contrast to Bâ, however, Djebar undertakes a more ambitious project. Beginning with the conquest of Algeria in 1830, depicted in *L'Amour, la fantasia*, her work spans two centuries; her protagonist

---

* Nous voici toutes deux en rupture de harem, mais à ses pôles extrêmes: toi au soleil désormais exposée, moi tentée de m'enfoncer dans la nuit resurgie (10).

† Au sortir de la longue nuit, l'odalisque est en fuite (169).

situates herself in relation to two historical moments, conquest and liberation in *L'Amour, la fantasia,* and present-day Algeria in *Ombre sultane.* The Algerian novelist depicts political turmoil upsetting sociocultural norms, thereby allowing women to wrest freedom, at least temporarily, from a besieged patriarchy. Bâ, in contrast, presents personal crisis as the sole catalyst for transformation.

In addition, Djebar explores her relationship to the colonial language and reveals her personal conflicts as an Algerian novelist writing in French. Although Djebar views the colonizer's language with ambiguity, Bâ does not. Writing in French evokes neither conflict nor ambiguity for the Senegalese novelist fluent in Wolof and French.

In conclusion, the two African women writers express shared commitments and present complementary voices. Bâ and Djebar consider female bonding essential to the struggle against male domination and view the act of writing as a process that leads to healing, liberation, transformation, and self-understanding. Viewing liberation as the goal, and the dual process of journey and writing as the means, both artists commit themselves to listening attentively to women speaking, at times loudly and clearly, more often in muffled whispers. They express individual and collective identities as they write to and for their sisters as well as themselves.

Chapter 6

▼▼▼▼▼▼▼

Women's Flight

KEN BUGUL, *Le Baobab fou*
LEÏLA SEBBAR, *Fatima ou les Algériennes au square; Shérazade, brune,
frisée, les yeux verts; Les Carnets de Shérazade*

A close reading of the texts of Bâ and Djebar reveals the importance
they attribute to the act of writing. In their respective works, it leads
to self-discovery, affirmation, and healing. Moreover, for Djebar,
writing frees her from the cultural and linguistic exile imposed by
colonialism. Listening to the whispers in the harem, she brings the
maternal language toward the paternal language by translating traditional women's Arabic into French and transcribing speech into
writing. I now propose to "listen" to the voices of women who have
left the harem. Examining novels that propose an outward trajectory
formerly denied women—the journey to a foreign land—I will be
seeking a response to the following question: In women's novels of
exile and flight, does the journey outward—and its concomitant
inner journey—end in self-discovery or in illusory escape?

The novels of Ken Bugul and Leïla Sebbar, published in the
1980s, share this common theme: they focus upon the female protagonist in an alien land. Bugul's autobiographical narrative describes
the physical and spiritual journey of a Senegalese woman in Belgium.
Sebbar portrays the struggle for identity of "Beurs," a generation of
North Africans who, having grown up in France, must come to
terms with the Maghrebian heritage of their immigrant parents and
the dominant European culture in which they risk the marginalization
that their parents have known in France.

The Orphan's Quest: Ken Bugul

In *Le Baobab fou*, Ken Bugul presents a traveling heroine. Granted a
scholarship to study in Brussels, the protagonist leaves Africa in
search of a better life, only to fall victim to drugs, prostitution, and
near-suicide before returning to her native village in Senegal. In

terms of theme and structure, the novel corresponds to the earlier
Senegalese fiction of Cheikh Hamidou Kane. The novel is an "ambiguous" adventure to the West. Ken, like Samba Diallo, experiences
alienation and loses her bearings when she makes the journey to the
Occident.

Although Kane gives his Poular name, Samba Diallo, to his
protagonist, he fictionalizes autobiographical elements in a third-
person narrative that emphasizes philosophical dialogue. Bugul, on
the other hand, adopts a first-person narrative, publishing this novel
in *Vies d'Afrique*, an autobiographical collection of Nouvelles Editions
Africaines. Ken Bugul is the *nom de plume* of Mariétou M'Baye. She
has explained that the editors, fearing scandal because of the sexual
disclosures in the novel, required her to hide her identity (Magnier,
"Ken Bugul" 153).

Ken Bugul means "the person no one wants" in Wolof and is a
name generally given to a child born after several stillborn babies in
the hope that death will spare this one. The name chosen by M'Baye
links her to African tradition, emphasizing the precarious nature
of the narrator's existence, and proposes a leitmotif of the novel:
orphanhood. Abandoned in Africa, the protagonist embarks upon an
outer journey in the attempt to put an end to solitude and start anew.
Flight from Africa involves a parallel spiritual journey in the course
of which Ken defines her relationship to gender and race and comes
to terms with personal trauma. Unlike Samba's sons, who search for
the key to their puzzling inheritance, and Aïwa, the orphan sent to
whiten the black cloth, Ken seeks to put together the pieces of a
fragmented self in an attempt to heal a wounded soul.

As an autobiographical novel, *Le Baobab fou* follows a tradition
that began with the earliest Senegalese francophone novel, Diallo's
Force-Bonté, published in 1927. Bugul, like Bakary Diallo and later
Cheikh Hamidou Kane, situates the protagonist in two geographical
settings: first Africa, then Europe. The trajectory of the three novels
is essentially the same: it is circular, beginning and ending in Africa.
Moreover, the journey from Africa to Europe gives rise to a binary
structure emphasizing the contrast between the African village
and the European capital. Travelling heroes (Bakary, Samba, and
Ken), become keenly aware of cultural differences that separate the
continents. Diallo's protagonist embraces Europe with enthusiasm
and hopes to remain in Paris. Kane's hero, however, evolves into an
anguished hybrid unable to find a place in either world. For Ken
Bugul, the journey presents a dimension not explored in the earlier

works. A woman as well as a colonial subject, she faces the dual constraints of colonialism and patriarchy.

Dealing specifically with alienation in exile, the colonized African adrift in Europe, Bugul's narrative differs from the works of Djebar and Bâ. Yet it grants the same importance to writing as a therapeutic activity. As enclosure leads to disclosure in Bâ's text and revolt in Djebar's, flight leads to the physical and spiritual exile of a protagonist struggling to define herself. Hence, self-understanding involves a dual process: the journey and its written record. Bugul has discussed the therapeutic dimension of her work:

> I began to write in a period of transition in my life. I was quite confused. I didn't know how to handle what I had lived through and it hung on. My life was dragging on.
>
> Since I really enjoy being alone and taking notes, I began to write what was going to become a book. As I began to write, I felt that my writing was becoming therapeutic. I had not intended to write a book, but to bear witness to my life, to get it out, put it before me on paper; and that released me. I could not confide in anyone and so I put it all down on paper. (Magnier, "Ken Bugul," 151)*

Ostensibly writing because she has no confidante, Bugul's point of departure differs from Bâ's. Unlike Ramatoulaye, Ken has no friend in whom to confide — except the reader; her autodiegetic narrator discloses her thoughts and feelings to an unknown narratee. Thus, the relationship between Ramatoulaye and Aïssatou in Bâ's *Une si longue lettre* and Isma and Hajila in Dejbar's *Ombre sultane*, which give rise to the doubling in both narratives, are absent from this work. As a result, Ken experiences greater solitude and only rarely female bonding.

In this work, Bugul combines a linear chronological narrative, her Brussels diary, with analepses, scenes of childhood and adolescence in Senegal of the late 1950s and early 1960s; she prefaces the two distinct but complementary spatial-temporal narratives with a

---

* J'ai commencé l'écrire dans une période de transition dans ma vie. Je ne savais plus où donner de la tête, je ne savais plus où aller avec tout ce vécu que je trainais en moi. Je trainais dans ma propre vie.

Comme j'aime beaucoup rester seule et prendre des notes, j'ai commencé à écrire ce qui allait devenir un livre. Au fur et à mesure que je l'écrivais, j'ai senti que ce que j'écrivais, c'était comme une thérapeutique. Je n'avais pas l'intention d'écrire un livre, mais de me prendre à témoin d'un vécu, le sortir de moi, l'avoir en face de moi, sur du papier et ça me dégageait. Je ne pouvais me confier à personne alors j'ai mis tout cela sur du papier.

"prehistory." The latter, a third-person narrative that describes the settling of her family in her birthplace, provides mythic context. Therefore, the narrator presents three narratives: a preface and two interwoven texts. Individually, each provides specific keys to self-understanding. Collectively, they recount her past and, most importantly, explore the role of memory in the journey to self-understanding.

The "prehistory" recounts three seemingly disconnected events which precede the narrator's birth: the unexpected arrival of a stranger from the north (Ken's ancestor), the accidental fire that almost destroys the village, the unintentional planting of a baobab seed. Accidental and unforeseen, the three events foreshadow and mirror important moments in the protagonist's life: migration, near destruction, rebirth. In effect, Ken's relocation corresponds to her ancestor's move to the village. The fire's devastation of the village suggests the near self-destruction of the protagonist. Finally, the baobab, symbolizing rebirth for the villagers, provides an important spatial and temporal referent. The image of the sturdy tree that Ken carries with her in memory maintains her bonds to the village. A symbol of strength and protection within the traditional context, the baobab serves the heroine adrift as a positive reminder of the past. Not until Ken's journey has come full circle, and she has gone back to the tree, is her journey to self-understanding complete. Upon her return, Ken discovers that the baobab has become a desolate remnant of that past, a dead trunk hollow at the core. The baobab thus functions as a metaphor for an African society that Bugul believes has also become an empty shell.[1]

Poetic, atemporal, and oneiric, the narrator's prehistory presents an etiological narrative that illustrates the importance of the "crazy" baobab to the narrator and the community. It begins with a young village boy snatching a baobab fruit. As he grabs the fruit, Fode Ndao shrieks with joy, anticipating the savor of *ndiambane*, the drink he will prepare from it. The baobab seed is watered by Fode's mother, who inadvertently drops a water jug when she is startled by the sudden appearance of a stranger on horseback. This seed grows to be a giant baobab which the narrator designates as the symbol of a new era: "It was the pit of the baobab fruit that Fode had spit out when answering his mother on the morning on the first day of the gods' creation of a new generation that would upset the times" (17).*

---

* C'était le noyau du fruit de baobab que Fode avait craché en allant répondre à la mère, le matin du premier jour de la conception par les dieux d'une génération nouvelle qui allait bouleverser les temps.

Spared by a fire that lays waste to the village, the tree protects the community now restored to its former prosperity.

One day, however, a small child playing in the shade of the baobab discovers an amber bead, which had fallen from the necklace of the stranger's wife and lay buried in the sand. Suddenly, the village reverberates with the scream of the frightened child who has plugged its ear with the bead. Harmony is shattered as a positive signifier gives way to a negative one: the amber bead, an instrument of pain, replaces the baobab seed, a portent of happiness. The child's piercing scream as the bead moves further into the ear concludes an episode that had begun with Fode's shout of joy as he snatched the ripened baobab fruit.

In the following chapter, Bugul reveals that she was that child. In effect, the incident that closes the prehistory marks the narrator's ejection from Eden, introducing her to vulnerability and pain. Thus, the prehistory not only functions as an etiological tale concerning the origin of the baobab in the village, it establishes the narrator's relationship to her community (of which the baobab is a synecdoche). Suffering occurs when protectors, mother and baobab, fail: "Oh, I wanted to tell the mother that she should not have left me alone at the age of two to play beneath the baobab! This naked baobab in this deserted village! The baobab and the sun. The sun and the baobab. The imagination and the consciousness that clash abruptly under the baobab, this huge and complicitous baobab" (30).* Here Ken reveals that language also fails, for silence follows the initial cry. Unable to verbalize the anger toward the mother who had left her unprotected, Ken later expresses the psychological pain of isolation and alienation through interior monologue. Her words remain within her until the process of writing sets them free.

This first traumatic incident foreshadows another, the departure of Ken's mother from the village. Childhood, the world that should offer security, becomes a threatening and dangerous space. Unlike nostalgic recollections of the African village that characterize Senghor's poem "Nuit de sine" and Camara Laye's novel *L'Engant noir*, Bugul depicts the fragmented, dislocated world of a child traumatized by the departure of its mother. She states, "All my life I will curse that

---

* Comme je voudrais dire à la mère qu'elle ne devait pas me laisser seule à deux ans jouer sous le baobab! Ce baobab dénudé dans ce village désert. Le baobab et le soleil. Le soleil et le baobab. L'imagination et la conscience qui s'entrechoquaient sous le baobab brusquement, ce baobab complice et immense (30).

day that robbed me of my mother, destroyed my childhood, reduced me to that little five-year-old child standing alone on the train platform long after the train had gone" (81).*

As the narrative progresses, it becomes clear to the reader that Ken suffers from a double loss within her family. On the one hand, the sudden physical absence of her mother has psychological consequences; on the other hand, despite her father's physical presence, he too is psychologically absent. Obsessed with the sense of abandonment brought on by her mother's departure, Ken does not fully acknowledge the strains of a distant relationship with her father until the aged patriarch has died. Only toward the end of the novel, after having probed the past, does Ken realize that her mother's departure was made traumatic in part by its suddenness but also by the void that was never filled. She asks poignantly, "When the mother left, why didn't father clasp me tightly in his arms? Father devoted himself entirely to prayers and God" (143).†

Although Ken asks time and again why her mother left, the question is never clearly answered. The reader may speculate whether the woman was repudiated by a polygamous Muslim patriarch or chose to divorce. When she left, Ken's mother assumed other family obligations. The narrator explains that her mother's destination was the home of an older daughter who, at the age of fifteen, needed help in caring for her child. In other words, Ken's mother appears to have left her five-year-old daughter in order to care for her two-year-old grandchild. Yet, in the belief that this child, her niece, has taken her place in her mother's heart, Ken is unable to reestablish the earlier bonds when she and her mother are reunited the following year: "And so when I arrived, *my* mother no longer existed. Only *the* mother remained. There was silence" (emphasis mine) (130).‡ Replacing the possessive adjective with the definite article, the narrator chooses a linguistic marker to express distance from her mother. She uses the French language not only to record the actions and dialogue

---

* Je maudirai toute ma vie ce jour qui avait emporté ma mère, qui m'avait écrasé l'enfance, qui m'avait réduite à cette petite enfant de cinq ans, seule sur le quai d'une gare alors que le train était parti depuis longtemps.

† Lors du départ de la mère, pourquoi père ne m'avait-il pas serrée fort dans ses bras? Ce père entièrement consacré à la prière et à Dieu.

‡ Ce fut ainsi que quand je suis arrivée, ma mère n'était plus. Il ne me restait plus que la mère. Ce fut le silence.

of *wolof* speakers, but to judge—and condemn.[2] Bugul recounts her childhood in Senegal to justify her "descent into Hell" in Brussels. She blames her parents (her mother directly and her father indirectly) for subsequent alienation. Aware that the narrator is telling her story as much to justify her actions as to struggle free from the nightmarish past, the reader is prompted to question—Is Ken a trustworthy narrator?

Given Ken's initially close relationship with her mother and distant one with her father, Nancy Chodorow's study *The Reproduction of Mothering* is pertinent to an understanding of the protagonist-narrator despite its focus on the Western nuclear family. According to Chodorow, the object relations between a girl and her mother result in a basic feminine sense of self that is connected to the world. Unlike men, women develop relational abilities and preoccupations (169). In the text, Ken confirms the very close ties with her mother: "My mother, I felt her presence every evening in the bed I shared with her. Exhausted from a day's work, her body collapsed half-naked, as soft as a feather nest" (79—80).* With intimacy shattered when the child is suddenly bereft of the primary nurturer, the protagonist experiences an acute sense of loss and bears the scars of abandonment even though she is later reunited with her mother. Following Chodorow's analysis, I suggest that the loss of Ken's connection to the prime nurturer at an early age results in a self that has poor relational abilities. Although Ken presents herself as a victim of family and society, the reader is obliged to qualify her judgments and self-analysis. Ken's solitude stems in large measure from her inability to connect with the world and form stable personal relationships. Following this line of reasoning, Ken's mother is the catalyst for her daughter's subsequent alienation, but not the villain in the piece.

The structuring device in the autobiographical narrative is the journey: *Le Baobab fou* sets in motion two temporal-spatial journeys that confirm and reinforce the protagonist's sense of alienation. Ken's mother leaves one African village for another when the child is approximately five years old. Ken, at the age of twenty, travels to Belgium. Mirroring the incident of the amber bead, the first journey ejects Ken from Eden. Promising an end to solitude, the second

---

* Ma mére, je la sentais tous les soirs, dans le lit que je partageais avec elle. Son corps, repu d'une journée de besogne, s'abandonnait à demi découvert, doux comme un nid de plumes.

results in further alienation. Separated by time (fifteen years) and by space (one journey to a distant Senegalese village, the other to a European capital), both voyages are linked to the presence of the colonial school in Africa. Ken's mother does not leave her daughter behind because she lacks maternal affection. She does not want to interrupt her child's education: "But you were attending school, that's why I didn't take you with me" (114).* As she continues her education, Ken moves from place to place, living with one relative and then another, growing all the while more distant from her family. When Ken finally embarks upon her journey to a distant land, she does so because she has been awarded a scholarship in recognition of her fine school record. By thwarting Ken's first journey and facilitating the second, the colonial school becomes a crucial alienating factor through the narrator's childhood, adolescence, and young adult years.

Once Ken enters school, she (like Kane's Samba Diallo) follows a trajectory that makes reintegration difficult, if not impossible. Most importantly, she acknowledges that her apprenticeship to Westernization results in her subsequent rejection of her mother. The tables are turned: having been abandoned, Ken in turn, abandons:

> I learned Western songs by heart and wanted to live them. The gap widened despairingly. Africa came back to me through its spirit, its moments of poetry, and its rites. But I held tight to the link with the values that colonization had brought. I could not backtrack, nor even glance backward.
>
> From time to time, the mother wished to grab hold of me, but I refused. I could not accept her nor could I be satisfied with the emotional prop of compromise. Plunged into my phantasms, I rejected the mother through my Western references. (143)†

Echoing Assia Djebar, Bugul expresses the belief that her French education has isolated her from the maternal sphere. For example, Ken states that her grandmother came to dislike her because of her schooling. Thus, the narrator reveals that the acquisition of a French

---

* "Mais tu allais à l'école, c'est pour cela que je ne t'ai pas amenée avec moi."

† J'apprenais par coeur les chansons occidentales et voulais les vivre telles. De plus en plus le fossé se creusait, désespérément. L'Afrique me rappelait à elle par ses élans, ses instants de poésie et ses rites. Mais je tenais bon le lien avec les valeurs apportées par la colonisation. Je ne pouvais plus retourner sur mes pas, ni même jeter un coup d'oeil en arrière.

Par moments, la mère avait voulu m'accrocher et je refusais. Je ne pouvais pas accepter et me satisfaire d'un secours émotionnel de compromis. Plongée dans mes fantasmes, je rejetais la mère par mes références occidentales.

education results in alienation within her community and increases her sense of orphanhood. Through the narrator, Bugul reiterates the position of many francophone African writers educated during the colonial period. They accuse the colonial educational system of ignoring indigenous culture and transmitting a false heritage. Teaching African children that their ancestors were the Gauls, the colonial educational system subverted the foundations of a social structure in which their true African ancestors held an important place. Therefore, the imported system prepared an elite to imitate European tastes and manners and adopt European materialism. Whereas Bâ defends education under colonialism as a liberating force for women, Bugul attacks it as an alienating one. In contrast to Bâ's sympathetic portrait of the French school directress who inspired her with moral values, Bugul depicts a sadistic African schoolmaster who delivers corporal punishment indiscriminately.

Although Ken's "ambiguous adventure" leads to growing isolation and alienation, her French education provides a screen against a world in which she functions as an outsider; then, it allows her to escape. Moreover, Ken uses the success in her studies to compensate for rejection at home. Scarcely acknowledged by her family, Ken is rewarded at school. For example, she receives numerous prizes for her outstanding record at the closing exercises each year. Finally, by providing the young woman with a scholarship to further training in Brussels, education becomes a passport to a new world.

Ken acknowledges education as a means of escape. She embarks upon her journey to the "promised land" in the hope that it will put an end to solitude. Paradoxically, when granted the possibility to begin a new life, Ken imprisons herself by her subsequent choices. The protagonist who defines herself as a victim of rejection in Africa becomes an agent of rejection in Europe. Deciding that the university program is inappropriate to her needs, she abandons her studies. Discovering that she is pregnant, she breaks off with her Belgian lover and has an abortion. As she begins her "descent into Hell" via alcohol, drugs, and finally prostitution, Ken moves into a world of dimly lit night clubs where faces remain largely anonymous. The daughter of a *marabout* (a Muslim holy man) finds herself spiritually a long way from home.

Elisabeth Mudimble-Boyi notes, in her study of the novel, that memories of a stolen childhood stand as a metaphor for Ken's stolen cultural heritage ("Ken Bugul" 7). In Ken's self-analysis, she builds a significant case for the two overwhelming losses: the departure of her mother in Africa; the end of the dream of assimilation in Europe. Ken attributes her initial solitude to her mother's abandonment and her "descent into Hell" to the loss of the dream of assimilation:

> Solitude followed me everywhere, silently. I fled it and yet it pursued me. I smoked a lot of marijuana and took more and more opium, searching truly for shelter, as if on the train platform in the village when the mother had gone away. I recovered this solitude painfully, with the shock of having lost, here, my Gallic ancestors. The reflection in the mirror, the face, the look, this color that characterized me and yet disowned me. I found this solitude in the bedsheets of the one-night stands with my lovers, in that painful need of others beyond my grasp. (110)*

Another contributing factor to alienation is Ken's abortion, which takes place during her first winter in Brussels. It is a disorienting experience which, by conflicting with traditional African values, accelerates the protagonist's fall. Ken exclaims: "If I had stayed there, as it was before the amber bead in my ear, I would never have had an abortion." (64−65)† Grouped with other women in the doctor's waiting room, Ken states: "I realized that women, all women, shared the same fate" (56).‡ I concur with Houedanou that this experience is the protagonist's first step toward a new feminist identity (166) and is crucial to Ken's process of defining the self, but believe that it does so with respect to race as well as gender. The episode marks a significant encounter with racism: the doctor who performs the abortion cautions his client against the mixing of races. Moreover, this experience initiates the protagonist's downward trajectory. After refusing to marry Louis and bear his child, Ken falls under the influence of a malevolent intercessor, Jean Wermer, a Belgian artist who introduces her to a dissolute life in Brussels.

The two interwoven threads of narrative — childhood and adolescence in Africa, young adulthood in Europe — form a binary construct. Both worlds remain physically, temporally, and in part

---

* La solitude me suivait silencieusement partout. Je la fuyais et elle me poursuivait. Je fumais beaucoup de marijuana et prenais de plus en plus de sirop d'opium, pour chercher vraiment abri, comme sur le quai de la gare, au village, au depart de la mère. Cette solitude que j'avais retrouvée durement, avec le choc d'avoir perdu, ici, mes ancêtres les Gaulois. Le reflet dans le miroir, le visage, le regard, cette couleur qui me distinguait en me niant. Cette solitude jusque dans les draps des amants d'un soir; ce besoin lancinant des autres, introuvables.

† "La-bas, si j'y étais restée, comme avant la perle d'ambre dans l'oreille, je n'aurais jamais eu a subir un avortement.

‡ Je me rendais compte que les femmes, toutes les femmes avaient le même destin.

thematically distinct through most of the narrative. Temporally, Africa represents the distant past, Europe the immediate past. Spatially, individuals of one world never enter the other. Ken, who makes the initial journey outward alone, is neither visited in Brussels by Senegalese family nor do Europeans accompany her on her trips to Africa. Finally, the alienation that the protagonist experiences in both Africa and Europe takes a different form in each place. Ken considers herself to be an orphan in one world, an object in the other. Invisible in Africa, where she is largely ignored, Ken is too visible in Europe, where she is coveted as an exotic sexual commodity.

The boundaries of Ken's binary world dissolve, however, and both worlds conflate when the outer journey approaches its nearly self-destructive end. Figuratively—if not literally—in Hell, Ken, contemplating suicide, calls out to her mother. As she ejects a drunken client from her room and drags him down a flight of stairs, Ken cries, "Oh mother, what have I done to you? What have you done? Oh, if you could see me at this moment, I would die!" (176).*
Ken subsequently locks herself in her room:

> I stayed in my room for two days and two nights. I was neither hungry nor thirsty.
> But whether I wanted it or not, my life was waiting for me just behind the door, and I cried abundantly, with deep sobs that came from my bursting bowels. At this moment, the scream rang out. A piercing cry that shattered the harmony, under the naked baobab in the deserted village. (180)†

Enclosed space becomes Ken's refuge from the painful present; self-imposed confinement allows her to break free of her nightmare. Simulating childbirth—"l'éclatement des entrailles"—the young woman, confined to her room, painfully gives birth to a new self. At the same time, her voluntary memory, which has consciously explored the past, is displaced by involuntary memory. As it reaches her from the far distant past, the piercing cry of the child struggling

---

* "Oh mère, que vous ai-je fait? Qu'avez-vous fait? Ah, si vous me voyiez en ce moment, comme je voudrais mourir."

† Je suis restée enfermée pendant deux jours et deux nuits. Je n'avais plus ni faim, ni soif.
Mais, le voulant ou non, la vie m'attendait juste derrière la porte et je pleurais très fort, en des sanglots profonds précipités dans l'éclatement des entrailles. A ce moment-là, le cri jaillit. Un cri perçant qui venait briser l'harmonie, sous le baobab dénudé, dans le village désert.

with the amber bead releases Ken from her nightmares in preparation for her final encounter with the baobab.

The journal of Ken's experience in Brussels concludes with the narrator's failure to create a new identity in the promised land. From a psycho-political perspective, the attempt is destined to fail. Ken cannot flee from her original personal trauma, nor can she shed her African identity in the world that views her as an exotic object. Marginalized in Africa by orphanhood and in Europe by race and gender, Ken must come to terms with all the components of her identity: "To be a woman, a rigid woman, to be a child without the notion of one's parents, to be black, and to be colonized" (110).* The protagonist's journey must be circular, for it has to lead the narrator back to the baobab tree where the child's piercing cry was first uttered.

Does Ken's journey result in victory or defeat? In other words, does the narrator return to her village with a heightened sense of self-understanding, or does she flee from Europe as she once fled from Africa? The final chapter not only confirms her victory but attests to the power of the word. Throughout her narrative, Ken uses the process of writing as therapy. She focuses on loss—the loss of maternal love in Africa, the broken dream of assimilation in Europe—as her life spirals downward. Although she gropes for a way out of emotional distress, Ken does not find it until she completes two final rituals: self-imposed confinement in Brussels and then a return to the baobab, the original site of trauma and alienation. The journey and its written record come together at the same point. The protagonist attains lucidity and conquers solitude by concluding the written record of her physical and spiritual journey.

Upon her return to the village, Ken learns that the baobab died because she did not return to the tree. As witness and accomplice to the death of the baobab which, in turn, was witness and accomplice to her mother's departure, Ken is now able to conclude her story where it first began. She recognizes that she, not the "crazy" baobab, came close to losing her sanity, as a result of her flight from identity. Returning to the point of departure, in order to recapture the promise of stability represented by the sturdy tree, Ken is now ready to assume the identity that she first sought to escape. Hence, the protagonist's

---

* Être une femme, une femme rigide, être une enfant sans notion de parents, être noire et être colonisée.

outer and inner journeys have led to self-knowledge and perception; writing has resulted in self-affirmation and healing.

Running Away: Leïla Sebbar

Set in the urban ghettos of France, the novels of Leïla Sebbar focus on the North African diaspora with which she shares the common bond of Maghrebian ancestors. Born in Algeria and now living in France, Sebbar is the daughter of a French mother and an Algerian father. Positioned between two cultures, Sebbar chooses to write about marginalized immigrants and in so doing to lessen her personal sense of exile. She uses French, her maternal language, to depict a reality that is not absolutely French nor entirely North African. In an exchange of letters with the Canadian writer Nancy Huston, Sebbar writes:

> I am there at the crossroads, serene at last, finally in my place; for I am the crossroads seeking a connection, writing within a lineage, one that is always the same. It is tied to history, to memory, to identity, to tradition, and to transmission, by which I mean the search for ascendants and descendants, seeking a place in the history of a family, a community, a people with regard to History and the universe. It is in fiction that I feel that I am a free subject (free of father, mother, clan, dogma) and strengthened by the burden of exile. Only there do I muster body and soul to span the two banks, both upstream and downstream...(138)*

In contrast to Bugul, who recounts her autobiography in her adopted language (the legacy of colonialism), Sebbar writes fiction in her mother tongue. Unlike most francophone African writers, Sebbar is monolingual. The language of her home as well as school was always French. Therefore, the choice of writing in either Arabic or French, an option for some Maghrebian writers — the Algerian Rachid Boudjedra, the Moroccan Tahar Ben Jelloun, and Assia Djebar as well — was never available to Sebbar, a writer of mixed French and Algerian heritage. As she explains, "My father's language remains

---

* Je suis là, a la croisée, enfin sereine, à ma place, en somme, puisque je suis une croisée qui cherche une filiation et qui écris dans une lignée, toujours la même, reliée à l'histoire, à la memoire, à l'identité, à la tradition et à la transmission, je veux dire à la recherche d'une ascendance et d'une descendance, d'une place dans l'histoire d'une famille, d'une communauté, d'un peuple, au regard de l'Histoire et de l'univers. C'est dans la fiction que je me sens sujet libre (de père, de mère, de clan, de dogmes...) et forte de la charge de l'exil. C'est là et seulement là que je me rassemble corps et âme et que je fais le pont entre les deux rives, en amont et en aval.

foreign to me, so near and yet at a distance" ("La Littérature et l'exil" 39).*

Sebbar's *Fatima ou les Algériennes au square* (1981), *Shérazade, brune, frisée, les yeux verts* (1982), and *Les Carnets de Shérazade* (1985) share a common preoccupation with Bugul's novel, *Le baobab fou*. Novels of initiation, they depict the psychological evolution of young women torn between conflicting cultures. I propose to discuss Sebbar's three works, presenting them in chronological order, because each represents a separate stage of the maturation process. Sebbar's protagonists, Dalila and Shérazade, grope toward a new definition of self, a process that involves the decision to leave home, live independently, and then travel, with the intention of returning to North Africa to reestablish ties that were broken when their families emigrated to France. The first, *Fatima ou les Algériennes au square*, presents the psychological and cultural conflicts within the Maghrebian family that lead Dalila, a high school student in Paris, to leave home. *Shérazade* chronicles the adventure of a runaway; she shares a *squatt* (an abandoned dwelling) with a group of friends who, for various reasons, have also left home. Finally, *Carnets de Shérazade* recounts Shérazade's adventure on the open road. Intending to return to Algeria, the young woman hitchhikes through France. Thus, Sebbar, like Bugul, proposes a circular journey, a voyage out and a journey home. Although the Senegalese novelist leads her fleeing protagonist from exile back to the baobab tree, the Franco-Algerian writer tantalizes the reader with an unattained goal. Closure eludes Shérazade; the traveling heroine expresses the desire to return to Algeria but nevertheless remains on the road.[3]

In their search for identity and their active response to life, Sebbar's protagonists, Dalila and Shérazade, resemble the heroines of Djebar, Bâ, and Bugul. They refuse a passive role. To borrow a phrase from Djebar, they are *odalisques en fuite*,[4] women fleeing confined space. However, in contrast to Djebar's *porteuses de feu* — women who become visible and vocal in a history in which they had previously been mute and invisible, one from which they had been excluded — Sebbar's runaways "drop out" of society to become invisible and silent to the established authorities, that is, to the law, as well as to their own families. Throughout Shérazade's wanderings, she anxiously awaits the identity card that will give her a false name

---

* La langue de mon père me reste étrangère, proche à distance.

and false French nationality. It will hide her Maghrebian origin as well as her status as a minor: "I will call myself Rosa, Rosa Mire and I will be eighteen years old, an adult" (179).*

Why do these young women choose *la fugue*? Why do they run away from home? The answer lies in the conflict between the immigrant parents who attempt to impose a Maghrebian cultural and religious framework upon the transplanted family and the children who challenge parental, specifically patriarchal, authority. As Michel Laronde explains, the exiled parents' dream of a return to the country of origin is feared by their children; they view North Africa as exile and seek to construct a new identity in France, one that is French and Maghrebian.[5] The term "Beur" which currently designates this second generation of Maghrebians in France contains, on the one hand, a component of cultural blending, and on the other hand, an element of revolt. A legacy of colonialism, Beur culture must define itself in terms of its North African culture of origin and its European culture of domination. Yet political, religious, and linguistic referents of the once-colonized nations and the former colonial power often conflict. In the postcolonial era, the nations of the Maghreb — Algeria, Tunisia, and Morocco — are independent states that officially embrace the religion of Islam and the Arabic language. Beurs in France, however, are marginalized in a francophone secular culture that enforces strict separation of church and state. Their task is to carve a niche for themselves. By accepting some elements and rejecting others, they seek a balance between these two worlds.

Focusing on young women opposing the rule of their fathers, Sebbar explores the challenge to Maghrebian patriarchy. Her adolescent heroines, Dalila and Shérazade, feel stifled at home. As they try to affirm their independence as young women, they are thwarted and punished, often beaten by their fathers for trying to do so. For Dalila, "the belt whistled; the buckle hit her arm, her back, her thigh. She didn't scream, she didn't cry; she tried to avoid the blows but the room was small" (12).† The physical beatings that fathers inflict upon their daughters who disregard parental curfews represent the psychological conflict between fathers and daughters that results in the flight from home.

Scenes of physical brutality project a very different image from

---

* "Je m'appellerai Rosa, Rosa Mire et j'aurai dix-huit ans, je serai majeure."

† La ceinture sifflait; la boucle l'atteignait au bras, au dos, à la cuisse; elle ne criait pas, ne pleurait pas; elle essayait d'échapper aux coups mais la pièce était petite.

that of Djebar's father proudly leading his daughter to school as she begins her outward journey. At that point, however, Djebar was a child, not an adolescent.[6] It is the adolescent leaving childhood behind who poses the problem for the Algerian patriarch; she challenges his personal authority and, by extension, the patriarchal structure of Algerian society. As the traditional guardian of his daughter, the patriarch defines the parameters of her daily life; he manipulates her destiny. His role is to choose a husband for his daughter and assure that her virginity is preserved. Shérazade's father loses patience with a daughter who turns down proposals of marriage.

If violence — beating a daughter — can be traced to tradition, to upholding family honor within a patriarchy, it is also a response to and reflection of one's own impotence, the inability to control rebellious offspring and also to control one's life when one is marginalized in an alien and hostile world. Finally, physical abuse replaces verbal communication. Saddened by his daughter's disappearance, Shérazade's father is unable to verbalize his love for her: "He loved his daughter despite everything that happened, but she didn't know it" (133).*

In this transplanted Maghrebian world, bonds between mothers and daughters are stronger and less violent than those between fathers and daughters. Unable to challenge the patriarchy themselves, mothers support their daughters in secret. Although Dalila's mother cannot protect her daughter from being beaten by her father, she can treat Dalila's bruises with homemade remedies. Shérazade's mother keeps from her husband the fact that their daughter has run off with the family jewels, and by her complicity grants her daughter the financial security that will allow her to begin an independent life. In marked contrast to Bugul, Sebbar shows female bonding extending to mother-daughter relationships.

Fatima ou les Algériennes au square emphasizes the importance of women talking. Storytelling becomes a key element of initiation, female bonding, and empowerment. Unlike Feraoun's Khalti, who tells imaginative tales drawn from folk tradition, these women in the square tell their own stories and those concerning their friends, family, and neighbors. Many of Dalila's childhood memories in Paris are of hours spent clutching at her mother's skirts and listening to the women's conversations as they supervise their children playing in the open square. Invisible and silent in the Maghrebian ghetto in Paris as

---

* Il aimait sa fille, malgré ce qui arrivait, et elle ne le savait pas.

they had been (and would still be) in North Africa, these women affirm themselves by speaking their text.

Like Djebar's *porteuses de feu*, Dalila's mother, Fatima, and her friends tell their stories in their maternal language. Similar to Djebar, Sebbar becomes the scribe of an oral tradition, although the conversations she transcribes are imagined, unlike Djebar's recorded testimony of women freedom fighters. Moreover, for Maghrebian women in France, the relationship between *écriture* and *kalaam*, between the written word in French and the spoken word in Arabic (or Berber), is redefined. In the Parisian ghetto, the French language enters the home as both a written and spoken language. Living in France and attending French schools, Beur children loosen their hold on their maternal language and begin to favor French. Hence, a linguistic gap occurs between mothers and children. As a result, women loose their grip on the children moving culturally and linguistically beyond their realm.[7]

In Sebbar's work, orality attests to a strong sense of community and female bonding and at the same time expresses alienation and victimization. These women know that they are victims of poverty and the patriarchy. If Djebar's *porteuses de feu* reveal the courage to fight against colonial domination, Sebbar's Fatima and her friends in the square have the courage to endure in a world defined by the colonizer's culture. Sebbar uses oral narrative to mirror daily life and preoccupations. The novelist's ear is finely tuned to the ebb and flow of women's daily conversation. Their speech is sometimes lyrical, sometimes strident, sometimes hopeful, sometimes desperate. It becomes clear that Fatima and her friends are deeply attached to their children and loyal to their husbands. Dalila is witness to their struggle to gain control of their lives and to their encounter with obstacles: cramped quarters, illiteracy, unemployment, and health problems.

Initiated into her mother's world, Dalila's relationship with Fatima involves an important exchange. Receiving her mother's guidance and protection, Dalila, in turn, teaches Fatima to write. As a member of the generation that has gained the power of the written word and can in effect *write* its own story, Dalila initiates Fatima into the world of *écriture*, the written word in French, by teaching her first to write her name: "So this name that she so rarely heard, FATIMA, it was her name and she knew how to write it" (47).*

---

* Donc ce nom qu'elle entendait si rarement, *FATIMA*, c'était son nom et elle savait l'écrire.

Fatima's response to her new skill is to keep secret the notebooks in which she practices her penmanship under Dalila's supervision. Fatima hides them in her *armoire*, which in the cramped apartment is her own private space. Just as Fatima and her friends have claimed the square as a public space of their own, she has a private space of her own. Not quite a room of one's own (a private place in which to retire and think), Fatima has acquired space in which to secure her most valuable possessions. She alone touches her closet.

Ambivalent toward learning to write in French, Fatima expresses ambiguity with respect to the education which moves her children along the path of assimilation: "If there were an Arabic school in the neighborhood, she would send them there to learn their language, to read and write it, just like the French language which they spoke so well now that they were forgetting their mother tongue" (47).[*] Acknowledging that a French education opens doors to the future (provided that the family remains in France), Fatima nonetheless fears that it will simultaneously close the door to their Arabic and Muslim heritage. Perhaps Fatima also anticipates her daughter's eventual departure.

Dalila, whose French education in both its cultural and linguistic dimensions allows her the possibility of leaving home, moves into the situation faced by Djebar and Bugul. In order to free herself from the enclosure, Dalila must choose exile from both the maternal and paternal spheres. Although the latter represents unjust patriarchal domination, it nevertheless embodies affection that is misunderstood and rarely expressed; the former, on the other hand, provides the love and the female bonding that will be difficult to find in the outside world. As she flees from home, Dalila can say with Djebar, "The world beyond with its risks instead of the prison of my fellow sisters" (*L'Amour, la fantasia* 208). "The outdoors and the risk instead of the prison of my peers" (*L'amour, la fantasia*, 184).[†]

Among the tales that Dalila carries with her on her journey is the story of Mustapha. Severely beaten by his mother, Mustapha, the grocer's son, is subsequently taken from his family and placed temporarily in a French foster home. Dalila comes to understand that the

---

[*] Si une école arabe existait dans le quartier, elle les y enverrait pour apprendre leur langue, la lire et l'écrire, comme la langue des Français qu'ils parlaient maintenant si bien qu'ils en oubliaient la langue maternelle.

[†] Le dehors et le risque au lieu de la prison de mes semblables (208).

child is a victim of child abuse because his mother has become a prisoner of the enclosure. Her outburst of violence stems from her confinement in an alien environment. "The family lived in the back of the store. Two dark rooms...She spoke French poorly, she knew no one, she never went out. In six months, she never left the back room. Finally she began to beat the little ones who stayed in there with her" (74).* Through oral narrative, then, as well as personal experience, Dalila is initiated into the violence of a culture under strain. She comes to recognize that adult frustration (the pent-up rage of both her father and Mustapha's mother) can be vented unintentionally on children. The story assumes significance to Dalila, who is beaten by her father and who consequently becomes preoccupied with the threat of confinement and the possibility of escape.

In this story of enclosure and escape, Dalila, the child who is being initiated to the adult world, learns that Mustapha's mother's world represents to a heightened degree the confinement that each woman in the square experiences. Aïcha suffers more than they do because she is an accomplice to her sequestration as well as a victim of it. Because she is too timid to venture alone even to the *hammam*, she denies herself the support that exists among the women in the square. Unlike Dalila's mother, Fatima, and her friends, Aïcha, the grocer's wife, has no access to the female space which in this novel functions as the *hammam* does in Djebar's work; it leads to female bonding.

As she listens attentively to Mustapha's story, the suspense heightened because it is told episodically, Dalila realizes that his escape—and therefore hers—is possible. If Mustapha can be sent to Normandy to live with a French Catholic family, others may be able to leave voluntarily. Yet the choice is difficult; the journey outward may involve a break with one's community and ultimately a loss of identity. When Mustapha's family visits him in Normandy, he appears to be thriving in a bucolic paradise. Although he still speaks Arabic, he now speaks French with the regional accent of the Normandy.

Just before leaving home, Dalila locks herself in her room for

---

* La famille habitait l'arrière-boutique. Deux pièces sombres...elle parlaitt mal le francais, elle ne connaissait personne, elle ne sortait pas. Pendant six mois, elle n'avait pas quitté l'arrière boutique. A la fin elle s'était mise à battre les petits qui restaient avec elle (74).

several days. Self-imposed confinement allows her to recall the conversations in the square. As Dalila withdraws into herself and away from her family in preparation for leaving home, she is nourished by her maternal tradition; it gives her the understanding and the strength to revolt. Although Dalila's retreat into enclosure recalls Ken's self-imposed confinement in Brussels, it is quite different. Whereas Ken withdraws for a final catharsis and emerges when she has wrestled free of a haunting past, Dalila gathers oral fragments of her past — whispers of the harem — to take with her on her journey.

Sebbar begins Dalila's story with enclosure, her self-imposed confinement, and ends with flight. The final image of the novel, however, is that of Dalila's mother, Fatima. Seated on her traditional rug, the sobbing grief-stricken mother has just discovered that her daughter has run away from home. Hence, Sebbar represents the distance between generations in terms of space: the older woman remains confined; the younger woman abandons the enclosure and those who dwell within it. Setting Dalila on an outward journey, Sebbar leaves her reader to imagine the next phase of her life. If, as Sebbar maintains, the first phase of the journey of self-understanding calls for rupture and distancing, where does it lead? The novelist provides an interesting answer to this question in her subsequent work, *Shérazade*.

The work that may be considered a sequel to *Fatima ou les Algériennes au square* depicts the life of the runaway. For Shérazade, the journey outward calls for redefinition: the protagonist breaks with her family, the smaller unit, and seeks to find her place in a larger one, possibly in Algeria. In order to forge a new identity, Sebbar's protagonist must probe her dual legacy: Algerian patriarchy and European colonialism. This duality is indeed apparent in Shérazade's dress: an Algerian scarf at her neck, a walkman plugged into her ears. Shérazade also faces a dual challenge; she must acknowledge and understand her Algerian identity and acquire the survival skills necessary to live independently, away from her family, in Paris.

Living clandestinely in Paris, Shérazade protects herself in part by refusing to admit to the dangers that face a *fugueuse*, a runaway. For example, she and her friends turn crime into parody. Calling their robbery of a chic restaurant an "autoréduction," they view it as a comic prank. In addition, Shérazade rejects Ken Bugul's "descent into Hell." Although some members of the group deal in pornography, prostitution, drugs, and terrorism, Shérazade does not. Except for the robbery and occasional shoplifting, Shérazade remains detached from the truly seamy side of life.

If Sebbar's heroine, unlike several other members of the group, emerges unscathed from her adventures, it is because she, like her namesake of the *Arabian Nights*, lives by her wits and imagination. A participant in the life of the *squatt*, Shérazade is also a keen observer. Aware that the group attempts to offer the comfort and stability of a caring family and tries to turn the *squatt* into a refuge, she acknowledges the limitations. The family, be it nonconventional or traditional, cannot save a troubled soul from self-destructive impulses. Salvation is in the hands of the individual.

Fiercely independent, Shérazade is the only member of the group to use intellectual activity to help her in her individual search for self-understanding. She writes, filling secret notebooks with personal entries and poems, but refuses to share her writing with anyone. A voracious reader, she spends a great deal of time in libraries, reading Algerian literature — works by Dib, Feraoun, Kateb, and Djebar.

In the library at Beaubourg, Shérazade encounters Julien, a *pied-noir* intellectual fifteen years her senior. Profoundly interested in Algeria's past and present, Julien is fluent in dialectical Arabic and skilled in written Arabic. As Shérazade copies into her notebooks numerous Arabic inscriptions that she finds on the walls in Paris, signs of the Maghrebian presence in the French capital, Julien, the descendant of French colonizers, deciphers them for the Beur adolescent. He and Shérazade sometimes speak Arabic together.

As with Fatima and Dalila, an important exchange occurs between Shérazade and Julien. She tells him stories of popular Algerian culture (such as the adventures of mad Djeha) and thereby initiates him into the realm of oral tradition. He, in turn, introduces her to nineteenth-century Orientalist painting. Shérazade begins to share Julien's passion for art. Together they visit the Louvre to view Delacroix's painting *Femmes d'Alger*, and discover that Shérazade resembles one of the odalisques; both women have the same green eyes. Shérazade recalls that green is the color of her original homeland: "Speaking among themselves, the women said that green is the color of Algeria" (203).* Delacroix granted Djebar an Orientalist's view of patriarchal confinement. He provides Shérazade with the same key.

---

* Le vert, disaient les femmes entre elles, c'est la couleur de l'Algérie.

At first an abstraction, Algerian history takes on personal significance for the young woman who would not be in France if the colonial power had not conquered her nation. Thus, Julien becomes the intercessor who leads Shérazade back to her origins. By initiating Shérazade to Orientalist painting and sharing in her exploration of the effects of Algeria's initial encounter with colonialism, Julien introduces the ambiguous relationship between the Beur and the *odalisque*. Having fled one enclosure, the restricting walls of her immigrant home, Shérazade encounters another in the pictorial representation of an Algerian harem. Yet, by studying the painting, Shérazade becomes a viewer, an observer. In so doing, she distances herself from the imprisoned and draws closer to the painter, empowered and free.

Julien, the intercessor, is also an observer. He studies Shérazade, the runaway, as Delacroix observed the women confined to the harem in Algiers. Whereas the *odalisques* led the French painter into the enclosure, the Beur adolescent encourages Julien to journey outward. First fleeing home—like Dalila, who runs from the maternal realm—Shérazade moves into the *squatt*; she subsequently leaves. When Shérazade takes to the open road to return to Algeria, Julien follows, pursuing her in her quest.

Before embarking upon her new journey, Shérazade, like the protagonist of Bugul's *La Baobab fou* and Sebbar's *Fatima ou les Algériennes au square*, seeks temporary refuge in the enclosure. Although Ken and Dalila move into the private space, their rooms, and then emerge resolute and transformed, Shérazade sequesters herself in public space; she hides at Beaubourg. Shérazade, who had been a frequent visitor to the Beaubourg library collection, hides in the building one night. She awakens to spend the hours before the museum opens gazing intently at one canvas, *L'Odalisque à la culotte rouge*, painted by Matisse in 1922. This work evokes within her the same emotional response as Delacroix's painting of 1834, *Femmes d'Alger*. In *Les Carnets de Shérazade*, the narrator explains the link between Delacroix and Matisse: "Delacroix taught her about light, in a long dark corridor. After that, she ran looking for it everywhere; she was seeking this light. That was what she was thinking about when she arrived at the Matisse Museum in Cateau-Cambresis" (238).[8]*

---

* Delacroix lui a appris la lumière, dans un long couloir sombre. Après, elle a cherché partout, en courant, cette lumière, c'est ce qu'elle pense lorsqu'elle arrive au musée Matisse au Cateau-Cambresis.

Without acknowledging her emotional response to the work, Shérazade enters an objective description of the painting in her notebook. The protagonist attempts to translate visual representation into words and does so by writing objectively. Her notebooks, which reappear and assume greater importance in the novel's sequel, *Les Carnets de Shérazade*, contain two distinctly different forms of entries: intimate poetry and objective description and facts (details of Rimbaud's life in Abyssinia and Flora Tristan's political activity in France, in addition to her descriptions of paintings of *odalisques*).

The intense personal experience that occurs within the enclosure, the museum at Beaubourg, has a practical end. It results in the protagonist's decision to return to Algeria, the source of the painters' inspiration. At the end of the novel, Shérazade has left Paris and is heading south, bound for the Mediterranean and North Africa. Escaping death in a car explosion that kills Pierrot, a companion of the *squatt*, Shérazade is presumed dead by the French police. She can therefore embark upon another journey, one that will allow her, now free and anonymous, to forge a new identity.

When Sebbar's previous heroine, Dalila, left maternal space, she, like Djebar's protagonists Isma and Hajila, carried with her echoes of women's voices, whispers from the harem. What of Shérazade? She too leaves home with memories. Unlike Dalila, however, Shérazade is nurtured by recollections of her grandfather in Algeria. This first intercessor taught her the rudiments of reading and writing in Arabic, recounted folktales and legends, and instructed her and her sister in the history of the Algerian struggle for independence. Shérazade's desire to return to Algeria is inspired by fond memories of her grandfather. After leaving home, Shérazade maintains tenuous contact with the world from which she has fled. Before leaving Paris, she sends her sister a postcard of the Matisse painting. Although Shérazade refuses to let her family know of her exact whereabouts, she keeps them informed of her movements.

In the two novels, Sebbar proposes several forms of expression which offer the possibility of restoring links of communication as they lead the *fugueuse*, the fleeing heroine, to self-understanding. They are orality, painting, and writing. Muted voices in the harem, which Dalila carries with her on her journey, are essential to the first novel. Visual representations of *odalisques* within the enclosure are crucial to the second. *Shérazade* also introduces the importance of writing; the protagonist keeps a series of private notebooks which she refuses to share with anyone. In the third work, as the title suggests, the traveling heroine records her adventures on the road. Does Sebbar follow Djebar, Bâ, and Bugul in placing the act of writing at the center of the process of self-discovery, affirmation and healing? Do the heroine's notebooks affirm her place in the world? *Les Carnets de Shérazade* reveals the extent to which Sebbar, who sets her protagonist on the journey to self-understanding, presents writing, both the process and the product, as an integral part of that journey.

In an interview with Monique Hugon, Sebbar explains her interest in the *fugueur*. For the novelist, the flight of the adolescent runaway reflects dual movement: the closing of one door, the opening of another. On the one hand, the runaway flees the enclosure; on the other hand, she or he accepts the challenge of new encounters. Sebbar states:

> It is not by accident that all the heroes I choose and like are *fugueurs*, runaways; *fuguer* means to escape the ghetto, and it means *rencontrer*, or encounter, often meeting situations of conflict. But situations of conflict also carry other things as well; they are not only destructive.
>
> To run away is to go toward the crossing; running away is the movement that characterizes exile.
>
> The children reenact their parents' exile by running away from home, and they do so to escape the ghetto and go toward the other. The other is very important. (Hugon 37)*

As the sequel to *Shérazade*, *Les Carnets de Shérazade* places the protagonist in a new setting and introduces new encounters. No longer sharing the *squatt* in Paris, she is now on the road. Although open to new adventures, Shérazade follows a precise itinerary that she has mapped out in advance; she traces the path of the Beur March. This march of demonstrators calling for equality and an end to racism began in Marseilles in October 1983 and ended in Paris two months later. The marchers chose a route through French cities of large immigrant populations.

Rather than return to Algeria, the home of her beloved grandfather and all her ancestors, and come to terms with the colonial past, the protagonist confirms her commitment to the present, fol-

---

* Ce n'est pas un hasard si tous les héros que je choisis et que j'aime sont des fugueurs; "fuguer," cela veut dire sortir du ghetto, cela veut dire "rencontrer," souvent dans des situations de conflit; mais des situations de conflit sont aussi porteuses d'autre choses, elles ne sont pas seulement destructrices.

Fuguer c'est aller vers le croisement, la fugue est le mouvement de l'exil.

Les enfants rejouent l'exil parental à travers la fugue pour sortir du ghetto, et pour aller vers l'autre. L'autre est très important.

lowing the path traced by her fellow Beurs. With this decision, Shérazade opts for Beur rather than Algerian identity. She keeps the project secret, however, from Gilles, the truck driver with whom she has hitched a ride: "She would not say that she was following at a distance the itinerary of the Beur march that had gone from Marseille to Paris via Lyon, Strasbourg, Lille" (21).* Her decision reveals a personal rather than a public manifestation of solidarity and commitment.

Although Shérazade's attempt to retrace the route of the Beur March attests to an affirmation of identity, her journey takes her towards the "other" and results in a new and different contact with France. Unlike Julien, the *pied-noir* whom Shérazade first met at the library at Beaubourg, Gilles, the French truck driver she encounters in Marseilles has no intellectual interest in Algerian history and culture nor particular attachment to the Maghreb. Gilles never projects a colonizer's fantasy upon the stranger he finds asleep in his truck parked at the Marseilles docks.

From the moment Gilles speaks to Shérazade, his relationship with her differs from Julien's. The latter not only cherishes the shared cultural bond with Shérazade but is captivated by a fantasy. Looking at the young girl through a lens tinged with exoticism, Julien situates her within a specific sociocultural context; she is his *odalisque* of the 1980s. Gilles, in contrast, exhibits curiosity but no preconceived ideas. He is fascinated by the young girl's independent spirit and by the qualities attributed to her namesake of the *Tales of the Arabian Nights* — intelligence, imagination, and the power of the word.

Having mastered the art of storytelling, Shérazade spins yarns in exchange for free transportation just as the legendary Shéhérazade invented tales for the Sultan in exchange for her life. Hence, two voices are intercalated in the novel: the narrator relates one journey, the adventures of Gilles and Shérazade traveling north by truck in eastern France, while Shérazade recounts another, her voyage on foot in western France as she heads for Marseilles. In addition, Shérazade reads to Gilles from her notebooks, attempting to interest him in two historical figures: one a political activist, the other a poet.

Shérazade is fascinated by the life of Flora Tristan, who, in the mid-nineteenth century, entered the French political arena with a

---

* Elle ne dirait pas qu'elle suivait à distance l'itinéraire de la marche des Beurs qui avait eu lieu de Marseille à Paris par Lyon, Strasbourg, Lille.

utopian vision of society. Although interested in Tristan's struggle for social justice for the working class, Shérazade is most taken by the woman's commitment to a universal community: "An intrepid and impassioned voyager who proclaims, because she doesn't have a country, that her nation is the universe" (113).* Rimbaud captivates Shérazade's imagination as the *fugueur* who experienced an extreme form of exile, the artist who supposedly abandoned literary aspirations and even linguistic powers in his nomadic wandering to the far reaches of Abyssinia. Tristan and Rimbaud reflect distinctly different forms of exile and nomadism. Both rebelled against the constraints of bourgeois France: Rimbaud fled from Europe to Africa, creating "le mythe de Rimbaud chez les nègres";[9] Tristan traveled from city to city within France attempting to organize workers in the creation of a new society. Both inspire the exiled nomad, Shérazade, in her quest for identity.

Speaking and writing, Shérazade takes on two roles: storyteller and scribe. Gilles, in turn, becomes Shérazade's audience and another intercessor. Replacing Julien, who initiated the young Beur into Algerian history and French painting, Gilles facilitates her contact with *la France profonde*, the French heartland which she had begun to discover alone on her journey south. By accompanying Gilles, Shérazade discovers more of the French countryside and its rural inhabitants and rekindles her earlier memories of the rural Algeria of her childhood.

Sebbar first introduced the encounter between rural France and urban ghetto in *Fatima ou les Algériennes au square* with the story of Mustapha, the battered child sent to live on a farm in Normandy. In this novel, she develops specific affinities between these seemingly different worlds, for each, in its way, represents marginality and confinement. If colonialism has created an impoverished immigrant population primarily in French cities, industrialization has marginalized a French rural population. Shérazade learns that the walls of enclosure which imprison Maghrebian women in urban ghettos reappear in rural France. In her travels, Shérazade encounters a runaway farm girl, Francette, who has stolen her family's tractor in her attempt to escape from the enclosure, and who expresses to Shérazade her loneliness, frustration, despair: "I was alone all the time with the

---

* Une voyageuse intrépide et passionnée qui proclame, parce qu'elle n'a pas de terre, que sa patrie, c'est l'univers.

animals, the pitchfork, and the tractor, and all the rest, even Saturday, Sunday, vacations, with the stench of raw milk, stable cows, the smell of the farm boys. I no longer wanted to wash. I would go to bed completely dressed, wearing the same clothes, one of my brother's overalls, one of my brothers' sweaters, rubber boots, always the same; on TV I would see women and girls my own age, and me apart" (227).* Francette comes close to reacting like Mustapha's mother, Aïcha, who transforms frustration into violence: "I took the sharpened pointed meat cleaver. I would have killed everything, the chickens, the rabbits, the pigs, the cows, the calves, all of them, everything! A massacre. Death, blood everywhere" (228).† The young girl refrains from violence, however, by turning her energy towards escape. Francette, unlike Mustapha's mother, finds a refuge; a farmer has asked her to marry him. Will escape from one enclosure lead only to another?

Shortly before Shérazade and Francette separate, the two young *fugueuses* bathe together in a stream. Then, Shérazade gives Francette a new set of clothes from her own knapsack. As a representation of female bonding, this episode is significant in several respects. First, Shérazade, an independent but solitary figure, reveals empathy and compassion. She listens attentively to Francette's story just as Dalila committed to memory the tales of Fatima's friends, the women in the square. Secondly, as they wash each other's backs in the stream, the young women reenact the traditional ritual of bathers in the *hammam*. In contrast to confined Muslim women who, in Djebar's writings, find refuge in the traditional enclosure of the steambath, these two adolescents, one French, the other Beur, move the ritual of cleansing and bonding to the outdoors. Open space is indeed a more appropriate setting for young women breaking free of confinement.

As she travels to Marseilles, on the first journey, Shérazade moves further from the enclosure and experiences a series of chance encounters along the route. Travelling with Gilles, on the second

---

* "J'étais seule tout le temps avec les bêtes, la fourche et le tracteur, et tout le reste, même le samedi, même le dimanche, même les vacances, avec toujours l'odeur du lait cru, des vaches de l'étable, l'odeur des garçons de ferme, je voulais plus me laver, je me couchais tout habillée, les mêmes habits, un pantalon de mes frères, un pull de mes frères, des bottes en caoutchouc, toujours pareil; à la télé je voyais des femmes, des filles de mon âge, et moi à côté."

† "J'ai pris le couteau à viande pointu, bien aiguisé. J'aurais tout tué, la volaille, les lapins, les cochons, les vaches et les veaux, tout, tout, tout. Un massacre. De la mort, du sang partout."

journey, she follows an established itinerary, tracing the Beur march. Although both protagonists travel, Gilles's displacements are deliberate, predictable, routine. Sherazade's trajectory, as illustrated by her accounts of traveling alone on foot, is spontaneous, unpredictable, out of the ordinary.

Listening to the account of Shérazade's encounters on the open road, Gilles challenges the authorial voice:

> "I know France better than you do... You are barely out of the suburbs... And you are going to teach me?"
> "I'm telling you that's all," said Sherazade. "And all that is true. I didn't invent anything... Do you believe me?"
> "I believe you." (235)*

Yet Gilles does not believe her tales of consistent triumph over adversity. For example, Shérazade tells of robbing a band of thugs who had tried to rape her and discovering a country cabin where, like Goldilocks, she finds the door unlocked, soup simmering on the stove, and a cozy mattress by the fire. She attributes success in the first instance to her possession of a loaded pistol and the second to good fortune. Moreover, Shérazade blantantly interjects fantasy into her narrative. Introducing encounters with novelist V. S. Naipaul, diva Jessye Norman, and film director Jean-Luc Godard, she erases the distinction between fact and fiction.

Just as Gilles questions the veracity of Shérazade's tales, the reader is prompted to pose the question raised initially with respect to Ramatoulaye's discourse in *Une si longue lettre*. Does the narrative function as a portrait or a mask? The answer must take account of the protagonist's intent. Clearly, Shérazade does not tell her stories to keep Gilles from ejecting her from his truck. Why then does Shérazade narrate? Sebbar emphasizes the importance of storytelling in *Fatima ou les Algériennes au square*; it is a source of initiation, female bonding, and empowerment. Invisible and silent in their ghettos, Fatima and her friends affirm themselves by speaking their text. I believe that Shérazade, who has chosen to become invisible and silent by "dropping out," by leaving her family and community, uses orality in the same way as the women in the square.

---

* "La France, je connais mieux que toi... Tu sors à peine de la banlieue... Et tu vas m'apprendre?"
"Je te raconte, c'est tout," dit Shérazade. "Et tout ça, c'est vrai. J'ai rien inventé... tu me crois?"
"Je te crois."

During the seven days in which Shérazade and Gilles travel together, she succeeds in winning Gilles's ear. Her stories replace the radio as the truck driver's favorite form of distraction. Moreover, the tales of Shérazade empower her. As she perfects her technique as storyteller, she gains control of her narrative, choosing what she will reveal, conceal, and/or invent. Although Gilles, the driver, appears to control the route (physical space), and Shérazade, the storyteller, controls language (mental space), she directs both, coercing him unwittingly to follow the route of the Beur march.[10] Hence, mastery of the word, empowering to the women in the square, is crucial to Shérazade's success in emerging from the enclosure and taking her place in the new world. Oral narrative leads Sebbar's heroine to self-affirmation. Writing, an activity unavailable to the women in the square, who lack the young Beur's oral and written skills in French, empowers her as well. Although her false identity serves Shérazade as a mask in society, her narrative functions as a portrait. Therefore, one may view the novel as a *Künstlerroman*, a portrait of the artist as a young woman.

We may recall that Shérazade's notebooks contain objective and subjective entries, objective description and historical facts as well as intimate poetry. Gilles allows her to read him selections of the former, but not the latter:

> "Do you want me to read you a poem?" Sherazade, obstinate, asked again. She saw that he grimaced beneath his mustache and gave a light shrug with his left shoulder.
> "I really don't care very much, I told you that." As he leaned towards the radio, Sherazade began to speak more loudly.
> "So, I can never read them to you?"
> "Not to me. To others. Some folks like poetry, don't they?" (41)*

By refusing to listen to Shérazade's poetry, Gilles renders her portrait incomplete. Although the *fugueuse* uses both the journey and self-expression to situate herself in the world, the reader is denied access to an important domain, Shérazade's creative writing. As a result, Shérazade, like Kateb Yacine's Nedjma, remains illusive and mysterious to the reader.

---

* "Vous voulez que je vous lise un poème?" demanda à nouveau Shérazade, obstinée. Elle le vit faire une moue sous sa moustache et hausser légèrement l'épaule gauche.
"J'y tiens pas tellement, je vous l'ai dit." Comme il se penchait vers la radio, Shérazade se mit à parler plus fort.
"Alors, je pourrai jamais vous les lire?"
"Pas à moi. Vous les lirez à d'autres. Ça existe des gens qui aiment la poésie, non?"

In this study, I have noted three forms of expression — orality, painting, and writing — that serve as links of communication and as paths to self-understanding. Sebbar follows Bugul (Djebar and Bâ as well) in making self-expression an integral part of the journey to self-understanding. She departs from them, however, by placing orality, not writing, at the center of the process. In effect, the title, *Les Carnets de Shérazade*, is misleading, for the protagonist's tales, far more than her notebooks, affirm her place in the world.

In conclusion, Bugul and Sebbar affirm that the journey outward — and its concomitant inner journey — lead to self-discovery, not illusory escape. Ken returns to her point of departure with greater understanding of the world and her place in it. Writing results in self-affirmation and liberates her from the ghosts of the past. Sebbar sets her *fugueuses*, Dalila and Shérazade, on similar paths. In contrast to Bugul, she does not bring her runaways home. By keeping them on the road, Sebbar suggests that they may eventually enter into dialogue with the world they left behind but will surely forge a new identity; reintegration for the runaway appears to be impossible. Most important, Bugul and Sebbar share the commitment to the empowerment of the individual through self-expression: Ken, as scribe; Shérazade, as *griote*.[11]

Conclusion

▼▼▼▼▼▼▼▼▼

I began this study of the journey motif with the conviction that fiction written by male African writers represents a conquest of outer space, the political space formerly reserved for the colonizer, whereas fiction of African women writers presents the journey inward, a response to enclosure. Hence, the proverb "Man is the outer lamp; woman is the inner lamp" became a referent in my work. In the course of my personal journey through the texts, the initial premise was refined; it took on nuances. I discovered that although *L'Enfant noir* charts the journey from the paternal village hut to the airport in Paris, depicting an African youth sufficiently equipped with European technology to claim access to public space, the trajectory of Laye's successors (male literary offspring of male novelists) reveals *contact with* but not necessarily *conquest of* this outer space. For example, Kane's protagonist, Samba Diallo, leaves the European capital to return home to his African village in confusion and defeat. Beti's Denis, however, cannot choose to seek refuge in his village where he is in danger of being conscripted into the road gang. Whether or not Denis has acquired the skills to conquer public space successfully, his only chance is to set out for the world beyond the village and hope that with luck he will survive.

The outer journey leads the protagonist to clarity of vision; it results in understanding one's place in the world as a colonial or postcolonial subject, and most importantly, as a human being. The novelist grants lucidity, not necessarily happiness. More often than not, the traveling hero's triumph is in the journey, not the destination. Kourouma's Fama and Mammeri's Mourad meet death but not defeat. Having gained lucidity via the journey both protagonists reaffirm their initial choice—marginality rather than hypocrisy under a repressive regime.

Having initially formulated a distinction between outer and inner journeys in terms of gender, I discovered fluid boundaries where I expected to find clear demarcations. Although the prohibition to travel leads female protagonists to invent a world beyond the closed door, to "women's escape through imagination" (Pratt 177), African womens' writing (as illustrated in the works of Bâ, Djebar, Bugul, and Sebbar) reveals the increased movement of women into public space. The door that was firmly shut is not wide open, but it is ajar. Whereas Delacroix's painting *Femmes d'Alger dans leur appartement* depicts confined women lost in reverie, prisoners who can only escape through imagination, African fiction presents enclosure as refuge, not prison. In Bâ's novel *Une si longue lettre*, enclosure leads to disclosure, and writing — while in the enclosure — to liberation. Concurrently, African women's fiction attests to the importance of the outer journey in the process of self-affirmation. Bâ and Djebar insist that women need public space, freedom to discover the world, as well as private space (refuge such as the *hammam*) in which to withdraw from it. Hence, Djebar uses open and closed space metaphorically, depicting Hajila, a traditional woman, embarking upon an outward journey, and portraying Isma, an emancipated women, undertaking an inward journey.

A parallel can be drawn between the inner and outer journeys of contemporary francophone African fiction and those recorded in nineteenth-century Afro-American slave narratives. Harriet Jacobs's *Incidents in the Life of a Slave Girl*, the account of the author's life as a slave and her escape to freedom, reveals her successful use of enclosure. Unlike her male counterpart, Frederick Douglass, who gains freedom by physically overpowering his master and then fleeing to the North, Jacobs escapes through enclosure, by living concealed in a crawl space in an attic for seven years. Thus, the female slave uses enclosure both as refuge and as a stage of the liberation process. Jacobs achieves final liberation, however, when she, like Douglass, crosses into a free state. The female fugitive slave reaches freedom via an outer journey, but her trajectory, which includes enclosure, differs from that of her male counterpart; her successful escape takes significantly longer than that of Douglass. In addition, Jacobs acknowledges the support she received from family and friends, thus echoing Djebar's affirmation of female bonding.[1]

The most dramatic example of women's outward trajectory in this study is the concluding one, Shérazade's flight. As invisible to the French police as the runaway slave to antebellum Southern authorities, Shérazade revolts against patriarchal authority. As a consequence of having studied Orientalist paintings, Shérazade becomes an *odalisque* in flight, a runaway fleeing all forms of confinement. In her quest for freedom, Shérazade takes to the open road; choosing her route, Shérazade sets out to gain mastery of movement.

In her search for self-understanding, she turns to language—to orality and writing. As she crafts her stories, deciding what she will reveal, conceal, and/or invent in her narrative, Shérazade gains control of language. Sebbar's protagonist is thereby empowered through freedom of movement and self-expression, both denied Delacroix's *Femmes d'Alger*, archetypal prisoners of patriarchy.

Expressed as the journey and its accompanying record, empowerment through movement and language is a recurrent process in the African fiction examined in this study. In *L'Enfant noir*, the African child who is progressively distanced both physically and psychologically from his traditional world by his parents' decision to send him to the colonial school is molded by a new, imported structure: the colonial school replaces the traditional forge. When he is far removed in space and time from the initial scenes of childhood, the son of the village blacksmith proves, by writing, that he can function successfully in public space away from his father's forge. Moreover, the process of writing his autobiographical novel confirms that the narrator has appropriated European language. Hence, Camara Laye empowers his protagonist through language as well as movement; the written record confirms the outer journey.

As he acquires a French education (language and technology), Laye loses the sense of mystery that permeates his traditional world. In an attempt to compensate for the loss of mystery, the young man who has admired his father's skill as an artisan turns to writing; he counters European rationality with poetic intuition. A new *griot*, master of the written word, Laye records his journey to self-understanding with an eloquence that would confound and impress Marlow and Kurtz.

Although separated by gender (the male vs. the female *Bildungsroman*), *L'Enfant noir* and *Shérazade* (and its sequel *Les Carnets de Shérazade*) are novels of initiation that contain elements of the *Künstlerroman*, the portrait of the artist reaching maturity. Two storytellers, Laye and Shérazade, master their craft as they struggle to forge an individual identity against the backdrop of a society in which traditional beliefs are challenged by Western ideology. Sebbar's heroines share Laye's quest for lucidity and self-definition and mirror the African child's attempt to synthesize two cultures. Shérazade, a child of migration, faces the challenge of a dual legacy: Algerian patriarchy and French colonialism.

In the three decades between the publication of *L'Enfant noir* and Sebbar's novels portraying the heroine in flight, the locus has shifted from village to city. This spatial transformation results in a new relationship between orality and writing. In the original trajectory from village to city, protagonists born into an oral culture acquire the written word as they move through the colonial school system. In pursuit of a French education, Laye, Samba, Ramatoulaye, and Ken are encouraged to leave the village for the city. Journeying forth into public space, Samba carries memories of Thierno's glowing hearth. Living far from home, Ken recalls the village baobab. At the end of her journey, she discovers that the baobab has become an impotent remnant of an irretrievable past, but during her voyage the tree functions as a powerful symbol of security and protection.

Only memories of her grandfather's tales link Shérazade to the Algerian village. Her reality is the city; the village is a fleeting souvenir. Shérazade faces no physical displacement in acquiring an education, although her Beur identity bears the stamp of psychological dislocation and exile. Moreover, Shérazade's aborted attempt to return to Algeria reflects the adolescent's quest for an identity that is inextricably bound to maternal language — to *kalaam*, not *écriture* — to the spoken word in Arabic as opposed to the written word in French.

Empowerment by means of a dual process — movement and language — occurs in all the texts under study, including Conrad's colonialist novella. Marlow's journey up the Congo River and subsequent narrative result in self-affirmation as well as self-understanding. As storyteller, Marlow acquires the eloquence he recognizes first in Kurtz. Moreover, by withholding language from the Africans, Marlow feeds the colonialist fantasy of shrieking, grunting natives and projects a colonial voice that appears all the more powerful by contrast.

I began this study with Conrad's novella because I wished to show that African novelists counter the depersonalization of colonized Africans that occurs in colonialist fiction. As they affirm and validate their culture, African writers portray protagonists who are the authentic voices — and scribes — for a society they know intimately from within. Beginning with *L'Enfant noir*, the eloquence of African writers destroys the stereotype of the inarticulate savage.

Happily, the exotic veils that obscured colonialist perception have for the most part disappeared. Hence, the Western reader who ventures forth into the less charted waters of emerging African literature does not repeat Marlow's journey. More akin to the reader's experience is the journey of Samba's perplexed sons seeking an answer to their puzzling legacy. Like them, the reader of contemporary

African fiction is encouraged to embrace the wisdom of Kem Tanne, the venerable sage who teaches the three travelers to probe surface reality. Concluding on a personal note, I wish to say that as I journey through the texts I too find myself repeating with Samba's sons: "Qui marche longtemps, voit beaucoup."

Notes

▼▼▼▼▼

Introduction

1. For a more complete study of the relationship between writing and the spoken word see the works of Jack Goody, Ian Watt, and Walter J. Ong.

2. In Robert's view, Don Quijote represents the self-searching and self-questioning protagonist, whereas Robinson Crosue gives the novel the stamp of the mercantile middle class (19).

3. For an extensive evaluation of Kane's study, see Irene d'Almeida ("The Making of an African Literary-Critical Tradition," 159–178).

4. For a more detailed study of oral techniques, see Eileen Julien, "Orality through Writing: *Les Contes d'Amadou Koumba*" and "Oral Styles in Birago Diop's Tales: Excerpts from a Study of Language in *Les Contes d'Amadou Koumba.*"

5. These may be songs of woe and misfortune, of exile, of warning, of adoration. (See Mildred Mortimer, Introduction to *Contes africains*, x–xiii.)

6. See Gilles Deleuze and Félix Guattari (29–30) and George Joseph.

7. Cited by Jean Déjeux ("Regards sur la litterature maghrébine d'expression française," 17). According to Jean Déjeux (*Littérature Maghrebine de langue française*, 21), two works precede Fikri's novel: Slimane Ben Ibrahim (with Etienne Dinet), *Kahdra, danseuse des Ouled Naïl* (1910); and Caïd Ben Cherif, *Ahmed Ben Mostapha, goumier* (1920). The works that follow the Fikri novel are Chukri Khodja, *El Eudj, captif des Barbaresques* (1929); Robert Randau and Abdelkader Fikri, *Les Compagnons du jardin* (1933); Mohammed Ould Cheikh, *Myriam dans les palmes* (1936); Ali Belhadj (pseudonym for Mohammed Sifi), *Souvenirs d'enfance d'un blédard* (1941); Aïssa Zehar, *Hind à l'âme pure ou l'histoire d'une mère* (1942); the brothers Zenati, *Bou el Nouar, le jeune Algérien* (1945).

8. Guy Ossito Mediouhouan has drawn my attention to the writings of Lamine Senghor of the same period that were discovered in the 1970s. Senghor opposed Diallo's assimilationist stance. See his "Lamine Senghor (1889–1927): Précurseur de la prose nationaliste négro-africaine."

9. With the founding of the *Bulletin de l'enseignement de l'Afrique Occidentale française* in 1913, the *Bulletin du Comité d'études historiques et scientifiques de l'A.O.F.* in 1916, and the *Organe de l'Association des Instituteurs d'origine indigène en Algérie* in 1921, French-educated "évolués" had vehicles for self-expression and were encouraged by the colonial administration to do anthropological and sociological research on indigenous culture.

10. There is a growing interest in Algeria in the literature of this period. See Christiane Achour and Abdelkader Djeghloul.

11. In his historical study of the early Senegalese novel, Fredric Michelman ("The Beginnings of French-African Fiction") discusses the protagonist's fascination with writing as a portent of later fiction.

12. In her study of the novel, Ronnie Scharfman emphasizes the ambiguity of Sembène's conclusion. She notes that the women who have been catalysts for change either disappear or are recuperated by the patriarchal structure.

13. Although sub-Saharan African women of all religious persuasions (Muslim, Christian, and followers of indigenous African religions) are not veiled and are generally allowed greater freedom of movement within their villages and/or urban neighborhoods, they rarely have the liberty to undertake long journeys. For a discussion of the position of women in Muslim societies of sub-Saharan Africa, see Fatou Sow.

14. Florence Stratton takes Gilbert and Gubar's book as a point of departure for her analysis of three novels of the Nigerian novelist Buchi Emecheta and Mariama Bâ's *Une si longue lettre*. Uncovering archetypes, Stratton suggests the possibility of a female literary tradition that, in its response to patriarchy, transcends all cultural boundaries.

15. In a more recent study, *Chahrazad n'est pas marocaine—autrement, elle serait salariée!*, Mernissi discusses the gains made by Moroccan women in the workplace in recent years.

16. I would like to see a study of the diverse forms that rupture or "deter-ritorialization" has taken in the Maghreb and sub-Saharan francophone Africa. Such a study should take note of the historical difference between north/south colonial stereotypes and the negativity of Orientalism that Edward Said documents compared to the "blank darkness" of Africanist discourse that Christopher Miller uncovers.

17. The sole exception is Bâ's *Une si longue lettre*, in which enclosure, not travel, is the thematic and structuring device that results in self-discovery.

Chapter 1. From the Colonialist to the African Novel

1. Page references in this text are to the 1974 Everyman's Library edition of Conrad's works.

2. A note of the Everyman edition of *Heart of Darkness* reads: "Crews of steamers on the Upper Congo were mostly Bangalas, who were cannibals" (cf. W. Holman Bentley, *Pioneering on the Congo*, 1900 t. I. 210, 213) (351).

3. Miller 169–183.

4. Nazareth calls attention to Marlow's fascination with a "white patch" on the map (which was Africa before colonialists arrived) and suggests that Conrad reverses images of blackness and whiteness in this passage and several others to work against the racism inherent in the English language (177).

5. Jean-Aubry (fn. 170) writes that this is confirmed by the manuscript at Yale University Library: "In the interior you will no doubt meet Mr. Klein..." (55).

6. Watt states: "The total disconnection in Kurtz between words and reality reflects a general tendency in Western culture to place an exorbitant cultural emphasis on the verbal aspects of collective life; and this inevitably involves a disparity between verbal expression and the actual behavior much deeper than exists in most other societies" (235).

7. For a further study of the differences in the portrayal of the two women see Busia: ("Miscegenation as metonymy" 361): "The two women are both essentially trapped where their men find them, as fixed points of conflicting desires, and the century of drama enacted between the spaces they each occupy has been one in which they have been pawn and prize; both of them."

8. All the translations are from the 1965 edition of *The African Child*.

9. When he published *L'Enfant noir*, the novelist adopted the inverted form of his name customary in the French colonial school. I am following other critics in maintaining the inverted name. In point of fact, Camara is the writer's surname.

10. Raskin states: "The Congo Conrad saw in 1890 with its factories, plantations, missionaries, and commercial firms was a more highly organized and 'civilized' region than the Congo of *Heart of Darkness*, which is presented in the rudimentary stages of development" (117). Watt notes that "at what Marlow calls the Company Station, Matadi, there were actually some 170 Europeans present, and much commercial activity in which German, Dutch, French, and English concerns were involved; and contrary to the impression given by Marlow, the railway to Kinshasa was in fact being built" (140).

11. For further study of the symbolism of circumcision, see Durand (191–94).

Chapter 2. Cultural Conflict During the 1950s and 1960s

1. All page references in this text are to the 1976 edition of *Le Pauvre Christ de Bomba*, published by Présence Africaine, and to the 1985 translation by Gerald Moore.

2. Melone states: "Mongo Beti insistera beaucoup sur l'inaptitude de Drumont à pénétrer l'âme africaine, sur l'importance des valeurs africaines héritées de la tradition, sur l'existence des religions antérieurement à l'avènement du christianisme en Afrique et sur l'attachement quasi cosmologique de l'Africain à sa tradition et à son passé" (*Mongo Beti: l'homme et le destin*, 36).

3. Wilfred Cartey and Eloise Brière view the sorcerer as the ultimate winner. Brière also acknowledges that in Beti's symbolism the river, claimed by Sanga Boto as his weapon against the missionary, represents tradition (193). Melone, on the other hand, views the shaming of Sanga Boto as the sorcerer's defeat. He states: "Même l'impressionnant Sanga Boto, dont tout le monde craint la terrible puissance, finira par s'incliner devant le missionnaire, et par déclarer publiquement l'inefficience de ses fétiches devant les oeuvres de Dieu et du R.P.S., son fidèle serviteur" (*Mongo Beti: l'homme et le destin*, 67–68). Melone concludes that the river alone,

not Sanga Boto, is responsible for the missionary's accident (*Mongo Beti, l'homme et le destin*, 129—30).

4. Missionaries accompanied the Portuguese in the fifteenth century to the Kingdom of Kongo. The Christian presence resulted in local artists creating crucifixes for chiefs who used them as power tokens, not as devotional objects ("African Art in the Life Cycle," exhibit at the National Museum of African Art [Smithsonian Institution, Washington, D.C.], Winter 1988).

5. All page references in this text are to the 1961 edition of *L'Aventure ambiguë*, published by Julliard, and to the translation by Katherine Woods.

6. Tidjani-Serpos objects to this training: "Certes, cette méthode avait le don de développer la mémoire; elle s'adaptait peut-être aussi au caractère oral de la production textuelle africaine; mais en fait cette mémorisation, sans explication aucune, correspondait parfaitement bien à un autre trait de la culture africaine; la science est d'autant plus prisée qu'elle est ésoterique et qu'elle demande des années d'errances et de misères avant d'être acquise. Le savoir, dans sa clarté, ne peut être confié de manière inconsidérée à la jeunesse. Il ne peut être possédé qu'au bout de la traversée d'un long tunnel et durant ce temps il faut faire aveuglement confiance au maître et le mimer au maximum" (191).

7. One well-known exception to the rule is El Haj Saidou Nourou Tall, a descendant of Umar Tall, who as clan leader and *marabout* became an important political leader, using his position among the Toucouleur to deal with the French and then with the independent Senegalese government (Behrman 33).

8. Raymond Okafor views the Knight as a spokesman for Senghorian Negritude, a protagonist defending the thesis that Africans must retain traditional values to preserve African dignity (203).

Chapter 3. Catalyst for Change

1. Page references in the text are to *Les Bouts de bois de Dieu* (Paris: Le Livre Contemporain, 1960; Presses Pocket, 1979) and to the translation by Francis Price.

2. Martin T. Bestman notes: "Le déplacement des personnages dans l'univers romanesque de Sembène est lié à une certaine conception du monde: ceux qui aiment les habitudes séculaires ne se déplacent guère, tandis que les personnages qui veulent reconquérir leur liberté sont en constant mouvement" (294).

3. Léopold Sédar Senghor (ed.) "Souffles," *Anthologie de la nouvelle poésie nègre et malgache de langue française* (Paris: Presses Universitaires de France, 1969) 145.

4. Soundjata Keïta (1210—1260). His successive conquests transformed the kingdom of Kangaba into the Empire of Mali. Soundjata challenged and defeated his adversary Sumanguru (also called Soumaoro) at the battle of Kiringa in 1235. Mali prospered under Soundjata's rule because of the centralized monarchy, its location on the trans-Saharan trade route, and its control of the gold market. For the legend of Soundjata, see Niane.

5. Hamon provides an illuminating study of realism's emphasis upon conveying information to the reader and attempting to convince the reader of its authenticity. Schipper uses this approach in her analysis of *Les Bouts de bois de Dieu* in "Toward a Definition of Realism in the African Context."

6. In Sembène's interview with Moore, he states that he personally presented Malraux with a copy of *Les Bouts de bois de Dieu* when it was published but had not read *La Condition humaine* before writing his first novel, *Le Docker noir*, published in 1956 ("Evolution of an African Artist," 223).

7. Critics differ with respect to Bakayoko's importance in the novel. Case views Penda, not Bakayoko, as the principal character (287). Bestman emphasizes the extreme dependency of Tiémoko, Doudou, and others upon the strike leader. Chemain calls the dependency a form of "doubling" (duplication of the hero) that recalls the epic tradition; he gives as an example in French literature the relationship between Roland and Olivier le Preux (176).

8. "The women meet in the open air and never in a building, whereas the men, dependent as they are on the institutional structure of their organisation, invariably assemble within a union building" (Case 287).

9. For a discussion of the *griot*'s interpretation of oral narrative, see my introduction to *Contes africains* and Eileen Julien, "Orality through Writing."

10. Scharfman believes that Penda is too subversive to remain alive. "Ayant préparé la voie, il faut que Penda et sa route substitutive soient réabsorbées par le discours paternal, avant qu'elles n'aillent trop loin" (142).

11. "Le déplacement fréquent de la caméra renforce le mouvement symphonique qui revêt une signification sociale symbolique: l'architecture triptyque laisse apparaître la solidarité qui relie les hommes devant une communauté de destin, les joies et souffrances individuelles se mêlent à celles de la collectivité" (Bestman 223).

12. In West Africa, the slaughter of large animals is traditionally done by men (Sow 563–70).

13. Kateb Yacine prefers to invert his name as he was taught to do as a schoolboy in French Algeria.

14. Named for the year in which the Algerian war began. The group of Algerian novelists includes Mouloud Feraoun, Mouloud Mammeri, Mohammed Dib, Malek Haddad, Mourad Bourboune, Assia Djebar, Marguerite Taos-Amrouche, Henri Kréa, Malek Ouary.

15. See Gontard's comparison of Nedjma with Faulkner's *The Sound and the Fury* (*Nedjma de Kateb Yacine* 48) and the dissertation (D.E.S.) of Hocine Menasseri. Aresu also finds parallels between the Algerian work and Faulkner's *Absalom, Absalom!* and *Light in August*. He states: "The motif of the road and of nomadic displacement, with their ordalic and initiatory symbolism, are made to play equally significant roles in *Light in August* and *Nedjma*" ("Elaborative Fiction," 13).

16. Page references in the text are to *Nedjma* (Paris: Seuil, 1956) and to the translation by Richard Howard.

17. In the penultimate scene, Richard Howard keeps the verbs *apparaître* and *relever* in the present tense, but I have used the past tense to remain closer to the original text.

18. "If the fictional characterization of woman, on the one hand, remains incomplete, mono-dimensional, often sketchily perceived through the unreliable eye of a protagonist throughout a narrative pattern of inter-personal division and antagonism, the symbolic extensions of female characterization, on the other, provide Kateb's writings with a tremendous sense of mythical and structural unity. One can discern in the symbolic use of the figure of woman a double, antithetical impulse of valorization whose dominant elements of an alternately negative and positive nature are brought to a point of resolution in the dramas" (Aresu, "Female Characterization" 371).

19. In her study *La littérature maghrébine de langue français: II Le cas de Kateb Yacine*, Jacqueline Arnaud views Lakhdar and Mustapha as naive nationalists, representative of Kateb at the age of sixteen (302).

20. For more on the folk hero in the works of Mohammed Dib, Rachid Boudjedra, and Kateb Yacine, see Jean Déjeux, *Djoh'a: héros de la tradition*.

21. Although I have emphasized the colonial jail, Djaider and Khadda view the *chantier* (construction yard) as the space of alienation, confrontation, and the implantation of the colonizer (75−86).

22. Gontard notes: "En compagnie d'un écrivain public, Rachid se délivre, dans une sorte d'exorcisme verbal, de sa névrose et de l'échec: échec de l'idéal nationaliste, échec de la passion amoureuse, échec dans l'élucidation du meurtre paternel" (*Nedjma de Kateb Yacine* 31).

23. In *L'Amour, la fantasia* and *Ombre sultane*, Assia Djebar explores the relationship between women's silence and enclosure, focusing on three traditional forms of enclosure in the Muslim world: *harem* (women's secluded quarters), *haïk* (veil), and *hammam* (Moorish bath). See chapter 5.

Chapter 4. Independence Acquired — Hope or Disillusionment?

1. See Roland Oliver and Michael Crowder, eds., *The Cambridge Encyclopedia of Africa* (200−202).

2. See Jean-Claude Vatin, "Désert construit et inventé, Sahara perdu ou retrouvé: le jeu des imaginaires" (107−31).

3. Page references in the text are to *Les Soleils des independances* (Paris: Seuil, 1970) and to the translation by Adrian Adams.

4. Fredric Michelman views the negative imagery of the sun — "les soleils des indépendances maléfiques" (the evil suns of independence) (9) — in contrast to a traditional beneficial sun as an example of this reversal ("Independence and Disillusion" 93). In so doing, Kourouma ironically returns to the negative sun imagery of Pierre Loti's *Le Roman d'un Spahi*.

5. As Rosemary Schikora explains, "Death, in African ontology, represents

a journey, a passing on and, at the same time, *rapprochement* with those who preceded one in time. Having once existed, a being never ceases to exist" ("African Fiction in French" 196).

6. For a discussion of time in the novel, see K. R. Ireland.

7. Calling Fama "la stérilité faite homme," M. M'Lanhoro views the harmattan, a dry, sterile Saharan wind, as a metaphor for Fama's condition (52).

8. For a study of animal imagery in the novel, see Roger Chemain, 35–55.

9. The protagonist's insistence upon predetermined fate leads Aloysius O. Ohaegbu to view him as a tragic figure—"livré au destin hostile, implaccable, qui l'écrase" (255).

10. Eileen Julien ("Oral Styles in Birago Diop's Tales" 3) notes that Birago Diop frequently uses the following techniques of oral art: dialogue, repetition, questioning the narratee, listing, songs and refrains, etiological endings. She explains that Diop does not incorporate all these elements into every tale. His success lies in the selection of techniques.

11. George Joseph believes that the *narrataire* (receiver in the narrator) is not a reader but a listener in an oral situation such as a dialogue between two isolated persons, or a gathering around a *griot* (71).

12. See Schikora, Lavergne, Sellin ("Ouologuem, Kourouma"), and Emeto-Agbasière for a discussion of the role of proverbs in the novel, and Ruth Finnegan (390–425).

13. Ruth Finnegan attributes frequent comparisons with nature to rural culture rather than to some mystical affinity to African flora and fauna (405).

14. Eric Sellin concludes that this kaleidoscope effect is due to the African writer's predilection for episodes: "Récemment cette prédilection pour l'épisodique semble avoir assumé une forme plus ou moins autochtone ou l'ontologie africaine l'emporte sur la tradition française sous une forme toutefois romanesque ou auparavant l'Africain se contentait peu ou prou d'adapter sa vision créatrice aux formes épisodiques déjà traditionalisées, pour ainsi dire, par Voltaire, Lesage, Gide et tout un lignage littéraire d'oeuvres épisodiques, épistolaires et qui tenaient du journal" "Ouologuem, Kourouma" 38).

15. Citing Niane's *Sounjata* and Ouologuem's *Le Devoir de violence* as examples of works that use the *griot*-narrator, Michelman states that Kourouma is the first to do so in a sustained manner ("Independence and Disillusion" 95).

16. See also Malek Haddad, Tahar Djaout, and Albert Memmi, as well as a comparative study of Haddad's novel with *La Traversée* in Mildred Mortimer, "The Desert in Algerian Fiction."

17. André Gide, *Les Nourritures terrestres* (Paris: Gallimard, 1944) and *L'Immoraliste* (Paris: Mercure de France, 1902). Ernst Psichari, *Les Voix qui crient dans le désert* (1920) in *Oeuvres complètes*, vol. 11 (Paris: Conard, 1948). For a study of the colonial experience in the French novel, see Alec G. Hargreaves, Martine Astier-Loutfi, and Léon Fanoudh-Siefer.

18. In "L'Hôte," Camus plays upon the dual meaning in French of the word *hôte*, both host and guest. In this short story, the term applies both to the French colonial school teacher who is host and to the Arab prisoner whom Daru treats as his guest.

19. Mammeri writes of his own reaction: "Aux portes du désert je me présentais sans préjugés particuliers: ni peur mythique ni non plus appétit d'un exotisme facile, avec simplement le désir de rencontrer des hommes qui, comme toujours, ne seraient ni tout à fait les mêmes ni vraiment différents" ("Ténéré atavique" 214).

20. See Mouloud Mammeri, *L'Ahellil du Gourara*, in which Mammeri has transcribed and translated into French the songs of the festivals.

21. Mammeri writes: "Quand l'écho répercuta plusieurs fois l'appel du guide, que les rochers jouaient à se renvoyer, je ne peux pas dire que, ce qui soudain me serra la gorge à l'étouffer, ce fut l'immense soulagement du naufragé perdu et retrouvé" ("Ténéré atavique" 215).

22. Following riots in October 1988, the Algerian government proposed a new constitution granting greater political freedom for its citizens. Two days after Algerians voted to approve the constitution Mammeri was killed in an automobile accident. We will never know whether future political events would have tempered Mammeri's pessimism expressed in *La Traversée*.

Chapter 5. Women's Voice

1. For Scheub's study of women as performers see *The Khosa "Ntomsi."*

2. See Elinor C. Flewellen, "Assertiveness vs. Submissiveness in Selected Works by African Women Writers," and Femi Ojo-Ade, "Still a Victim? Mariama Bâ's *Une si longue lettre.*"

3. Page references in the text are to *Une si longue lettre* (Dakar: Les Nouvelles Editions Africaines, 1980) and to the translation by Modupe Bode-Thomas.

4. Discussing *mirasse*, Mbye Boubacar Cham writes: "Mirasse, therefore, becomes the principle that legitimizes and regulates Rama's act of systematic personal revelation which simultaneously constitutes a systematic analysis of some of the most pressing socioeconomic and cultural issues challenging women and society" ("The Female Condition in Africa" 33). In contrast to Cham's socioeconomic emphasis, I will focus on the personal development that results from disclosure. Geneviève Slomski, on the other hand, writes that the Islamic custom allows Ramatoulaye to launch into a series of torments she has endured as Modou's wife (140). I will examine disclosure to see whether it leads exclusively to victimization or results in self-understanding.

5. Cham calls Aïssatou the stable reference point for a temporarily unstable Ramatoulaye ("The Female Condition in Africa" 35).

6. Florence Stratton believes that Ramatoulaye's feelings toward her friend become increasingly ambivalent. Praising Aïssatou's courage, Ramatoulaye belittles her choice, and she betrays her by retaining Mawdo as a confidant and doctor (163).

7. For a more detailed discussion of the role of the wicked stepmother, see Sonia Lee. Lee notes that often the orphan's virtues win her the supreme reward—marriage. Her husband then brings about the stepmother's downfall ("The Image of the Woman in the African Folktale from the Sub-Saharan Francophone Area," 22).

8. Abena Busia criticizes Djebar for excluding the servant from her discussion.

9. Page references in the text are to *Fantasia: An Algerian Cavalcade* (London: Quartet Books, 1989), translation by Dorothy S. Blair of *L'Amour, la fantasia*.

10. For a study of Djebar's writing in terms of open and closed space, see Mildred Mortimer, *Assia Djebar*.

11. Djebar has written about her ancestor Malek Sahraoui El Berkani in the poem entitled "Un Pays sans mémoire," published in *Poèmes pour l'Algérie heureuse* (Alger: SNED, 1969) 39–40.

12. Hédi Abdel-Jaouad notes: "But this audacious act of breaking away from tradition is and can only be made in the conqueror's language. Hence the contradictory appeal and ambivalent status of this foreign (imposed) but liberating (cathartic) medium" (29). He adds that the parental cultural transgressions were of important psychological significance to their adolescent daughter who recalls the incident at the time of her marriage.

13. For an interview that focuses on the writer's relationship to the French language, see Marguerite LeClézio.

14. The translation of *Ombre sultane* is *A Sister to Sheherazade*, translated by Dorothy S. Blair (London: Quartet Books, 1987).

15. Blair omitted the phrase "Nous voici toutes deux en rupture de harem, mais à ses pôles extrêmes." Although I refer the reader to Blair's translation, I have modified it, inserting the phrase that had been omitted.

Chapter 6. Women's Flight

1. Dorothy S. Blair makes this point in her study *Senegalese Literature: A Critical History* (121–22).

2. Lucien Houedanou notes that this narrative is not neutral: "En même temps qu'elle se raconte, Ken Bugul se justifie" (166).

3. Although Sebbar has not yet sent Shérazade back to Algeria, she has written in *Lettres parisiennes*, her correspondence with Nancy Huston: "C'est Shérazade qui ira en Algérie, dans l'Algérie contemporaine, sans moi...Parce que j'ai comme une peur d'aller où je n'ai plus rien à faire, où je ne trouverai pas ce que j'ai aimé dans l'état où je l'ai quittée parce que l'éternité des maisons et des écoles, ça n'existe pas..." (80).

4. *Odalisque en fuite* was the title that Djebar intended at first for *Ombre sultane*.

5. See Michel Laronde, "L'Apport de la culture d'origine."

6. Djebar illustrates this point in *Ombre sultane* (145–49). The same father who proudly accompanied his six-year-old daughter to school punishes

her years later when, as an adolescent, she inadvertently lifts her skirt in public.

7. Sebbar develops this theme further in her novel *Parle mon fils, parle à ta mère*.

8. Denise Brahimi considers *Shérazade* and *Les Carnets de Shérazade* "la description de cette course vers la lumière que la jeune Shérazade situe d'abord en Algérie avant de comprendre l'illusion de son projet" ("Orientalisme et conscience de soi" 32).

9. Christopher L. Miller (139–65) discusses the distinction between the "mythe du nègre chez Rimbaud" and the "mythe de Rimbaud chez les nègres."

10. I thank Sonia Lee for pointing this out to me.

11. Henry Louis Gates, Jr. explores the distinction between the "speakerly" text and the novel of letters, citing Zora Neale Hurston's *Their Eyes Were Watching God* and Alice Walker's *The Color Purple*. He notes: "Whereas Janie's moment of consciousness is figured as a ritual speech act, for Celie it is the written voice which is her vehicle for self-expression and self-revelation" (245). Although Gates shows evidence of "signifyin(g)," of Walker's rewriting Hurston's speakerly text, I do not make that claim for Bugul and Sebbar.

Conclusion

1. For a detailed discussion of the slave narrative, see Valerie Smith, *Self-Discovery and Authority in Afro-American Narrative*.

Works Consulted

▼▼▼▼▼▼▼▼▼▼▼▼▼

Primary Sources

Bâ, Mariama. *So Long a Letter*. Trans. Modupe Bode-Thomas. London and Nairobi: Heinemann, 1981.

———. *Une si longue lettre*. Dakar: Les Nouvelles Editions Africaines, 1980.

Beti, Mongo. *Le Pauvre Christ de Bomba*. Paris: Editions Robert Laffont, 1956.

———. *Le Pauvre Christ de Bomba*. Paris: Présence Africaine, 1976.

———. *The Poor Christ of Bomba*. Trans. Gerald Moore. 1971. London, Ibadan, and Nairobi: Heinemann, 1985.

Boudjedra, Rachid. *La Répudiation*. Paris: Denoël, 1981.

Bugul, Ken. [Mariétou M'Baye]. *Le Baobab fou*. Dakar: Les Nouvelles Editions Africaines, 1984.

Camus, Albert. *L'Exil et le royaume*. Paris: Gallimard, 1957.

Chraibi, Driss. *Le Passé simple*. Paris: Denoël, 1954.

Conrad, Joseph. *Heart of Darkness*. London: Penguin Books, 1973.

———. *Heart of Darkness and the Secret Sharer*. New York: Signet Classic-American Library, 1950. 65–158.

———. *A Personal Record*. New York: Harper and Row, 1912.

———. *Youth, Heart of Darkness, and the End of the Tether*. 1958. London and Melbourne: Everyman's Library-Dent, 1974. 45–162.

Diallo, Bakary. *Force-Bonté*. Paris: F. Rieder, 1927.

Dib, Mohammed. *La Grande maison*. Paris: Seuil, 1952.

Diop, Birago. *Les Contes d'Amadou Koumba*. Paris: Présence Africaine, 1961.

Djaout, Tahar. *L'Invention du désert*. Paris: Seuil, 1987.

Djebar, Assia. *L'Amour, la fantasia*. Paris: Jean Lattès, 1985.

———. *Fantasia: An Algerian Cavalcade*. Trans. Dorothy S. Blair. London: Quartet Books, 1989. Trans. of *L'Amour, la fantasia*.

———. *Femmes d'Alger dans leur appartement*. Paris: Editions des Femmes, 1980.

———. *Ombre sultane*. Paris: Jean Lattès, 1987.

———. *A Sister to Scheherazade*. Trans. Dorothy S. Blair. London and New York: Quartet Books, 1987. Trans. of *Ombre Sultane*, 1987

Feraoun, Mouloud. *Le Fils du pauvre*. Paris: Seuil, 1954.

Haddad, Malek. *Je t'offrirai une gazelle*. Paris: Julliard, 1959.

Kane, Cheikh Hamidou. *Ambiguous Adventure*. Trans. Katherine Woods. Intro. Wilfred G. O. Cartey. New York: Collier Books, 1969.

———. *L'Aventure ambiguë*. Paris: Julliard, 1961.

Kateb, Yacine. *Le Cercle des représailles* ("Le Cadavre encerclé"; "La Poudre d'intelligence"; "Les Ancêtres redoublent de férocité"; "Le Vautour"). Paris: Seuil, 1956.

———. *Nedjma*. Paris: Seuil, 1956.

————· *Nedjma.* Trans. Richard Howard. New York: George Braziller, 1961.

————· *L'oeuvre en fragments.* Inédits littéraires et textes retrouvés, rassemblés et présentés par Jacqueline Arnaud. Paris: Sinbad, 1986.

————· *Le Polygone étoilé.* Paris: Seuil, 1966.

————· "Un Rêve dans un rêve." *Terrasses* I (1953): 28−37.

KOUROUMA, AHMADOU. *Les Soleils des indépendances.* Paris: Seuil, 1970.

————· *The Suns of Independence.* Trans. Adrian Adams. New York: Africana Publishing Company, 1981.

LAYE, CAMARA. *The African Child.* Trans. James Kirkup. Intro. William Plomer. London and Glasgow: Fontana Books, 1965.

————· *The Dark Child.* Trans. James Kirkup and Ernest Jones. New York: Noonday Press, 1954.

————· *L'Enfant noir.* Paris: Presses Pocket, 1976.

LOTI, PIERRE. *Le Roman d'un Spahi.* Paris: Calmann-Lévy, 1949.

MAMMERI, MOULOUD. *La Colline oubliée.* Paris: Plon, 1952.

————· *La Mort absurde des Aztèques: Le Banquet.* Paris: Librairie Académique Perrin, 1973.

————· *L'Opium et le bâton.* Paris: Plon, 1965.

————· *Le Sommeil du juste.* Paris: Plon, 1955.

————· *La Traversée.* Paris: Plon, 1982.

MEMMI, ALBERT. *Le Désert.* Paris: Gallimard, 1977.

————· *La Statue de Sel.* Paris: Gallimard, 1954.

OYONO, FERDINAND. *Une Vie de boy.* Paris: Julliard, 1956.

RANDAU, ROBERT, and ABDELKADER FIKRI. *Les Compagnons du jardin.* Paris: Domat-Montchrestien, 1933.

SAINT-EXUPÉRY, ANTOINE DE. *Terre des Hommes.* Paris: Gallimard, 1939.

SEBBAR, LEÏLA. *Les Carnets de Shérazade.* Paris: Stock, 1985.

————· *Fatima ou les Algériennes au square.* Paris: Stock, 1981.

————· "La Langue de l'exil." *La Quinzaine littéraire* 436 (16−31 mars 1985): 8, 10.

————· "La Littérature et l'exil." *Magazine Littéraire* (juillet−août 1985): 39−40.

————· *Parle mon fils, parle à ta mère.* Paris: Stock, 1984.

————· *Shérazade, brune, frisée, les yeux verts.* Paris: Stock, 1982.

SEBBAR, LEÏLA, and NANCY HUSTON. *Lettres parisiennes.* Paris: Bernard Barrault, 1986.

SEMBÈNE, OUSMANE. *Les Bouts de bois de Dieu.* Paris: Le Livre Contemporain, 1960. Reedited. Paris: Presses Pocket, 1979.

————· *God's Bits of Wood.* Trans. Francis Price. London, Ibadan, and Nairobi: Heinemann, 1970.

————· *L'Harmattan.* Paris: Présence Africaine, 1964.

SENGHOR, LÉOPOLD SÉDAR, ed. *Anthologie de la nouvelle présie negre et malgache de langue française.* Paris: Presses Universitaires de France, 1945. Reprinted 1969.

ZENATI, A., and R. ZENATI. *Bou-el-nouar, le jeune algérien.* Alger: La Maison des Livres, 1945.

Secondary Sources

ABDEL-JAOUAD HÉDI. "*L'Amour, la fantasia*: Autobiography as Fiction."

CELFAN Review 7:1—2 (1987—88): 25—29.

ACCAD, EVELYNE. *Veil of Shame: The Role of Women in the Contemporary Fiction of North Africa and the Arab World.* Sherbrooke: Naaman, 1978.

ACHEBE, CHINUA. "An Image of Africa." *Research in African Literatures* 9 (1978): 1—15.

ACHOUR, CHRISTIANE. *Abécédaires en devenir: idéologie coloniale et langue française en Algérie.* Algiers: ENAP, 1985.

ADAM, JEANNE. "Le Jeune Intellectuel dans les romans de Mouloud Mammeri." *Revue de l'Université d'Ottawa* 46 (avril—juin 1976): 278—87.

AIRE, VICTOR O. "Mort et devenir: Lecture thanato-sociologique de *L'Aventure ambiguë.*" *The French Review* 55.6 (1982): 752—60.

ALESSANDRA, JACQUES. "Pourquoi Kateb Yacine a-t-il abandonné l'écriture française?" *Présence Francophone* 24 (Spring 1982): 5—8.

ALLOULA, MALEK. *Le Harem colonial.* Paris: Garance, 1981.

———. *The Colonial Harem.* Trans. M. Godzich and W. Godzich. Minneapolis: University of Minnesota Press, 1986.

AMROUCHE, JEAN. "L'Eternel Jugurtha." *Arche* 13 (fevrier 1946): 58—70.

ARESU, BERNARD. "Elaborative Fiction: Kateb and Faulkner." *CELFAN Review* 5.3 (1986): 10—16.

———. "Female Characterization and Mythmaking in the Dramas of Kateb Yacine." *Neophilologus* 67.3 (1983): 368—76.

———. "Polygonal and Arithmosophical Motifs: Their Significance in the Fiction of Kateb Yacine." *Research in African Literatures* 9.2 (1978): 143—75.

———. "The Fiction of Kateb Yacine: A Study in Afro-Occidentalism." Diss. University of Washington, 1975.

ARNAUD, JACQUELINE. *La Littérature maghrébine de langue français.* Vol. 2, *Le cas de Kateb Yacine.* Paris: Publisud, 1986.

———. "Sur *Nedjma* de Kateb Yacine." *Oeuvres et critiques* 4.2 (1979): 37—49.

ASTIER—LOUTfi MARTINE, *Littérature et colonialisme: l'expansion coloniale vue dans la littérature romanesque française, 1871—1914.* Paris: Mouton, 1971.

AUDEN, W. H. *The Enchafed Flood or The Romantic Iconography of the Sea.* London: Faber and Faber, 1951.

AURBAKKEN, KRISTINE. *L'Étoile d'araignée: une lecture de* Nedjma *de Kateb Yacine.* Paris: Publisud, 1986.

BADDAY, MONCEF. "Ahmadou Kourouma, écrivain africain." *Afrique Littéraire et Artistique* 10 (June 1970): 2—8.

BEHRMAN, LUCY C. *Muslim Brotherhoods and Politics in Senegal.* Cambridge: Harvard University Press, 1970.

BERNARD, PAUL R. "Individuality and Collectivity: A Duality in Camara Laye's *L'Enfant noir.*" *French Review* 52.2 (December 2, 1978): 313—24.

BERQUE, JACQUES. *Le Maghreb entre deux guerres.* Paris: Seuil, 1962.

BESTMAN, MARTIN T. *Sembène Ousmane et l'esthétique du roman négro-africain.* Sherbrooke, Québec: Editions Naaman, 1981.

BETI, MONGO [ALEXANDRE BIYIDI]. "Le Pauvre Christ de Bomba expliqué!. . ." *Peuples Noirs, Peuples Africains* 19 (1981): 104—32.

BIYIDI, ALEXANDRE (alias MONGO BETI). "Afrique noire, littérature rose." Présence Africaine (Apr.—July 1955): 133—45.

BLAIR, DOROTHY S. *Senegalese Literature: A Critical History.* Boston, Twayne,

1984.

BLAKE, SUSAN L. "Racism and the Classics: Teaching *Heart of Darkness.*" *CLA Journal* (June 1982): 396–404.

BLANZAT, JEAN. *Le Figaro littéraire.* 6 March 1956: 16–17.

BOL, VICTOR P. "Les Formes du roman africain." *Actes du colloque sur la littérature africaine d'expression française.* Dakar: Publications de la Faculté des Lettres et Sciences Humaines, Collection Langue et Littérature, 14, 1965.

BONN, CHARLES. "Histoire et production mythique dans *Nedjma.*" *Le Roman algérien de langue française.*

———. *Le Roman algérien de langue française.* Paris: L'Harmattan, 1985.

BOURAOUI, HEDI. "L'Afrique francophone des deux côtes du Sahara: problématiques et perspectives littéraires." *Présence Francophone* 27 (1985): 101–11.

———. "Plus que jamais africain." *Notre librairie* 96 (1989): 42–43.

BRAHIMI, DENISE. "Orientalisme et conscience de soi." Guy Dugas. *Littérature maghrébine d'expression française de l'écrit à l'image.* Meknès: Faculté des Lettres, Université Sidi Mohamed Ben Abdallah, 1987. 29–36.

BRIÈRE, ELOISE. "Résistance à l'acculturation dans l'oeuvre de Mongo Beti." *Canadian Journal of African Studies* 15.2 (1981): 181–99.

BUSIA, ABENA P. A. "Erasing Black Women: Reading Black Women; or Feminist Discourse on Edge." African Literature Association Meeting, Dakar, Senegal, March 1989.

———. "Miscegenation as Metonymy: Sexuality and Power in the Colonial Novel." *Ethnic and Racial Studies* (July 1986): 360–72.

BUTOR, MICHEL. "L'Espace du roman." *Essais sur le roman.* Paris: Gallimard, 1969. 48–58.

CADI-MOSTEFAI, MÉRIEM. "L'Image de la femme algérienne pendant la guerre 1954–1962, à travers les textes paralittéraires et littéraires." D.E.A. thesis. Université d'Alger, Instutit des Langues Vivantes, 1977.

CAILLER, BERNADETTE. "*L'Aventure ambiguë*: autobiographie ou histoire d'un peuple?" *French Review* 55.6 (1982): 743–51.

CAMPBELL, JOSEPH. *The Hero with a Thousand Faces.* New York: Pantheon, 1949.

CARTEY, WILFRED. *Whispers from a Continent.* New York: Random House, 1969.

CASE, F. "Workers Movements: Revolution and Women's Consciousness in *God's Bits of Wood.*" *Canadian Journal of African Studies—Revue Canadienne des Etudes Africaines* 15.2 (1981): 277–92.

CASSIRER, THOMAS. "The Dilemma of Leadership as Tragi-Comedy in the Novels of Mongo Beti." *L'Esprit Créateur* 10 (1970): 223–33.

CHAM, MBYE BABOUCAR. "Contemporary Society and the Female Imagination: A Study of the Novels of Mariama Bâ." *African Literature Today* 15 (1987): 89–101.

———. "Ousmane Sembène and the Aesthetics of African Oral Traditions." *Africana Journal* 13.1–4 (1982): 24–40.

———. "The Female Condition in Africa: A Literary Exploration by Mariama Bâ." *Current Bibliography on African Affairs* 17.1 (1984–86): 29–52.

CHARTIER, MONIQUE. "L'Eau et le feu dans *L'Aventure ambiguë* de Cheikh

Hamidou Kane." *Présence Francophone* 9 (1974): 15–25.

CHEMAIN, ROGER. *L'Imaginaire dans le roman africain.* Paris: L'Harmattan, 1986.

CHEVRIER, JACQUES. "Elles sont soeurs et pourtant ..." *Notre librairie* 95 (1988): 30–40.

———. "Les Romans coloniaux: enfer ou paradis?" *Notre libraire* 90 (1987): 61–72.

CHODOROW, NANCY. *The Reproduction of Mothering: Psychoanalysis and the Sociology of Gender.* Berkeley and Los Angeles: University of California Press, 1978.

CIXOUS, HÉLÈNE. "Le Rire de la Méduse." *L'Arc* (1975): 39–54.

———. "The Laugh of the Medusa." Trans. Keith Cohen and Paula Cohen. *Signs: Journal of Women in Culture and Society* 1.4 (1976): 875–93.

COE, RICHARD. *When the Grass Was Taller.* New Haven: Yale University Press, 1984.

CORNEVIN, ROBERT. *Littératures d'afrique noire de langue française.* Paris: Presses Universitaires de France, 1976.

COULON, CHRISTIAN. *Le Marabout et le Prince (Islam et pouvoir au Senegal).* Paris: Pédone, 1981.

CREIGNOU, HOURIA. "Le Sentiment de la terre dans les romans de Mammeri." Actes du colloque de Paris (4–5 mai 1974). *Aspects de la littérature maghrébine.* Paris: Edition de la Francité, 1974. 41–47.

DADIÉ, BERNARD. "Le Pagne noir." *Le Pagne noir.* 1955. Paris: Présence Africaine, 1970. 18–22.

D'ALMEIDA, IRENE ASSIBA. "The Concept of Choice in Mariama Bâ's Fiction." Davies and Graves. 161–71.

———. "The Making of an African Literary-Critical Tradition." Diss. Emory University, 1987.

DAVIES, CAROLE BOYCE, and ANNE ADAMS GRAVES, eds. *Ngambika: Studies of Women in African Literature.* Trenton: Africa World Press, 1986.

DÉJEUX, JEAN. *Assia Djebar.* Sherbrooke: Naaman, 1984.

———. *Djoh'a: héros de la tradition orale arabo-berbere, hier et aujourd'hui.* Sherbrooke, Québec: Editions Naaman, 1978.

———. "Kateb Yacine ou l'éternel retour." *Littérature maghrébine.* 209–46.

———. *Littérature Maghrebine de langue française.* 1973. 3rd ed. Sherbrooke, Québec: Editions Naaman, 1980.

———. "Les Structures de l'imaginaire dans l'oeuvre de Kateb Yacine." *Revue de l'Occident Musulman et de la Méditerranée* 13–14 (1973): 267–92.

———. "Regards sur la littérature maghrébine d'expression française." *Cahiers nord-africains* 61 (October–November 1957): 120.

DELEUZE, GILLES, and FÉLIX GUATTARI. *Kafka: Pour une littérature mineure.* Paris: Minuit, 1975.

DE MAGNY, OLIVIER. "Panorama d'une nouvelle littérature romanesque." *Esprit* (July–August 1958): 3–16.

DJAIDER, MIREILLE, and NAGET KHADDA. "L'écriture en chantier." *Visions du Maghreb.* Aix-en-Provence: Publisud, 1987. 75–86.

DJAOUT, TAHAR. *Mouloud Mammeri: entretien.* Alger: Laphomic, 1987.

DJEGHLOUL, ABDELKADER. "Un Romancier de l'identité perturbée et de l'assimilation impossible: Chukri Khodja." *Revue de l'Occident Musulman et de la Méditerranée:* "Le Maghreb dans l'imaginaire français: la colonie, le désert, l'exil," 37 (1984): 81–96.

DOMOWITZ, SUSAN. "The Orphan in Cameroon Folklore and Fiction." *Research in African Literatures* 12 (1981): 350–58.

DURAND, GILBERT. *Les Structures anthropologiques de l'imaginaire. 1969. 6 ed.* Paris: Bordas, 1982.

EBOUSSI, FABIEN. *"L'Aventure ambiguë* de Cheikh Hamadou Kane; quelques instants d'entretien avec Cheikh Hamidou Kane." *Abbia* 6 (1964): 207–15.

ECHENIM, KESTER. "La structure narrative de *Soleils des indépendances.*" *Présence Africaine* 107 (1978): 139–61.

EDWARDS, PAUL, and KENNETH RAMCHAND. "An African Sentimentalist: Camara Laye's *The African Child.*" *African Literature Today* 4 (1970): 37–53.

ELIADE, MIRCEA. *Forgerons et Alchimistes.* Paris: Flammarion, 1977.

——. *Le Mythe de l'éternel retour: archetypes et répétition.* Paris: Gallimard, 1949.

EL NOUTY, HASSAN. "La Polysémie de *L'Aventure ambiguë.*" *Revue de Littérature Comparée* 48.3–4 (1974): 475–87.

EMETO-AGBASIÈRE, JULIE. "Le Proverbe dans le roman africain." *Présence Francophone* 29 (1986): 27–41.

ERICKSON, JOHN D. "Cheikh Hamidou Kane's *L'Aventure ambiguë.*" *Yale French Studies* 53 (1976): 92–101.

FANOUDH-SIEFER, LÉON. *Le Mythe du nègre et de l'Afrique noire.* Paris: Klincksieck, 1968.

FINNEGAN, RUTH. *Oral Literature in Africa.* Oxford: Oxford University Press, 1970.

FLAUBERT, GUSTAVE. "Un Coeur simple." *Trois contes.* Paris: Gallimard, Collection Folio. 1877. 19–61.

FLEWELLEN, ELINOR C. "Assertiveness vs. Submissiveness in Selected Works by African Women Writers." *Ba Shira: A Journal of African Languages and Literature* 12.2 (1985): 3–18.

FRANK, KATHERINE. "Feminist Criticism and the African Novel." *African Literature Today* 14 (1984): 34–48.

GADJIGO, SAMBA. "L'Image de l'école coloniale dans le roman d'Afrique noire francophone." Diss. U of Illinois at Champaign-Urbana, 1988.

GAFAITI, HAFID. *Kateb Yacine: un homme, une oeuvre, un pays.* Alger: Laphomic, 1986.

GAKWANDI, SHATTO ARTHUR. *The Novel and Contemporary Experience in Africa.* New York: Africana Publishing Company, 1977.

GATES, HENRY LOUIS, JR. *The Signifying Monkey: A Theory of Afro-American Literary Criticism.* New York and Oxford: Oxford University Press, 1988.

GAVRONSKY, SERGE. "Linguistic Aspects of Francophone Literature." *French Review* (May 1978): 843–52.

GENETTE, GÉRARD. "Discours du recit." *Figures III.* Paris: Seuil, 1972. 67–273.

GÉRARD, ALBERT, and JEANNINE LAURENT. "Sembène's Progeny: A New Trend in the Senegalese Novel." *Studies in Twentieth Century Literature* 4.2 (1980): 133–45.

GETRY, JEAN. *L'Aventure ambiguë de Cheikh Hamidou Kane.* Paris: Editions Saint-Paul, 1982.

GILBERT, SANDRA, and SUSAN GUBAR. *The Madwoman in the Attic: The Woman Writer and the Nineteenth-Century Literary Imagination.* New Haven: Yale University Press, 1979.

GLISSANT, EDOUARD. "Le Chant profond de Kateb Yacine." Introduction to *Le Cercle des représailles.* Paris: Seuil, 1959. 9–13.

GONTARD, MARC. "Aux origines de *Nedjma,* l'absence, la déchirure." *CELFAN Review* 5.3 (May 1986): 20–24.

———· *Nedjma de Kateb Yacine: Essai sur la structure formelle du roman.* Paris: L'Harmattan, 1985.

GOODY, JACK, and IAN WATT. "The Consequences of Literacy." *Literacy in Traditional Societies,* ed. Jack Goody. Cambridge: Cambridge University Press, 27–84.

GORDON, DAVID C. *The Passing of French Algeria.* London: Oxford University Press, 1966.

GUÉRARD, ALBERT J. *Conrad the Novelist.* Cambridge: Harvard University Press, 1958.

HAMON, PHILIPPE. "Un discours contraint." *Poétique* 4.16 (1973): 411–45.

HARGREAVES, ALEC G. *The Colonial Experience in French Fiction: A Study of Pierre Loti, Ernest Psichari and Pierre Mille.* London: Macmillan, 1981.

HARRELL-BOND, BARBARA. "Interview: Mariama Bâ." *African Book Publishing Record* 6 (1980): 209–14.

HARROW, KENNETH. "*L'Aventure ambiguë* and the Wedding of Zein." *African Studies Review* 30.1 (1987): 63–77.

———· "Ideology and Technique in *Les Bouts de bois de Dieu.*" Unpublished paper.

HENRY, JEAN-ROBERT. "Le Désert nécessaire." *Autrement,* hors series 5 (1983): 17–34.

HOBSON, J. A. *The Psychology of Jingoism.* London: G. Richards, 1901.

HOUEDANOU, LUCIEN. "Islam et société dans la littérature féminine du Sénégal." *Nouvelles du Sud* 7 (1987): 159–70.

HUANNOU, ADRIEN. "La Technique du récit et le style dans *Les Soleils des indépendances.*" *L'Afrique littéraire et artistique* 38 (1975): 31–38.

HUGON, MONIQUE. "Leïla Sebbar ou l'exil productif." *Notre Libraire* 84 (1986): 32–37.

IRELAND, K. R. "End of the Line: Time in Kourouma's *Les Soleils des indépendances.*" *Présence Francophone* 23 (Autumn 1981): 79–89.

IZEVBAYE, DAN. "Reality in the African Novel: Its Theory and Practice." *Présence Africaine* 139.3 (1986): 115–35.

JACCARD, AMY-CLAIRE. "Visages de l'Islam chez Mariama Bâ et Aminata Sow Fall." *Nouvelles du Sud* 7 (1987): 171–82.

JACOBS, HARRIET A. *Incidents in the Life of a Slave Girl.* Introduction by Valerie Smith. London: Oxford University Press, 1988.

JANMOHAMED, ABDUL R. *Manichean Aesthetics: The Politics of Literature in Colonial Africa.* Amherst, Mass.: University of Massachusetts Press, 1983.

JEAN-AUBRY, GÉRARD. *The Sea Dreamer: A Definitive Biography of Joseph Conrad.* Trans. Helen Sebba. Garden City, N.Y.: Archon Books, 1967.

JOSEPH, GEORGE. "Free Indirect Discourse in *Les Soleils des Indépendances.*"

American Journal of Semiotics 6.1 (1988—89): 69—84.

JULIEN, EILEEN. "A Narrative Model for Camara Laye's *Le Regard du roi.*" *French Review* 45.6 (1982): 798—803.

———. "Oral Styles in Birago Diop's Tales: Excerpts from a study of language in *Les Contes d'Amadou Koumba.*" Unpublished paper presented at the African Studies Association Meeting, San Francisco, October 29—November 1, 1975.

———. "Orality Through Writing: *Les Contes d'Amadou Koumba.*" Diss. University of Wisconsin, Madison, 1978.

KA, AMINATA MAIGA. "Ramatoulaye, Aïssatou, Mireille et. . ." *Notre librairie* 81 (1985): 129—34.

KANE, MOHAMADOU. "Document pédagogique: *L'Héritage* de Birago Diop." *Annales de la faculté des lettres et sciences humaines de Dakar* 2 (1972): 26—38.

———. "*Les Paradoxes du roman africain.*" *Présence Africaine* 139.3 (1986): 74—87.

———. *Roman africain et tradition.* Dakar: Nouvelles Editions Africaines, 1982.

———. "Structures: sur les formes traditionnelles du roman africain." *Revue de littérature comparée* 48.3—4 (1974): 536—68.

"Kateb Yacine à la croisée des chemins." *Révolution Africaine* 178 (24 juin—1 juillet 1966): 24—25.

KATEB, YACINE. "Une Interview." *Témoignage Chrétien* 1223 (14 December 1967). Rpt. in *Review de Presse* 121 (January 1968).

———. "La Situation de l'Ecrivain Algérien." Public Lecture at Temple University, Philadelphia, March 21, 1988.

KERN, ANITA. "On *Les Soleils des indépendances* and *Le Devoir de violence.*" *Présence Africaine* 85 (1973): 209—30.

KING, ADELE. *The Writings of Camara Laye.* London: Heinemann, 1980.

KOTCHY, BARTHÉLÉMY. "Interview de M. Cheikh Hamidou Kane, écrivain sénégalais." *Etudes Littéraires* 7 (1974): 479—86.

———. "Signification de l'oeuvre." *Essai sur* Les Soleils̈ es indépendances. Adibjan: Nouvelles Editions Africaines, collection la girafe, 1977. 81—93.

KUNENE, DANIEL. "Journey as Metaphor in African Literature." *African Literature Studies: The Present State/L'Etat Present* (Stephen Arnold, ed.). Annual Selected Papers of the ALA, special unnumbered volume. Washington, D.C.: Three Continents Press, 1985. 189—215.

LAMBERT, FERDINAND. "L'Ironie et l'humour de Mongo Beti dans *Le Pauvre Christ de Bomba.*" *Etudes Littéraires* 7 (1974): 381—94.

———. "Narrative Perspectives in Mongo Beti's *Le Pauvre Christ de Bomba.*" *Yale French Studies* 53 (1976): 78—91.

LARONDE, MICHEL. "L'Apport de la culture d'origine dans la recherche identitaire beure: Le rôle de la mère maghrébine dans *Parle mon fils, parle à ta mère* de Leïla Sebbar." Unpublished paper delivered at the African Literature Association meeting, Cornell University, April, 1987.

———. "Leïla Sebbar et le roman 'croisé': histoire, mémoire, identité." *CELFAN Review* 7.1—2 (1987—88): 6—13.

LAVERGNE, EVELYNE. "*Les Soleils des indépendances*: Un roman authentiquement africain." *Revue de littérature et d'esthétique Négro-Africaines* 3 (1981): 15—25.

LeCLÉZIO, MARGUERITE. "Assia Djebar: Ecrire dans la langue adverse." *Contemporary French Civilization* 9.2 (1985): 230—44.

LEE, SONIA. *Camara Laye.* Boston: Twayne Publishers, 1984.

———. "The Image of the Woman in the African Folktale from the Sub-Saharan Francophone Area." *Yale French Studies* 53 (1976): 19—28.

———. "Le Thème du bonheur chez les romancières de l'Afrique occidentale." *Présence Francophone* 29 (1986): 91—103.

LEINER, JACQUELINE. "Interview avec Camara Laye." *Présence Francophone* 10 (1975): 157.

LESAGE, LAURENT. *The French New Novel.* University Park, Pa.: Pennsylvania State University Press, 1962.

LEZOU, GÉRARD-D. "Temps et Espace." *Essai sur* Les Soleils des indépendances. Adibjan: Nouvelles Editions Africaines, collection la girafe, 1977. 27—42.

LINKHORN, RENÉE. "L'Afrique de demain: Femmes en marche dans l'oeuvre de Sembène Ousmane." *Modern Language Studies* 16.3 (Summer 1986): 69—76.

LIPPERT, ANNE. "Cultural Mix and Personal Integrity in Leïla Sebbar's *J. H. cherche âme soeur." CELFAN Review* 7.1—2 (1987—88): 2—5.

LY, AMADOU. "Quelques réflexions sur la forme des *Les Soleils des indépendances* de Kourouma." *Annales de la faculté des lettres et sciences humaines:* Université de Dakar 11 (1981): 117—34.

MADELAIN, JACQUES. *L'Errance et l'itinéraire.* Paris: Sinbad, 1983.

MAGNIER, BERNARD. "Ahmadou Kourouma." Interview. *Notre librairie* 87 (1987): 11—15.

———. "Ken Bugul ou l'écriture thérapeutique." *Notre librairie* 11 (1985): 151—55.

MAHOOD, M. M. *The Colonial Encounter: A Reading of Six Novels.* Totawa, N.J.: Rowman and Littlefield, 1977.

MAKWARD, EDRIS. "Marriage, Tradition and Woman's Pursuit of Happiness in the Novels of Mariama Bâ." Davies and Graves 271—81.

MAMMERI, MOULOUD. *L'Ahellil du Gourara.* Paris: Edition de la Maison des Sciences de L'Homme, 1984.

———. "Ténéré atavique." *Autrement,* hors série 5 (1983): 213—21.

MARIE-CÉLESTE [SOEUR]. "Le Mysticisme chez Cheikh Hamidou Kane." *Présence Africaine* 101/102 (1977): 216—26.

———. "Le Prophétisme chez Cheikh Hamidou Kane." *Afrique littéraire et artistique* 46 (1977): 36—50.

MAYER, JEAN. "Le Roman en Afrique noire francophone: tendances et structures." *Etudes Françaises* 3 (1967): 169—95.

MEDIOUHOUAN, GUY OSSITO. "Lamine Senghor (1889—1927): Précurseur de la prose nationaliste négro-africaine." Paper delivered at the African Literature Association meeting, Dakar, Senegal, March 1989.

MELONE, THOMAS. "Mongo Beti, l'homme et le destin." *Présence Africaine* 70 (1969): 120—36.

———. *Mongo Beti: l'homme et le destin.* Paris: Présence Africaine, 1971.

MEMEL, H. "La Bâtardise." *Essai sur* Les Soleils des indépendances. Abidjan:

Nouvelles Editions Africaines, collection la girafe, 1977. 53–65.

MENASSERI, HOCINE. "William Faulkner: *The Sound and the Fury*. Kateb Yacine: *Nedjma*." Diss. (D.E.S.) Algiers: Faculty of Letters, 1968.

MERNISSI, FATIMA. *Beyond the Veil: Male-Female Dynamics in a Modern Islamic Society*. Cambridge: Schenkman, 1975. Revised ed. Bloomington and Indianapolis: Indiana University Press, 1987.

———. *Chahrazad n'est pas marocaine — Autrement, elle serait salariée!* Casablanca: Editions Le Fennec, 1989.

———. *Le Harem politique: Le Prophète et les femmes*. Paris: Albin Michel, 1987.

———. *Sexe, idéologie, Islam*. Paris: Editions Tierce, 1983.

MICHELMAN, FREDERIC. "The Beginnings of French-African Fiction." *Research in African Literatures* 2.1 (1971): 5–17.

———. "Independence and Disillusion in *Les Soleils des indépendances*: A New Approach." *Design and Intent in African Literature*. Annual Selected Papers of the ALA. Ed. Stephen H. Arnold. Washington, D.C.: Three Continents, 1982. 91–95.

MILLER, CHRISTOPHER L. *Blank Darkness: Africanist Discourse in French*. Chicago: University of Chicago Press, 1985.

M'LANHORO, M. "Fama." *Essai sur* Les Soleils des indépendances. Abidjan: Nouvelles Editions Africaines, collection la girafe, 1977. 43–52.

MOORE, CARRIE DAILEY. "Evolution of an African Artist: Social Realism in the Works of Sembène Ousmane." Diss. Indiana University, 1973.

MOORE, GERALD. "Camara Laye: Nostalgia and Idealism." *Seven African Writers*. London: Oxford University Press, 1962. 25–38.

———. "Sembène Ousmane: The Primacy of Change." *Twelve African Writers*. Bloomington, Ind.: Indiana University Press, 1980. 69–83.

MORTIMER, MILDRED. *Assia Djebar*. Philadelphia: CELFAN Monographs, 1988.

———. *Contes africains*. Boston: Houghton Mifflin, 1972.

———. "The Desert in Algerian Fiction." *L'Esprit Créateur* 36.1 (1986): 60–69.

———. "Entretien avec Assia Djebar, écrivain algérien." *Research in African Literatures* 19.2 (1988): 197–205.

———. "The evolution of Assia Djebar's feminist conscience." *Contemporary African Literature*. Eds. Wylie, Houchins, Julien, Linneman, Shelton. Washington, D.C.: Three Continents Press, 1983. 7–14.

———. "A Feminist Critique of the Algerian novel of French Expression." *Design and Intent in African Literature*. Eds. Dorsey, Egejuru, Arnold. Washington, D.C.: Three Continents Press, 1982. 31–38.

———. "The Feminine Image in the Algerian Novel of French Expression." *Ba Shiru* 8.2 (1977): 51–62.

———. "La Femme algérienne dans les romans d'Assia Djebar." *French Review* 49.5 (1976): 759–63.

———. "The Isefra of Si Mohand-ou-Mhand: Songs of a Berber Poet Interpreted by Mouloud Mammeri." *Towards Defining the African Aesthetic*. Washington, D.C.: Three Continents Press, 1982. 31–38.

———. "L'Itinéraire de lucidité dans le roman africain francophone: *Le Sommeil du juste* de Mouloud Mammeri et *L'Aventure ambiguë* de Cheikh

Hamidou Kane." *Ecriture Française dans le Monde* 17—18.6 (1984): 5—13.

———· "Kateb Yacine in Search of Algeria." *L'Esprit Créateur* 12.4 (Winter 1972): 274—88.

———· "Language and Space in the Fiction of Assia Djebar and Leïla Sebbar." *Research in African Literatures* 19.3 (1988): 301—11.

———· *Mouloud Mammeri: écrivain algérien.* Sherbrooke: Editions Naaman, 1982.

M'RABET, FADÉLA. *La Femme algérienne.* Paris: Maspero, 1966.

MUDIMBE, V.Y. *The Invention of Africa. Gnosis, Philosophy, and the Order of Knowledge.* Bloomington, Ind.: Indiana University Press, 1988.

MUDIMBE-BOYI, ELISABETH. "Evangelization and Culture: *The Poor Christ of Bomba.*" Guest lecture, Haverford College, March, 1987.

———· "Ken Bugul." *Fifty African and Caribbean Women Writers,* ed. Anne Adams, Westport, Conn.: Greenwood Press (forthcoming).

NADEAU, MAURICE. "De Keblout à Kateb." *La Quinzaine Littéraire* 11 (1 September 1966): 9

———· Kateb Yacine juge l'islamisme." *France-Observateur* 327 (16 August 1956): 13.

NAZARETH, PETER. "Out of Darkness: Conrad and Other Third World Writers." *Conradiana: A Journal of Joseph Conrad Studies* XIV/3 1982: 173—87.

NEGANDU NKASHAMA, PIUS. *Kourouma et le mythe: Une lecture de* Les Soleils des indépendances. Paris: Silex, 1985.

NIANE, D. T. *Soundjata ou l'épopée mandingue.* Paris: Présence Africaine, 1960.

NISBET, ANNE-MARIE. *Le Personnage féminin dans le roman maghrébin de langue française des l'indépendance à 1980.* Sherbrooke: Naaman, 1982.

OBIECHINA, EMMANUEL N. *Culture, Tradition and Society in the West African Novel.* Cambridge: Cambridge University Press, 1972.

———· "Transition from Oral to Literary Tradition." *Présence Africaine* 63 (1967): 140—61.

OHAEGBU, ALOYSIUS U. "*Les Soleils des indépendances* ou le drame de l'homme écrasé par le destin." *Présence Africaine* 90 (1974): 253—60.

OJO-ADE, FEMI. "Still a Victim? Mariama Bâ's *Une si longue lettre.*" *African Literature Today* 12 (1982): 71—87.

OKAFOR, RAYMOND. "Cheikh Hamidou Kane: à la recherche d'une certaine synthèse. L'acculturation dans *L'Aventure ambiguë.*" *Annales de l'Université d'Abidjan,* Série D. Littérature (1972): 195—217.

OLIVER, ROLAND, and MICHAEL CROWDER. *The Cambridge Encyclopedia of Africa.* Cambridge: Cambridge University Press, 1981.

OLNEY, JAMES. "Ces pays lointains." *Tell Me Africa: An Approach to African Literature.* Princeton: Princeton University Press, 1973. 124—56.

ONG, WALTER J. *Orality and Literacy: The Technologizing of the Word.* London: Methuen, 1982.

ORTOVA, JARMILA. "Les Femmes dans l'oeuvre littéraire d'Ousmane Sembène." *Présence Africaine* 71 (1969): 69—77.

PALMER, EUSTACE. "Camara Laye: The African Child." *An Introduction to the African Novel.* New York: Africana Publishing Company, 1972. 85—95.

PARRY, BENITA. *Conrad and Imperialism: Ideological Boundaries and Visionary*

Frontiers. London: Macmillan, 1983.

PORTER, ABIOSEH MIKE. "The Child−Narrator and the Theme of Love in Mongo Beti's *Le Pauvre Christ de Bomba." Design and Intent in African Literature.* Ed. Dorsey, Egejuru, Arnold. Washington, D.C.: Three Continents Press, 1982. 103−7.

POULET, GEORGES. *Les Métamorphoses du cercle.* Paris: Plon, 1961.

PRATT, ANNIS; with Barbara White, Andrea Loewenstein, Mary Wyer. *Archetypal Patterns in Women's Fiction.* Bloomington: Indiana University Press, 1981.

RASKIN, JONAH. "Imperialism: Conrad's *Heart of Darkness." Journal of Contemporary History* (Apr. 1967): 113−31.

RAYBAUD, ANTOINE. "Poème(s) éclaté(s) de Kateb Yacine." *Revue de l'Occident Musulman et de la Méditerranée* 22 (1976): 119−28.

RIMMON-KENAN, SHLOMITH. *Narrative Fiction: Contemporary Poetics.* London and New York: Methuen, 1983.

RIPAULT, GHISLAIN. "Les Soleils de Kourouma brillent pas leur présence." *Notre librairie* 87 (1987): 6−10.

ROBBE-GRILLET, ALAIN. *Pour un nouveau roman.* Paris: Editions de Minuit, 1963.

ROCHE, ANNE. "Tradition et subversion dans l'oeuvre de Mouloud Mammeri." *Revue de l'Occident Musulman et de la Méditerranée* 22 (1976): 119−30.

ROBERT, MARTHE. *Origins of the Novel.* Trans. Sacha Rabinovitch. Bloomington, Ind.: Indiana University Press, 1980.

SAID, EDWARD. *Joseph Conrad and the Fiction of Autobiography.* Cambridge: Harvard University Press, 1966.

———. *Orientalism.* New York: Random House, 1979.

SCHARFMAN, RONNIE. "Fonction romanesque féminine: Rencontre de la culture et de la structure dans *Les Bouts de bois de Dieu." Ethiopiques* 1.3−4 (1983): 134−44.

SCHEUB, HAROLD. *The Khosa "Ntomsi."* Oxford: Clarendon Press, 1979.

SCHIKORA, ROSEMARY G. "African Fiction in French, 1961−1977: A Study of Narrative Techniques." Diss. Wayne State University, 1979.

———. "Narrative Voice in Kourouma's *Les Soleils des indépendances." French Review* 55.6 (May 1980): 811−17.

SCHIPPER, MINEKE. "Oralité écrite et recherche d'identité." *Research in African Literatures* 10 (1979): 40−58.

———. "Toward a Definition of Realism in the African Context." *New Literary History* 16.3 (Spring 1985): 559−75.

———. "Who Am I?: Fact and Fiction in African First-Person Narrative." *Research in African Literatures* 16.1 (Spring 1985): 53−79.

SCHOLES, ROBERT, and ROBERT KELLOGG. *The Nature of Narrative.* London: Oxford University Press, 1966.

SELLIN, ERIC. "Alienation in the Novels of Camara Laye." *Pan-African Journal* 4 (1971): 455−72.

———. "Les Eléments classiques dans les romans de Mouloud Mammeri." *CELFAN Review* 3.2 (1984): 26−30.

———. "Ouologuem, Kourouma et le nouveau roman africain." *Littératures ultramarines de langue française, genèse et jeunesse.* Eds. T. H. Geno and R.

Julow. Ottawa: Naaman, 1974. 37−50.

SÉNAC, JEAN. "Kateb Yacine et la littérature nord-africaine." *Entretiens sur les lettres et les arts* (février 1957): 60−66.

SERREAU, GENEVIÈVE. "Situation de l'écrivain algérien: Interview de Kateb Yacine." *Les Lettres nouvelles* 40 (July−August 1956): 109.

SHERRY, NORMAN. *Conrad's Western World*. Cambridge: Cambridge University Press, 1971.

SHIVER, WILLIAM S. "A Summary of Interior Monologue in Cheikh Hamidou Kane's *Ambiguous Adventure*." *Présence Africaine* 101/102 (1977): 207−15.

SHOWALTER, ENGLISH, JR. *Exiles and Strangers*. Columbus: Ohio State University Press, 1984.

SLADE, RUTH. *King Leopold's Congo*. New York: Oxford University Press, 1962.

SLOMSKI, GENEVIÈVE. "Dialogue in the Discourse: A Study of Revolt in Selected Fiction by African Women." Diss. Indiana University, 1986.

SMITH, VALERIE. *Self-Discovery and Authority in Afro-American Narrative*. Cambridge: Harvard University Press, 1987.

SOW, FATOU. "Muslim Families in Black Africa." *Current Anthropology* 26.5 (December 1985): 563−70.

STAUNTON, CHERYL ANTOINETTE. "Three Senegalese Women Novelists: A Study of Temporal/Spatial Structures." Diss. George Washington University, 1986.

STORZER, GERALD. "Abstractions and Orphanhood in the Novels of Mongo Beti." *Présence Francophone* 15 (1979): 93−112.

STRATTON, FLORENCE. "The Shallow Grave: Archetypes of Female Experience in African Fiction." *Research in African Literatures* 19.2 (1988): 143−69.

STRINGER, SUSAN. "Senegalese Women Writers." Diss. University of Colorado, 1988.

SZYLIOWICZ, IRENE L. *Pierre Loti and the Oriental Woman*. New York: St. Martin's Press, 1988.

TADROS, RAYMONDE GHATTAS. "Circularité, langage et mythe dans *Candide, L'education sentimentale, Nedjma*." Diss. University of California, Irvine, 1980.

TCHEHO, ISAAC-CELESTIN. "Un Pont au-dessus du Sahara." *Notre librairie* 96 (1989): 60−65.

TIDJANI-SERPOS, NOURÉINI. "De l'école coranique á l'école étrangère ou le passage tragique de l'Ancien au Nouveau dans *L'Aventure ambiguë* de Cheikh Hamidou Kane." *Présence Africaine* 101/102 (1977): 188−206.

TILLION, GERMAINE. *Le Harem et les cousins*. Paris: Seuil, 1962.

TINE, ALIOUNE. "Wolof ou français: le choix de Sembène." *Notre librairie* 81 (Oct.−Dec. 1985): 43−50.

TODOROV, TZVETAN. *La Conquête de l'Amérique*. Paris: Seuil, 1982.

———. *The Conquest of America*. Trans. Richard Howard. New York: Harper & Row, 1984.

TOURÉ, ABDOU. *La Civilisation quotidienne en Côte d'Ivoire: procès d'occidentalisation*. Paris: Karthala, 1981.

TREMAINE, LOUIS. "The Absence of Itinerary in Kateb Yacine's *Nedjma*." *Research in African Literatures* 10.1 (Spring 1979): 16−39.

————. "The Implied Reader in Kateb Yacine's *Nedjma.*" *Artist and Audience: African Literature As a Shared Experience.* Washington, D.C.: Three Continents Press, 1979. 149–58.

TURK, NADA. "Assia Djebar: Solitaire solidaire. Une étude de la lutte des Algériennes pour les libertés individuelles dans l'oeuvre d'Assia Djebar." Diss. University of Colorado, 1987.

————. "*L'Amour, la fantasia* d'Assia Djebar: chronique de guerre, voix des femmes." *CELFAN Review* 7.1–2 (1987–88): 21–24.

UMEZINWA, WILLIAM. "Révolte et création artistique dans l'oeuvre de Mongo Beti." *Présence Francophone* 10 (1975): 35–48.

VATIN, JEAN-CLAUDE. "Désert construit et inventé, Sahara perdu ou retrouvé: le jeu des imaginaires." *Revue de l'Occident Musulman et de la Mediterranée* 37 (1984): 107–31.

————. "Pour une sociologie politique des nouveaux désenchantements: à propos d'une lecture de *La Traversée* de Mouloud Mammeri." *Annuaire de l'Afrique du nord* 21 (1982): 814–39.

WALLACE, KAREN SMYLEY. "*Les Bouts de bois de dieu* and *Xala*: a Comparative Analysis of Female Roles in Sembène's Novels." *Papers in Romance* 5.3 (Autumn 1983): 89–96.

————. "A Search for Identity: The Alienated Female Persona in Some Francophone African Novels." *Rendezvous: Journal of Arts and Letters* 22.2 (Spring 1986): 32–38.

WATT, IAN. "Heart of Darkness." *Conrad in the Nineteenth Century.* Berkeley: University of California Press, 1978. 126–253.

WONDJI, CH.-G. "Le Contexte historique." *Essai sur Les Soleils des indépendances.* Abidjan: Nouvelles Editions Africaines, collection la girafe, 1977. 17–26.

YETIV, ISAAC. "Trois procès dans la littérature française: Etude comparée." *Présence Francophone* 14: 31–36.

ZELL, HANS. "The First Noma Award for African Publishing." *African Book Publishing Record* 6 (1980): 199–201.

ZIMRA, CLARISSE. "In Her Own Write: The Circular Structures of Linguistic Alienation in Assia Djebar's Early Novels." *Research in African Literatures* (Summer 1980): 206–23.

Index

▼▼▼▼▼

#21335879